Entrepreneurship in China

China has grown to become the world's second largest economy in merely three decades and entrepreneurship has been identified as a key driver of China's fast growth. Since the mid-2000s, the country has transitioned from a predominance of necessity-based entrepreneurship to that of an opportunity-based entrepreneurship.

The China Surveys of Global Entrepreneurship Monitor in the last fifteen years consistently indicate the country's high rate of entrepreneurship. Furthermore, more Chinese entrepreneurs have started setting their sights on business internationalisation. Against this backdrop of a thriving entrepreneurial economy, institutions and business environments are, however, not often viewed as "friendly" to private entrepreneurs and businesses. The "re-emergence" of entrepreneurship suggests a history of struggle to overcome opposition and obstruction, to survive and grow, including "rule ambiguities", rent-seeking, subsidies, and institutional constraints, such as industrial barriers, difficulties in getting access to critical resources, and weak property rights. China has also been experiencing economic slowdown, increase in inequality, and worsening environmental problems since the turn of the century, clearly indicating that the rapid development of entrepreneurship in China presents a lot of puzzling questions.

Entrepreneurship in China attempts to deal with these unanswered queries as well as provide an insightful and updated understanding of entrepreneurship development in China.

The chapters in this book were originally published as a special issue of the journal, *Entrepreneurship & Regional Development*.

Qihai Huang is Professor of Entrepreneurship and Management and Head of Department of Management at the University of Huddersfield, UK. He received his first degree in Sociology from Peking University, China, and both MSc and PhD from the University of Bristol, UK. He has been Director of Research at Keele Business School and Head of Department of Entrepreneurship and Strategy at Lancaster University Management School.

Xueyuan Liu is Professor of Management and had been the Assistant Dean at the Economics and Management School of Wuhan University, China. He received his first degree in English from Nankai University, China, and both MBA and PhD from the University of Salford, UK. He had been a visiting scholar at Columbia University Business School and Fisher College of Business at Ohio State University, and the founding president of Association of Supply Chain and Operations Management (ASCOM). Prior to his academic career, he had been a professional manager and a founder of a start-up in international business for over 12 years.

Jun Li is Senior Lecturer of Entrepreneurship and Innovation at Essex Business School, University of Essex, UK. He previously held post at Chinese Academy of Sciences and was the President of Chinese Economic Association (UK/Europe) in 2012–2013. He currently serves as Editor-in-Chief of *Journal of Entrepreneurship in Emerging Economies*.

Entrepreneurship in China

Edited by
Qihai Huang, Xueyuan Liu and Jun Li

LONDON AND NEW YORK

First published 2022
by Routledge
2 Park Square, Milton Park, Abingdon, Oxon OX14 4RN

and by Routledge
605 Third Avenue, New York, NY 10158

Routledge is an imprint of the Taylor & Francis Group, an informa business

© 2022 Taylor & Francis

British Library Cataloguing in Publication Data
A catalogue record for this book is available from the British Library

ISBN: 978-1-032-01239-1 (hbk)
ISBN: 978-1-032-01240-7 (pbk)
ISBN: 978-1-003-17783-8 (ebk)

DOI: 10.4324/9781003177838

Typeset in Myriad Pro
by Newgen Publishing UK

Publisher's Note
The publisher accepts responsibility for any inconsistencies that may have arisen during the conversion of this book from journal articles to book chapters, namely the inclusion of journal terminology.

Disclaimer
Every effort has been made to contact copyright holders for their permission to reprint material in this book. The publishers would be grateful to hear from any copyright holder who is not here acknowledged and will undertake to rectify any errors or omissions in future editions of this book.

At the time when this book was to be handed over to production, the three editors were very grieved to hear that the former editor-in-chief of *Entrepreneurship and Regional Development, an International Journal*, Professor Alistair Anderson, passed away suddenly.

We are deeply saddened by the loss of such a distinguished scholar, an exceptional mentor, and a close friend. Without Professor Anderson's inspiration, encouragement and support, this book, with most of the papers originated and re-edited from the special issue of the journal, would never have been possible.

Though you are no longer with us, Alistair, you will never be forgotten. May your memory be held on each page of this book forever.

Contents

Citation Information

The chapters in this book were originally published in the journal *Entrepreneurship & Regional Development*, volume 32, issue 5–6 (2020). When citing this material, please use the original page numbering for each article, as follows:

Chapter 1

Contextualization of Chinese entrepreneurship research: an overview and some future research directions
Qihai Huang, Xueyuan Liu and Jun Li
Entrepreneurship & Regional Development, volume 32, issue 5–6 (2020), pp. 353–369

Chapter 2

Entrepreneurial ecosystems: what we know and where we move as we build an understanding of China
Juanyi Chen, Li Cai, Garry D. Bruton and Naiheng Sheng
Entrepreneurship & Regional Development, volume 32, issue 5–6 (2020), pp. 370–388

Chapter 3

The impact of sub-national institutions on SMEs' diversification into new businesses: evidence from China
Dong Chen, Donghong Li and Yongsun Paik
Entrepreneurship & Regional Development, volume 32, issue 5–6 (2020), pp. 389–407

Chapter 4

Hear it straight from the horse's mouth: recognizing policy-induced opportunities
Weiqi Dai, Felix Arndt and Mingqing Liao
Entrepreneurship & Regional Development, volume 32, issue 5–6 (2020), pp. 408–428

Chapter 5

Should I stay or should I go? Job demands' push and entrepreneurial resources' pull in Chinese migrant workers' return-home entrepreneurial intention
Jinyun Duan, Juelin Yin, Yue Xu and Daoyou Wu
Entrepreneurship & Regional Development, volume 32, issue 5–6 (2020), pp. 429–448

Chapter 6

International networking and knowledge acquisition of Chinese SMEs: the role of global mind-set and international entrepreneurial orientation
Zhibin Lin, Xuebing Cao and Ed Cottam
Entrepreneurship & Regional Development, volume 32, issue 5–6 (2020), pp. 449–465

Notes on Contributors

Felix Arndt, Department of Strategic Management and Marketing, De Montfort University, Leicester, UK.

Garry D. Bruton, Department of Management, Entrepreneurship, and Leadership, Neeley School of Business, Texas Christian University, Fort Worth, TX, USA.

Li Cai, School of Management and State Key Laboratory of Automotive Simulation and Control, Jilin University, Changchun, Jilin, China.

Xuebing Cao, Keele Management School, Keele University, Staffordshire, UK.

Dong Chen, Department of Management, Loyola Marymount University, Los Angeles, CA, USA.

Juanyi Chen, School of Management, Jilin University, Changchun, Jilin, China.

Ed Cottam, Newcastle Business School, Northumbria University, Newcastle upon Tyne, UK.

Weiqi Dai, School of Business Administration, Zhejiang University of Finance & Economics, Hangzhou, Zhejiang, China.

Jinyun Duan, School of Psychology and Cognitive Science, East China Normal University, Shanghai, China.

Qihai Huang, Department of Management, University of Huddersfield, Huddersfield, UK.

Donghong Li, Department of Innovation, Entrepreneurship and Strategy, School of Economics and Management, Tsinghua University, Beijing, China.

Jun Li, Essex Business School, University of Essex, Colchester, UK.

Mingqing Liao, School of Business Administration, South China University of Technology, Guangzhou, Guangdong, China.

Zhibin Lin, Durham University Business School, Durham, UK.

Xueyuan Liu, Economics and Management School, Wuhan University, Wuhan, China.

Yongsun Paik, Department of Management, Loyola Marymount University, Los Angeles, CA, USA.

Naiheng Sheng, School of Management, Jilin University, Changchun, Jilin, China.

Daoyou Wu, College of Business Administration, Zhejiang University of Finance & Economics, Hangzhou, Zhejiang Province, China.

Yue Xu, International Business School Suzhou, Xi'an Jiaotong- Liverpool University, Suzhou, China.

Juelin Yin, Business School, Sun Yat-sen University, Guangzhou, China.

Contextualization of Chinese entrepreneurship research: an overview and some future research directions

Qihai Huang, Xueyuan Liu and Jun Li

ABSTRACT

In this article, we briefly identify seven evolving characteristics of Chinese entrepreneurship that capture either the essential contextual elements or the outcomes of the contextual influences in China and provide a fertile ground for entrepreneurship research in China. We then present three approaches to contextualization in Chinese entrepreneurship research and map extant research with these approaches to assess the current state of contextualization in Chinese entrepreneurship research. Following the discussion we introduce the five contributions to the Special Issue that advance a more nuanced understanding of entrepreneurship in China from five diverse perspectives. We finally argue that the next stage of entrepreneurship research in China needs to explore four contextual parameters.

Background

When the reform and opening up started in China in the late 1970s, entrepreneurship was an alien concept to Chinese people both as a practice and subject of academic inquiry. Yet, once the shackles were removed from the people with entrepreneurial instinct and zest, entrepreneurship in China took off and a private sector quickly emerged and thrived. The fast growth of the private sector has contributed substantially to China's rapid development over the last four decades (Huang 2003, 2010; Li, Ding, and Li 2015; Atherton and Newman 2017). The development of entrepreneurship could determine the overall success of China's economic transition (McMillan and Woodruff 2002) and sustainable development in the future too (Huang 2003). Indeed, Chinese entrepreneurship is not simply a phenomenon of its own but one that is of global relevance and impact. Chinese entrepreneurs have left their mark, firstly through their made-in-China exports, and lately through their shopping spree in cross-border merger and acquisition deals. Chinese entrepreneurs not only contribute to wealth creation but also market competition in the world. Their presence both at home and abroad has also forced a response from their counterparts across the world, where survivors have to be fitter.

Contextualizing entrepreneurship in China

The critical role of entrepreneurship to China as above mentioned is in sharp contrast against the background of its development, where institutions and business environment are seldom viewed as 'friendly' to private entrepreneurs and businesses (Huang 2010). The 'reemergence' of entrepreneurship is 'a history of struggle to overcome opposition and obstruction, to survive and grow'

(Huang 2003, 101), which included institutional constraints such as industrial entry barriers, difficulties in getting access to critical resources and weak property rights (Zhou 2011). It is therefore captivating to research entrepreneurship in China.

Increasing research, including special issues, has been dedicated to the topic of Chinese entrepreneurship (e.g., Wank 1996; Yang and Li 2008; Ahlstrom and Ding 2014; Su, Zhai, and Landström 2015; He, Lu, and Qian 2018). Based on publications in Social Science Citation Index and Chinese Social Science Citation Index databases over the period of 2003–2012, Su et al. (2015a) used bibliometric method to analyse entrepreneurship research in China, Europe and the USA. They found that Chinese entrepreneurship researchers study similar themes and use similar theoretical foundations like their western counterparts. However, the tendency of Chinese management research to focus on 'general theories' and pay little attention to contextual variables can constrain our understanding and theory development (Meyer 2007). The Chinese contextual environment manifests itself in the uniqueness of entrepreneurship phenomenon. Chinese scholars should therefore shift from theory application to the incorporation of context into theory refinement or development so as to make a novel contribution to the global discourse (Meyer 2007; Su et al. 2015a). The institutional context of China, like other emerging economies, is often characterized as weak institutional infrastructures, such as poor protection of property right. This has a profound impact on behaviours of entrepreneurs and SMEs (Wright et al. 2005; Peng, Wang, and Jiang 2008). More specifically, Ahlstrom and Ding (2014) argue that unpacking how entrepreneurs remove such institutional barriers is essential to understanding entrepreneurship in China. For example, entrepreneurs tend to rely on guanxi (Wank 1996;Zhang 2015a), or seek to build relationships, which have been shown to serve as an informal institution (Cai, Fang, and Xu 2011; Du, Guariglia, and Newman 2015; Zhang 2015a). Furthermore, entrepreneurs may feel compelled to use bribes to access resource controlled by government officials (Baron et al. 2018).

Therefore, Bruton, Ahlstrom, and Obloj (2008) suggest the importance to understand how the cultural and institutional forces can moderate the behaviour of entrepreneurs in emerging economies like China from social psychological and organizational behaviour perspectives. Similarly, in their literature review, He, Lu, and Qian (2018) argue that the unique institutional and cultural settings behind the Chinese economy have provided some distinct perspectives on the study of entrepreneurship in China. For example, China is featured by significant sub-national, cross-region variation (Peng, Wang, and Jiang 2008), and the marked differences between sub-national institutions can either facilitate or constrain entrepreneurship in a variety of ways (Zhou 2011).

Taking 'context' seriously (Johns 2006) may significantly advance the theoretical development of entrepreneurship (Zahra 2007). However, context is much richer than institutional and cultural elements, which have been dealt with by much research. Social norm may not change rapidly and institutional inertia can exist. However, rapid economic development, social change dynamics, and shift in government policies provide tremendous entrepreneurial opportunities, present new challenges, and create 'new contexts', which in turn have an impact on entrepreneurship. Such richness of context is well reflected by the annual surveys of the Global Entrepreneurship Monitor (GEM) China project, which offer indispensable data for a glimpse. China has been part of GEM's international entrepreneurship consortium since 2002 that was initiated by Babson College and London Business School in 1999. An analysis of China GEM survey data between 2002 and 2018 reveals seven stylised facts of entrepreneurship in China (see Table 1). The complex, evolving picture of entrepreneurship in China demands our full attention to the underlying causes and contexts.

First, China had seen growing entrepreneurial activities along the rapid and phenomenal economic development in the past few decades. During 2002–2011, about one-sixth of working-age adults were engaged in early-stage entrepreneurial activity (TEA).[1] In this period, the TEA rates for China were significantly higher than many other countries, and China was ranked the 7th in GEM's global TEA ranking.

Second, the Chinese society consistently values entrepreneurship highly in recent years. On average, 69% of the adult population in China consider starting a business as a good career choice,

Table 1. Overview of Chinese entrepreneurship, 2002–2018.

Year	Values, abilities and opportunities					Intentions	Motivation		Entrepreneurship				impacts	
	Perceived opportunities	Perceived capabilities	Fear of failure rate	High Status to Successful Entrepreneurs	Entrepreneurship as a Good Career Choice	Entrepreneurial intentions	Opportunity-motivated TEA	Necessity-motivated TEA	TEA China	Female TEA	Established Business Ownership	Entrepreneurial Employee Activity	High Job Creation Expectation	Innovation
2018	35.07	24.15	41.7	68.72	60.82	15.28	n/a	n/a	10.4	9.2	3.16	1.0	20.38	33.06
2017	35.21	27.24	41.46	74.57	66.35	15.29	67.2	32.4	9.9	8.6	6.83	1.36	24.32	25.51
2016	37.33	29.82	49.08	77.8	70.3	21.3	73.3	26.7	10.3	10.2	7.5	1.2	26.7	28.8
2015	31.71	27.42	39.96	77.62	65.94	19.52	64.3	34.7	12.8	14.2	3.12	1.36	35	25.82
2014	31.88	32.97	39.5	72.91	65.68	19.33	65.7	33.2	15.5	12	11.59	0.46	13.65	19.63
2013	33.07	36.29	34.3	73.53	69.61	14.42	66.1	33.9	14	11	11.04	0.6	22.94	21.7
2012	32.24	37.6	35.82	76.13	71.67	20.39	63	37	12.8	22.4	12.45	0.59	18.23	21.06
2011	48.84	43.9	35.64	73.41	73.12	42.81	59.4	40.6	24	n/a	12.67	2.09	34.87	14.06
2010	36.17	42.33	32.01	76.93	70.03	26.9	58	42	14.4	16.5	13.77	n/a	20	n/a
2009	25.32	35.23	32.07	77.49	66.12	22.58	52	48	18.8	n/a	17.16	n/a	19.22	n/a
2007	39.19	38.85	31.05	70.59	68.64	31.46	60.4	39.6	16.4	20.5	8.39	n/a	29.41	n/a
2006	31.2	36.39	31.7	71.54	69.49	24.71	59.2	38.7	16.2	n/a	12.92	n/a	21.78	n/a
2005	21.31	22.55	13.91	67.25	73.78	45.54	53.2	45.3	13.7	n/a	13.24	n/a	16.62	n/a
2003	32.06	37.53	28.26	71.41	73	29.46	47	53	12.9	n/a	13.82	n/a	17.98	n/a
2002	26.98	35.86	36.92	n/a	n/a	27.55	40	60	12.1	n/a	10.58	n/a	20.69	n/a

Sources: GEM data (https://www.gemconsortium.org/data), Gao et al. (2008)

and 74% believe that entrepreneurs are well respected and enjoy high status within the Chinese society. The adult population also consistently perceive entrepreneurial opportunities positively. In the meantime, the number of people who are confident with their entrepreneurial capabilities has gone down and those who are more fearful of entrepreneurial failure have gone up. Worryingly, China scored −0.15 in the Entrepreneurial Spirit Index and was in the bottom half of the global ranking (GEM Global Entrepreneurship Monitor 2018). The Entrepreneurial Spirit Index is designated to capture a country's relative standing of score derived from three underlying variables (entrepreneurial awareness, opportunity perception and entrepreneurial self-efficacy). Countries with higher factor score are those with high value of the three underlying variables. The low score of entrepreneurial spirit is likely to be a problem, as lower numbers of people think about starting businesses.

Third, however, the rate of entrepreneurial activities has been declining in recent years, apparently echoing the slowing-down of the country's economic growth as a whole. Specifically, 2015 turned out to be a watershed for Chinese entrepreneurship when the TEA rate for China fell below the global average TEA rate for the first time. China's ranking in the global TEA has since dropped to 25th among the 49 countries surveyed in 2018. In another measure of entrepreneurship, established business ownership, which indicates the sustainability of start-ups, peaked in 2009 at 17.2% and has since gone on a downward trend. Established business ownership in 2018 was only 3.2%.

Fourth, changes in the quality of Chinese entrepreneurship over time are mixed. On the one hand, opportunity-motivated entrepreneurship first overtook necessity-motivated entrepreneurship in 2005. After a few years' consolidation opportunity-motivated entrepreneurship has firmly taken hold and become the driving force of Chinese entrepreneurship since 2009. This change matters. People who pursue the entrepreneurial dream, because of opportunity rather than necessity, are found to be more prepared, growth-minded, and are more likely to create more jobs and have higher impact (Hessels, Van Gelderen, and Thurik 2008). In a sense, the change underlines the dynamism of the Chinese economy. Also, there has been a consistent improvement from 2011 to 2018 in the extent to which entrepreneurs are innovative, i.e., introducing products that are new to some or all customers and that are offered by few or no competitors. On the other hand, levels of high-growth entrepreneurship as measured by high job creation expectations are declining, dropping by about 15 percentage points from 35% in 2015 to 20.8% in 2018.

Fifth, women entrepreneurs are a force to be reckoned with, despite that men are more likely to be involved in entrepreneurial activity than women as observed in most countries. The percentage of female 18–64 population who are either a nascent entrepreneur or owner-manager of a new business in China, as divided by the equivalent percentage for their male counterparts, is consistently higher. As compared with their international counterparts, Chinese women are more entrepreneurial. Women in China are also proportionately as likely as men to be opportunity-motivated. However, the percentage of women starting businesses is alarmingly declining. It has gone down from the peak of 22.4% in 2011 to 9.2% in 2018.

Sixth, Chinese employees do not appear to play an important role in corporate entrepreneurship. The average rate of entrepreneurial employee activity (EEA), which measures employees' involvement in activities such as developing or launching new goods or services or setting up a new business unit, new establishment or subsidiary, was merely 1.15% in China from 2011 to 2018. Proper EEA is essential for business sustainability and renewal through the successful introduction of new products or services or setting up new businesses. China's EEA rates are not only consistently low but also substantially lower than the global average rate (1.0% compared with 3.85 in 2018).

Seventh, the strengths of China's entrepreneurial framework conditions, consisting of social, cultural, political and economic dimensions, are not consistent and balanced. As can be seen in Figure 1, the survey data of China in 2018 suggest that the country's entrepreneurship environment is strong in physical infrastructure, services and internal market dynamics but is only moderate in all other aspects, which have never scored higher than 3 in the range of 1–5.

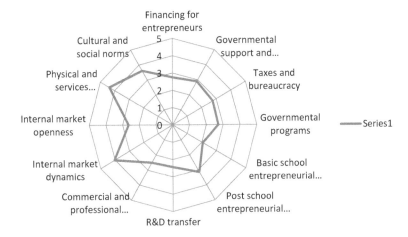

Figure 1. Entrepreneurship framework conditions in China in 2018.
Sources: GEM data (https://www.gemconsortium.org/data)

These seven facts, which are either essential contextual elements themselves or the outcomes of the contextual influences, provide a rich flavour of the development of entrepreneurship in China. Contextualization in Chinese entrepreneurship research echoes the recent calls to make the taken-for-granted background conditions or contexts of entrepreneurship visible in order to advance our knowledge of where and how entrepreneurship happens (Anderson and Gaddefors 2017; Welter 2011; Zahra 2007; Zahra, Wright, and Abdelgawad 2014b). Anderson and Gaddefors (2016), Anderson and Gaddefors (2017) argue that context offers potential for explaining the difficult questions around the 'how' issue of entrepreneurship and the entrepreneurial dynamics arising from the interplay between the entrepreneurial self and the circumstances they encounter.

Yet, context is a slippery term that may mean different things to different researchers. Welter (2011) defines context as situations or environments that are external to the respective phenomenon and enable or constrain it. He follows Johns (2006) to further distinguish the contexts for entrepreneurship into omnibus and discrete context dimensions. Omnibus context refers to a broad perspective, concerning who, what, when, where and why, while discrete context refers to specific contextual variables. Zahra et al. (2014b) define context in the broadest sense as the natural settings in which the researched enterprises origin, form, function and achieve outcomes. Similarly, Anderson and Gaddefors (2017) define contextualization as considering entrepreneurship 'in relation to the situation in which it happens or exists' (p.5).

While it is important to have a consensus on the definition of context in entrepreneurship research, it is equally important for entrepreneurship researchers to agree on framework and key components of context. In his influential paper, Welter (2011) draws on insights from Whetten (1989) to propose a framework for accounting for the entrepreneurial 'when' context and the 'where' context. 'When' refers to temporal and historical impacts on the nature and extent of today's entrepreneurship and changes in the respective contexts over time. 'Where' refers to the different locational contexts in which entrepreneurship happens. Welter (2011) further distinguished the 'where' dimension into four main types: business, social, spatial, and institutional. Alternatively, Zahra et al. (2014b) proposed a schema from a strategic entrepreneurship perspective that includes five dimensions of entrepreneurial context, namely temporal dimension, industry and market dimension, spatial dimension, social dimension, and organizational, ownership and governance dimension. From the Chinese management research perspective, Child (2009) makes an important point that 'an ability to compare national contexts through a common classificatory framework is essential for addressing the issue of how exclusively different China is and whether, therefore, a distinctive Chinese theory of management is required' (p.63). Consistent with his argument for cross-country comparison of context, Child (2009) proposes a framework that identifies components of the Chinese contexts in which management operates for purposes of comparing China with other countries. There are three contextual components in the framework, namely material systems (i.e. economic systems and technology systems), ideational systems (i.e. cultural values and rationales, religious values, and political values), and institutional outcomes (i.e. government, intermediate institutions, and conformity to international regulations and standards). The context frameworks that have been proposed thus far, despite inconsistency due to their respective standpoints, provide good templates for understanding how researchers have contextualized Chinese entrepreneurship in their studies.

An overview of approaches to contextualization in Chinese entrepreneurship research

Contextualization in Chinese entrepreneurship research is not without challenge. It has to reconcile the inherent tensions between the theorization and the contextualization of research arising from using 'borrowed' models that are grounded in assumptions often reflecting other phenomena (Zahra 2007). Not surprisingly there has been a similar debate on contextualization in Chinese management research. Consistent with insights from leading Chinese management scholars (e.g. Tsui 2006; Child 2009; Meyer 2015), there are three approaches to contextualization in Chinese entrepreneurship research. The first is the 'outside in' approach. It is to apply and test existing entrepreneurship theories in the Chinese context so as to ascertain whether a modified theory that is applicable to other parts of the world is capable of explaining Chinese entrepreneurship. Advances in entrepreneurship research over the past decades offer plenty of opportunities for the adoption of this approach. This is a necessary step for the development of the general theory of entrepreneurship. What is less satisfactory in Chinese entrepreneurship research, as Su et al. (2015a) revealed, is that researchers tended to adopt an existing theory without paying sufficient attention to a Chinese context where the concepts and relationships as stated in the theory do not necessarily apply. The second is the 'inside out' approach. This is to study either a China-specific entrepreneurship phenomenon or a phenomenon that is familiar to the non-Chinese scholar but manifests itself differently in the Chinese context. Additionally, this is an approach that draws inspiration from Chinese cultural heritages to theorise such entrepreneurship phenomena. This resonates with What Tsui (2004) advocates the 'indigenous research' approach. The third is the 'comparison' approach. This is to compare context and entrepreneurship between China and other countries so that claims of Chinese context uniqueness can be put to the test.

Central to these approaches is the question how entrepreneurship researchers can effectively use the Chinese context for their theoretical development and empirical research? Despite a number of literature reviews on Chinese entrepreneurship research (Li and Matlay 2006; Yang and Li 2008; Ahlstrom and Ding 2014; Su et al. 2015a; He, Lu, and Qian 2018), we have not yet seen one that comprehensively assesses the current state of contextualization in Chinese entrepreneurship research. Something similar to Jia, You & Du's (2012) review on Chinese context and theoretical contributions to management and organization research would do the Chinese entrepreneurship research community an excellent service. As a first small step, we use Welter's (2011) entrepreneurship context framework and carry out a mapping exercise. We do not suggest that this framework is superior to others. Nonetheless, the more generic entrepreneurship focus of the framework serves our purpose. The mapping exercise is not intended to be a systematic literature review but rather a snapshot of how extant research has addressed the context of entrepreneurship in China in the last 20 years. To achieve this, we first conducted a search of the electronic database Web of Science Core Collection over the period of 2000–2019, using the Boolean search terms 'chin* AND entrepreneur*' in the title of the papers in English. The search resulted in 346 papers. The number of papers reduced to 295 after conference proceeding papers were excluded. The abstracts of these papers were then read so to filter out sources that were not directly connected with contexts of entrepreneurship in China, namely the use of context-less China data to test an existing entrepreneurship theory. This led to the establishment of a sample of 69 papers. Each paper in this sample was then reviewed to identify the types of context it addresses. Table 2 presents the results of the assessment.

Not surprisingly, an outside-in approach dominates contextualization of Chinese entrepreneurship research with a focus on institutional context. Context that is considered a 'variable' or discrete context features strongly in the papers. Such discrete contexts include institutional profile (Tang and Tang 2012), ownership arrangements (Zhang et al. 2016b), political networks (Su et al. 2015b; Zhou 2013), political participation (Chen et al. 2012; Feng, Johansson, and Zhang 2014, 2015; Talavera, Xiong, and Xiong 2012), community-level institutional trust (Zhang 2015b), and institutional environments (Lin and Si 2014). Institutional context is also examined as an omnibus context. Interesting thematic institutional contexts include party-state-enterprise relations (Fuller 2010; Lu and Tao 2010; Sun, Wright, and Mellahi 2010; Cho 2011; Li et al. 2012; Liou and Tsai 2017); urban entrepreneurial states (Chien 2013); institutional entrepreneurship (Lee and Hung 2014; Liu et al. 2018b); policy entrepreneurship (Hammond 2013; Zheng and Hu 2018; Zhu 2013, 2016); institutional change (Eesley, Li, and Yang 2016; Zhang and White 2016); state-led strategic entrepreneurship (Sun 2015); institutional boundaries (Chen and Touve 2011); non-munificent institutional environment (Bhatt, Qureshi, and Riaz 2017); socialist imprinting (Dai et al. 2018); and compound (institutional) voids (Fish, Parris, and Troilo 2017).

Research on social context displays commendable efforts to apply the 'inside-out' approach to contextualizing. Such works include Confucian social model (Li and Liang 2015), Confucian Ren-Yi Wisdom (Zhu 2015) and Zhong-yong thinking (Ma, Gu, and Liu 2017). Intriguing studies have also introduced religion and faith into contextualization such as faith and trust of protestant

Table 2. Overview of contextualization in Chinese entrepreneurship research.

Social context
  Stage model of guanxi (Guo and Miller 2010); moral sentiment (Yiu et al. 2014b); Confucian social model (Li and Liang 2015); relational and institutional embeddedness (Avgerou and Li 2013); Confucian Ren-Yi Wisdom (Zhu 2015); religious and political involvement (Du 2017); prominent business association (Ma, Rui, and Wu 2015); reconfiguration of gender hierarchies (Wallis 2015); Zhong-yong thinking (Ma, Gu, and Liu 2017); mentoring (Ting, Feng, and Qin 2017); faith and trust of protestant entrepreneurs (Tong and Yang 2016)
Spatial context
  Urban entrepreneurial states (Chien 2013); regional institutions (Zhou 2014); local state entrepreneurial governance (Xue and Wu 2015); local government entrepreneurship (Xun et al. 2016); embeddedness in clusters (Fu 2016)
Institutional context
  State controlling ownership (Li et al. 2012); party affiliation (Lu and Tao 2010); urban entrepreneurial states (Chien 2013); entrepreneur-politician alliances (Sun, Wright, and Mellahi 2010); institutional entrepreneurship (Lee and Hung 2014); legal environments, political factors (Fuller 2010); co-evolution of entrepreneurial action and the institutional structure (Zhang and White 2016); policy entrepreneurship (Hammond 2013; Zheng and Hu 2018; Zhu 2013; Zhu 2016); institutional Change in Universities (Eesley, Li, and Yang 2016); dueling logics (Yiu et al. 2014a); state-led strategic entrepreneurship (Sun 2015); institutional boundaries (Chen and Touve 2011); a rent-seeking society (Dong, Wei, and Zhang 2016); network "fit by founding" (Zhang et al. 2016a); non-munificent institutional environment (Bhatt, Qureshi, and Riaz 2017); socialist imprinting (Dai et al. 2018); compound (institutional) voids (Fish, Parris, and Troilo 2017); the state-market complex (Cho 2011); universities as institutional entrepreneurs (Liu et al. 2018b); dual role of cadres and entrepreneurs (Liou and Tsai 2017); managerial task allocation (Guo, Jiang, and Xu 2017); contingency model of CSR (Song et al. 2016); property right (Wang 2012)
Temporal context
  Stage model of guanxi (Guo and Miller 2010); the role of early network events (Burt and Burzynska 2017; Burt and Opper 2017); dynamics of entrepreneurial emergence (Atherton and Newman 2016; Dai, Wang, and Liu 2019); changing role of guanxi (Liu et al. 2018b; Peng, Duysters, and Sadowski 2016); emergence of the digital entrepreneurial ecosystem (Du et al. 2018); entrepreneurship attributes (Cinar, Du, and Hienkel 2018)
Discrete
  Institutional profile (Tang and Tang 2012); ownership arrangements (Zhang et al. 2016b); political networking (Su et al. 2015b; Zhou 2013); political participation (Chen et al. 2012; Feng, Johansson, and Zhang 2014, Feng, Johansson, and Zhang 2015;Talavera, Xiong, and Xiong 2012); community-level institutional trust (Zhang 2015b); transitional stage (Bernhofer and Han 2014); guanxi networks (Su and Sohn 2015; Troilo and Zhang 2012); institutional environments (Lin and Si 2014); Chinese markets (Zhao and Parry 2012); local conditions (Li 2017); health insurance (Liu and Zhang 2018)
Comparison
  contrasting forms of network disadvantages in China and the West (Burt 2019); women entrepreneurship in China and Vietnam (Zhu et al. 2018)

entrepreneurs (Tong and Yang 2016) and religious and political involvement (Du 2017). Research has also touched upon the contexts of cultural values regarding embeddedness and gender such as relational and institutional embeddedness (Avgerou and Li 2013) and reconfiguration of gender hierarchies (Wallis 2015). However, contextualization in this regard remains limited.

With regards to spatial context, the papers we reviewed straddle the 'outside-in' and 'inside-out' approaches to some extent. Local government entrepreneurship (Chien 2013; Xue and Wu 2015; Xun et al. 2016) understandably features most strongly as research tries to capture the characteristics and impacts of decentralization of state capitalism in China. Furthermore, local governments can play an essential role in entrepreneurship and regional development (Liu and Huang 2018). The number of research on temporal context is modest and focuses on two separate themes, namely changing role of guanxi (Guo and Miller 2010; Peng, Duysters, and Sadowski 2016; Burt and Opper 2017; Liu et al. 2018c) and dynamics of entrepreneurial emergence (Atherton and Newman 2016; Cinar, Du, and Hienkel 2018; Dai, Wang, and Liu 2019). Du et al.'s (2018) recent research on emergence of the digital entrepreneurial ecosystem captures the impact of Internet revolution on entrepreneurship in China.

By far, the third approach, i.e. comparison between China and other countries in entrepreneurship context, is the most under-researched area. Nonetheless, Burt's (2019) eminent work that contrasts forms of network disadvantages in China and the West not only shows how this should be done in highest academic rigour but also points to a fertile area, in which this line of research can explore further.

Clearly, knowledge gap on Chinese entrepreneurship remains stubbornly large, in particular from the above mentioned three approaches concerning what specific Chinese contextual factors and how they impact entrepreneurial activities, behaviour and outcomes. Using China as an example, Bruton, Zahra, and Cai (2018) argue that scholars need shift from the US-dominated model of entrepreneurship in academic research to reflect better the variety and diversity of entrepreneurial activities around the globe. They further call for indigenous theory to investigate local settings of entrepreneurship, which not only researchers but also editors and reviewers should effort on. 'indigenous research', as Tsui (2004, 501) defines, is 'scientific studies of local phenomena using local language, local subjects, and locally meaningful constructs, with the aim to test or build theories that can explain and predict … phenomena in the local social cultural context'. By scientific studies, she emphasizes the need for high-quality indigenous research as judged by the scientific community. Indigenous Chinese management research is still at its initial stage of trial and formation (Zhang 2015a).

Preview of papers in the special issue

It is undoubtedly helpful to advocate 'indigenous research' (or the 'inside-out' approach) to develop the indigenous theories of entrepreneurship. Nevertheless, contextualization in Chinese entrepreneurship research has a much broader scope and the 'outside-in' and 'comparison' approaches to contextualization merit equal attention. Consequently, this special issue for Entrepreneurship and Regional Development is intended to plug a gap and advance our understanding of Chinese entrepreneurship towards the direction of contextualization by taking some specific contextual factors into consideration, which have largely been neglected by previous studies. Below we will explain the paper selection process and provide a brief preview of the five papers included in this special issue.

We received 47 submissions in the first round. After the initial review conducted by the three guest editors, 12 papers were selected and their authors were invited to attend the paper development workshop held at Wuhan University in April 2017. Professor Alistair Anderson, editor of Entrepreneurship and Regional Development, and Professor Garry Bruton were invited to give keynote speeches and provided insightful feedback and guidance for revisions to authors who participated the workshop, along with the three guest editors. After the workshop, we received 10 revised manuscripts from the participant authors by the set and extended deadlines. We also received two more manuscripts from authors who did not participate in the workshop. All 12 manuscripts went through rounds of double-blind review process, resulting in five papers being finally accepted.

These five papers help advance a more nuanced understanding of entrepreneurship in China from five diverse perspectives. Each article addresses a specific and significant aspect of Chinese entrepreneurship by using a unique conceptual framework and methodology or data set, respectively. More importantly, these articles achieve critical acclaims by enriching our understanding of various approaches to contextualization in Chinese entrepreneurship. They examine China's entrepreneurial ecosystems, sub-national institutions, entrepreneurs' global mindset and firms' international entrepreneurial orientation, migrant workers' entrepreneurship, and government entrepreneurship policies, respectively.

Li, Cai, Bruton and Sheng (this issue) provide probably a first systematic review of literature on entrepreneurial ecosystems in the leading international journals and also in the leading Chinese journals from the time period of 2000 to 2017. By employing an open code methodology to classify each of the identified 85 articles by theme, they find four principal themes in entrepreneurial ecosystem research: nature, networks, institutions, and dynamics. Articles in the nature theme address the definitions and component parts of entrepreneurial ecosystems. Articles in the networks theme examine interactions of components within the entrepreneurial ecosystem. Based on the institutional theory, the third theme of articles examine institutions and their central role in shaping entrepreneurial ecosystems. Articles in the fourth theme concern the dynamics of ecosystem with a particular focus on how structures can support and reinforce the ecosystem creation. Furthermore, they suggest four broad questions for future research in China. First, how do institutional variations in geographic regions affect entrepreneurial ecosystems? Second, what is the role of government in shaping the formation and evolution of entrepreneurial ecosystems? Third, how do entrepreneurial ecosystem components interact dynamically towards reconciled goals? Fourth, how can different entities develop coopetition relationship to create shared values in the entrepreneurial ecosystems.

Chen, Li and Paik (this issue) address an under-researched question as to how sub-national institutions affect the diversification of small and medium-sized enterprises (SMEs) into new businesses in China. Adopting an institutional framework, they assess the impact of sub-national institutions on SMEs' strategic behaviour. More specifically, they examine how two important aspects of sub-national institutions, the dominance of state-owned enterprises (SOEs) and development of market systems, influence diversification. Using data derived from both a large-scale national survey on SMEs and the National Economic Research Institute (NERI) Index of Marketization on China's provinces, they find that in provinces dominated by SOEs, SMEs were less likely to diversify into new businesses. They also find that the development of market systems tended to reduce the odds of diversification for SMEs that primarily served local markets and lower the likelihood of unrelated diversification. The study shed new light on the relationship between diversification and institutions in strategic entrepreneurship.

Lin, Cao and Cottam (this issue) respond to Chinese SMEs' increasing international networking and knowledge acquisition activities and set out to investigate the roles and joint influence of their leaders' global mindset and firms' international entrepreneurial orientation in those processes. Using survey data from a sample of 208 SMEs in China, they find that both leader's global mindset and firm's international entrepreneurial orientation have a direct and significantly positive impact on Chinese SMEs' international networking and knowledge acquisition activities. They also find that leader's global mindset has an indirect effect on the firm's internationalization activities through the mediation of firm entrepreneurial orientation, and eventually influences firm-level performance. These findings help advance knowledge of the role of business leaders in shaping organization-wide entrepreneurial orientation, behaviours and subsequent firm performance.

Duan, Yin, Xu and Wu (this issue) explore how the push factor of job demands and the pull factor of entrepreneurial resources influence the intention of Chinese migrant workers to return to their hometown and engage in entrepreneurial activities. From an analysis of a sample of 302 Chinese migrant workers, they find that job demands on migrant workers increase their job burnout and in turn increase return-home entrepreneurial intention. They also find that entrepreneurial resources of return-home migrant workers increase their entrepreneurial conviction that in turn positively influences their entrepreneurial intention. In addition, they find that intergenerational differences positively moderate the job demands–job burnout–entrepreneurial intention relationship and negatively moderate the entrepreneurial resources–entrepreneurial conviction–entrepreneurial intention relationship. Duan et al.'s study reveals the importance of examining push and pull factors concurrently, and emphasizes the intergenerational differences in explaining the return-home entrepreneurial intention of Chinese migrant workers.

Dai, Arndt and Liao (this issue) address the questions of what types of entrepreneurs are more likely to 'stay tuned' to government policies and whether it pays off to align with government policies. From the lenses of opportunity recognition and the institution-based view, they examine the link between the pursuit of policy-induced opportunities and firm performance. Based on an analysis of a sample of 3,284 privately owned Chinese firms in 31 regions/provinces in China, they find that entrepreneurs who have past working experience within the government are more likely to stay alert to government policies involving entrepreneurial opportunities, which leads to increased entrepreneurial activities and, ultimately, firm performance. This study enriches our understanding of the importance of policy-induced opportunities arising from changes in entrepreneurship framework condition and government intervention. It also sheds new light on how entrepreneurial alertness to government policies may influence firm performance.

Some future research directions

Despite the considerable progress, not least in the rapidly increasing volume of research on entrepreneurship in China, there still remain largely unanswered questions, and even 'puzzles' (Huang 2010; Zhou 2011; He, Lu, and Qian 2018; Bruton, Zahra, and Cai 2018) left unaddressed by the special issue papers. Some questions are related to the particular Chinese context, while others are associated with the new developments in China, both of which can have an impact on entrepreneurship as indicated earlier. Therefore, there is a need to broaden the scope by taking into consideration a more holistic and inclusive view of wider and richer contextual factors. We have identified four contextual parameters that are important to the next stage of entrepreneurship research. The research gap becomes prominent given the significance of these unique Chinese contextual factors in the entrepreneurial process and performance.

First, research needs to explore in greater depth the role of government in entrepreneurship (Liu and Huang 2018), as implied by Dai et al. (this issue). 'In China, the government is an integral part of the ecosystems that spawns and sustains entrepreneurship' (Bruton, Zahra, and Cai 2018). In recent years, the Chinese government has implemented a variety of policies to encourage and facilitate entrepreneurial activities as entrepreneurship is considered one key driving force of sustained economic development (He, Lu, and Qian 2018). Since 2015, 'mass entrepreneurship and innovation' has emerged as the new national economic development strategy. Entrepreneurship development in China has been applauded for entering a golden era (He, Lu, and Qian 2018, 1). However, it is not yet known if such policies have been effective.

China's stagnating TEA rate since 2015 as revealed by China GEM data is such a puzzling phenomenon. In his keynote speech at the 2014 Summer Davos held in Tianjin, China, Chinese Premier Li Keqiang first articulated the country's new initiative of mass entrepreneurship and innovation (MEI) as twin engines to revitalise economic growth. The Chinese government quickly beefed up its support to MEI in 'Opinions on Several Policy Measures to Boost Mass Entrepreneurship and Innovation (MEI)' issued by State Council in May 2015. Evidence is abundant that enthusiastic local governments have topped up central government's incentive measures with generous entrepreneurship support. Why have such policies and support not spurred more people in China into entrepreneurial action? In relevance to Dai et al.'s study (this issue), are the policies only effective on those entrepreneurs who have work experience in the government? Why do people feel less capable of exploiting entrepreneurial opportunities and more afraid of failure? Why are women less enthusiastic with entrepreneurship? To answer these questions, we need greater knowledge and understanding of how entrepreneurship policies are formulated and implemented. We need to open up the black box of policy-making in order to understand the context through which entrepreneurship policies are coordinated and impacts are trickled down.

Research on the role of government also needs to link it to the quality of entrepreneurship. One of the myths revealed in the GEM China surveys is the declining high-growth entrepreneurship. Entrepreneurs vary in their innovativeness (Li, Qu, and Huang 2018). In his provocative piece, Shane (2009) argues that encouraging more people to become entrepreneurs is a bad public policy. He contends that many entrepreneurship policies actually lead people to start marginal businesses that are likely to fail, have little economic impact, and generate little employment. China's MEI initiative is an entrepreneurship policy experiment on an unprecedented scale. Will MEI's outcomes prove Shane wrong or add more weight to Shane's argument? Does the stagnation of entrepreneurship hamper high-growth entrepreneurship in China? Does the unbalanced entrepreneurial ecosystem as revealed early on constrain high-growth entrepreneurship? Or does generous entrepreneurship support crowd out high-growth entrepreneurship? All these are intriguing questions that beg answers. The problems and obstacles identified could have implications for other countries that endeavour to promote entrepreneurship.

Second, research needs to explore the impact of the development of Chinese version of globalization on Chinese entrepreneurship. Chinese government has been vigorously promoting the 'Belt and Road Initiative' since 2013. Significantly, China's outbound FDI (foreign direct investment) since 2014 has overtaken inward FDI. Initially, Chinese FDI focused on natural resource-seeking in developing countries (Lehmann 2015). Chinese entrepreneurs are now setting up processing and production facilities to add value to raw materials in developing countries, for example, Africa (Ado and Osabutey 2018). Such international entrepreneurship can not only make important contributions to financial wealth creation (Coviello, McDougall, and Oviatt 2011) and economic development in these countries but also help upgrade Africa in the global value chain (Ado and Osabutey 2018) and even affect global sustainable well-being (Zahra, Newey, and Li 2014a). Nevertheless, most countries along the Belt and Road routes are least developed countries often coupled with underdeveloped institutional systems. Chinese entrepreneurs tend to lack country familiarity, defined as the sense of knowing about a country (Clark, Li, and Shepherd 2018) in these countries. In the meantime, more recent Chinese outbound FDI has gone in substantial sums to developed countries with focus on strategic resource-seeking, including in acquisitions of high tech and high brand companies (Lehmann 2015). How do Chinese entrepreneurs identify and explore opportunities? Do Chinese values influence their decision-making process? How do they overcome newness and liability as foreign firms? What determines their survival and success in unfamiliar countries?

Third, research needs to investigate the impact of urbanization on Chinese entrepreneurship. It has been argued that China's economic transition is a three-driver process, namely marketization, globalization, and decentralization. As a result, the dynamic institutional context is critical for entrepreneurial activities (He, Lu, and Qian 2018). In fact, this transition is coupled by the process of urbanization with a huge volume of population moving to the urban areas. According to Liu et al. (2018a), by 2013, more than 80% of the 240 million migrants in urban China were rural-to-urban migrants. However, there is little research, probably with the exception of Liu et al. (2018a), that specifically addresses internal migrant entrepreneurship. Using the 2012 and 2014 Chinese Labour-force Dynamics Survey (CLDS) data, they find that rural migrants in China are more likely to engage in entrepreneurial activities than their urban counterparts who live in cities and their rural counterparts who remain in the rural areas. However, available research seems to suggest that as 'outsiders' to the host locality (Rath and Kloosterman, 2000; Canello 2016), migrant entrepreneurs face significant disadvantages relative to local entrepreneurs, e.g., the active hostility of both the local government (Rath and Kloosterman, 2000) and local entrepreneurs (Canello 2016). This may have contributed to their further finding that migrant-owned businesses are over-represented in the mature sectors (wholesale, retail, and food) (Liu et al. 2018a). Indeed, as Liu et al. (2018a) admitted, little research has systemically examined migrant entrepreneurship dynamics in the Chinese context. Therefore, it would be interesting for future research to investigate how migrant entrepreneurs overcome barriers in the entrepreneurial process, from opportunity identification, resource acquisition to creation of new ventures towards success. Such research is not only important to China but also other emerging economies, such as India and Indonesia, which are witnessing large-scale movement of domestic migrants, many of whom have the potential to engage with entrepreneurial activities (Bhavnani and Lacina 2017).

Fourth, research is needed to examine the influence of digital technology on entrepreneurship in China. Digital technologies and infrastructure can be external enablers of new venture creation and growth (Nambisan 2017; von Briel, Davidsson, and Recker 2018; Autio et al. 2018). This is probably more significant in China (Du et al. 2018). China has the world's largest number of internet users and is already an internet leader in many ways. In addition, China has built considerable strengths in the IT industry with unique Chinese characteristics in terms of customer-focused and efficiency-driven (McKinsey Global Institute, 2015). China is also able to take advantage of having a minimal technology legacy and leapfrog into new technologies, mobile payments, on demand transportation, and social networks (China Daily, 16 November, 2016). In fact, China's technology industry, particularly its mobile businesses, has in some ways pulled ahead of the United States (New York Times, 9 January, 2019). For example, China is the world's leader in 'financial technology' (Fintech, internet-based banking and investment), which helps to build a more efficient banking system that benefits consumers and small businesses (Economist, 25 Feburary, 2017). Growing up as 'digital natives', the Chinese younger generation born after 1990 are constantly connected, and know information technology so well (Zhang et al. 2014). WeChat, a Chinese multi-purpose app developed by Tencent is the equivalent of WhatsApp plus Facebook plus PayPal plus Uber plus GrubHub plus many other things with more than 1 billion monthly active users around the world. Integrated, WeChat Pay provides merchants with an advanced mobile payment method and a platform which enables long-term communications and customized customer services for billions of Chinese consumers (New York Times, 9 January 2019). As the most widely used social network and one of the most popular mobile payment platforms among Chinese people, Wechat has 800 million monthly active users (China Daily, 23 January 2019). Against this background, how can and will such developments influence entrepreneurship? Will such extra-ordinary expansion of digital technology and online platform enable entrepreneurship by lowering market entry barrier and easier access to customers? Will this lead to development of informal economy, i.e., businesses are not registered with government regulatory authorities? Can such digital platforms facilitate cross-border businesses?

Note

1. Total early-stage entrepreneurial activity (TEA) is defined as the percentage of the adult population aged 18–64 years who are in the process of starting a business (a nascent entrepreneur) or started a business less than 42 months old before the survey took place (owner-manager of a new business) (GEM Global Entrepreneurship Monitor 2018, 21).

Acknowledgments

The guest editors would like to thank Alistair Anderson, Editor of *Entrepreneurship & Regional Development*, for his support of this special issue. We would like to express our appreciation to the Economics and Management School of Wuhan University and Lancaster China Management Centre for their sponsorship of the workshop held at Wuhan University. We also would like to thank Alistair Anderson, Garry Bruton and Xielin Liu for their keynote speeches at the workshop. We acknowledge valuable contribution from the reviewers, without whose kind help, this special issue would not have been possible: David Ahlstrom, Garry Bruton, Yunzhou Du, Wei Han, Shuangfa Huang, Caleb Kwong, Frank McDonald, Michael Mustafa, Lee Li, Xiaoying Li, Weiwen Li, Xielin Liu, Yipeng Liu, Yuan Lu, Danny Soetanto, Jing Su, and Haibing Yang.

Disclosure statement

No potential conflict of interest was reported by the authors.

References

Ado, A., and E. L. C. Osabutey. 2018. "Africa-China Cooperation: Potential Shared Interests and Strategic Partnerships?." *AIB Insights* 4.

Ahlstrom, D., and S. J. Ding. 2014. "Entrepreneurship in China: An Overview." *International Small Business Journal* 32 (6): 610–618. doi:10.1177/0266242613517913.

Anderson, A. R., and J. Gaddefors. 2016. "Entrepreneurship as a Community Phenomenon: Reconnecting Meanings and Place." *International Journal of Entrepreneurship and Small Business Development* 28 (4): 504–518. doi:10.1504/IJESB.2016.077576.

Anderson, A. R., and J. Gaddefors. 2017. "Entrepreneurship and Context: Is Entrepreneurship Research Out of Context? Dilemmas with (non) Contextualised Views of Entrepreneurship." *Journal of Asia Entrepreneurship and Sustainability* 13 (4): 3–9.

Atherton, A., and A. Newman. 2016. "The Emergence of the Private Entrepreneur in Reform Era China: Re-birth of an Earlier Tradition, or a More Recent Product of Development and Change?." *Business History* 58 (3): 319–344. doi:10.1080/00076791.2015.1122702.

Atherton, A., and A. Newman. 2017. *Entrepreneurship in China: The Emergence of the Private Sector*. London: Routledge.

Autio, E, S Nambisan, LDW Thomas, and M. Wright. 2018. "Digital Affordances, Spatial Affordances, and The Genesis Of Entrepreneurial Ecosystems." *Strategic Entrepreneurship Journal* 12 (1): 72-95. doi: 10.1002/sej.1266.

Avgerou, C., and B. Li. 2013. "Relational and Institutional Embeddedness of Web-enabled Entrepreneurial Networks: Case Studies of Netrepreneurs in China." *Information Systems Journal* 23 (4): 329–350. doi:10.1111/isj.2013.23.issue-4.

Baron, R. A., J. Tang, Z. Tang, and Y. Zhang. 2018. "Bribes as Entrepreneurial Actions: Why Underdog Entrepreneurs Feel Compelled to Use Them." *Journal of Business Venturing* 33 (6): 679–690. doi:10.1016/j.jbusvent.2018.04.011.

Bernhofer, L., and Z. Han. 2014. "Contextual Factors and Their Effects on Future Entrepreneurs in China: A Comparative Study of Entrepreneurial Intentions." *International Journal of Technology Management* 65 (1–4): 125–150. doi:10.1504/IJTM.2014.060955.

Bhatt, B., I. Qureshi, and S. Riaz. 2017. "Social Entrepreneurship in Non-munificent Institutional Environments and Implications for Institutional Work: Insights from China." *Journal of Business Ethics* 1–26.

Bhavnani, R. R., and B. Lacina. 2017. "Fiscal Federalism at Work? Central Responses to Internal Migration in India." *World Development*. 93:: 236–248. doi:10.1016/j.worlddev.2016.12.018.

Bruton, G. D., D. Ahlstrom, and K. Obloj. 2008. "Entrepreneurship in Emerging Economies: Where are We Today and Where Should the Research Go in the Future." *Entrepreneurship Theory and Practice* 32 (1): 1–14. doi:10.1111/j.1540-6520.2007.00213.x.

Bruton, G. D., S. A. Zahra, and L. Cai. 2018. "Examining Entrepreneurship through Indigenous Lenses." *Entrepreneurship Theory and Practice* 42 (3): 351–361. doi:10.1177/1042258717741129.

Burt, R. S. 2019. "Network Disadvantaged Entrepreneurs: Density, Hierarchy, and Success in China and the West." *Entrepreneurship Theory and Practice* 43 (1): 19–50. doi:10.1177/1042258718783514.

Burt, R. S., and K. Burzynska. 2017. "Chinese Entrepreneurs, Social Networks, and Guanxi." *Management and Organization Review* 13 (2): 221–260. doi:10.1017/mor.2017.6.

Burt, R. S., and S. Opper. 2017. "Early Network Events in the Later Success of Chinese Entrepreneurs." *Management and Organization Review* 13 (3): 497–537. doi:10.1017/mor.2017.30.

Cai, H., H. Fang, and L. C. Xu. 2011. "Eat, Drink, Firms, and Government: An Investigation of Corruption from the Entertainment and Travel Costs of Chinese Firms." *Journal of Law and Economics* 54 (1): 55–78. doi:10.1086/651201.

Canello, J. 2016. "Migrant Entrepreneurs and Local Networks in Industrial Districts." *Research Policy* 45 (10): 1953–1964. doi:10.1016/j.respol.2016.05.006.

Chen, Y., and D. Touve. 2011. "Conformity, Political Participation, and Economic Rewards: The Case of Chinese Private Entrepreneurs." *Asia Pacific Journal of Management* 28 (3): 529–553. doi:10.1007/s10490-009-9171-2.

Chen, Z., Y. Sun, A. Newman, and W. Xu. 2012. "Entrepreneurs, Organizational Members, Political Participation and Preferential Treatment: Evidence from China." *International Small Business Journal* 30 (8): 873–889. doi:10.1177/0266242611407534.

Chien, S. S. 2013. "New Local State Power through Administrative restructuring–A Case Study of post-Mao China County-level Urban Entrepreneurialism in Kunshan." *Geoforum* 46: 103–112. doi:10.1016/j.geoforum.2012.12.015.

Child, J. 2009. "Context, Comparison, and Methodology in Chinese Management Research." *Management and Organization Review* 5 (1): 57–73. doi:10.1111/j.1740-8784.2008.00136.x.

Cho, M. Y. 2011. ""we are the State": An Entrepreneurial Mission to Serve the People in Harbin, Northeast China." *Modern China* 37 (4): 422–455. doi:10.1177/0097700411400057.

Cinar, E. M., Y. Du, and T. Hienkel. 2018. "Chinese Entrepreneurship Attributes: A Comparative GEM Data Analysis." *Journal of Entrepreneurship in Emerging Economies* 10 (2): 217–248. doi:10.1108/JEEE-03-2017-0016.

Clark, D. R., D. Li, and D. A. Shepherd. 2018. "Country Familiarity in the Initial Stage of Foreign Market Selection." *Journal of International Business Studies* 49 (4): 442–472. doi:10.1057/s41267-017-0099-3.

Coviello, N. E., P. P. McDougall, and B. M. Oviatt. 2011. "The Emergence, Advance and Future of International Entrepreneurship research—An Introduction to the Special Forum." *Journal of Business Venturing* 26 (6): 625–631. doi:10.1016/j.jbusvent.2011.07.002.

Dai, S., Y. Wang, and Y. Liu. 2019. "The Emergence of Chinese Entrepreneurs: Social Connections and Innovation." *Journal of Entrepreneurship in Emerging Economies*. doi:10.1108/JEEE-02-2018-0021.

Dai, W., Y. Liu, M. Liao, and Q. Lin. 2018. "How Does Entrepreneurs' Socialist Imprinting Shape Their Opportunity Selection in Transition Economies? Evidence from China's Privately Owned Enterprises." *International Entrepreneurship and Management Journal* 14 (4): 823–856. doi:10.1007/s11365-017-0485-0.

Dong, Z., X. Wei, and Y. Zhang. 2016. "The Allocation of Entrepreneurial Efforts in a Rent-seeking Society: Evidence from China." *Journal of Comparative Economics* 44 (2): 353–371. doi:10.1016/j.jce.2015.02.004.

Du, J., A. Guariglia, and A. Newman. 2015. "Do Social Capital Building Strategies Influence the Financing Behavior of Chinese Private Small and Medium-sized Enterprises?." *Entrepreneurship Theory and Practice* 39 (3): 601–631. doi:10.1111/etap.2015.39.issue-3.

Du, W., S. L. Pan, N. Zhou, and T. Ouyang. 2018. "From a Marketplace of Electronics to a Digital Entrepreneurial Ecosystem (DEE): The Emergence of a Meta-organization in Zhongguancun, China." *Information Systems Journal* 28 (6): 1158–1175. doi:10.1111/isj.12176.

Du, X. 2017. "Religious Belief, Corporate Philanthropy, and Political Involvement of Entrepreneurs in Chinese Family Firms." *Journal of Business Ethics* 142 (2): 385–406. doi:10.1007/s10551-015-2705-2.

Eesley, C., J. B. Li, and D. Yang. 2016. "Does Institutional Change in Universities Influence High-tech Entrepreneurship? Evidence from China's Project 985." *Organization Science* 27 (2): 446–461. doi:10.1287/orsc.2015.1038.

Feng, X., A. C. Johansson, and T. Zhang. 2014. "Political Participation and Entrepreneurial Initial Public Offerings in China." *Journal of Comparative Economics* 42 (2): 269–285. doi:10.1016/j.jce.2014.03.005.

Feng, X., A. C. Johansson, and T. Zhang. 2015. "Mixing Business with Politics: Political Participation by Entrepreneurs in China." *Journal of Banking & Finance* 59: 220–235. doi:10.1016/j.jbankfin.2015.06.009.

Fish, R. J., D. L. Parris, and M. Troilo. 2017. "Compound Voids and Unproductive Entrepreneurship: The Rise of the "english Fever" in China." *Journal of Economic Issues* 51 (1): 163–180. doi:10.1080/00213624.2017.1287506.

Fu, W. 2016. "Industrial Clusters as Hothouses for Nascent Entrepreneurs? the Case of Tianhe Software Park in Guangzhou, China." *The Annals of Regional Science* 57 (1): 253–270. doi:10.1007/s00168-016-0776-3.

Fuller, D. B. 2010. "How Law, Politics and Transnational Networks Affect Technology Entrepreneurship: Explaining Divergent Venture Capital Investing Strategies in China." *Asia Pacific Journal of Management* 27 (3): 445–459. doi:10.1007/s10490-009-9149-0.

Gao, J., Y. Chen, X. B. Li, and Y. F. Jiang. 2008. *Global Entrepreneurship Monitor (GEM) China Report 2007: Entrepreneurial Transition and Employment*. Beijing: Tsinghua University Press.

GEM Global Entrepreneurship Monitor. 2018. *Global Report 2017/18*. Accessed 18 February 2019. http://www.gemconsortium.org/report

Guo, C., and J. K. Miller. 2010. "Guanxi Dynamics and Entrepreneurial Firm Creation and Development in China." *Management and Organization Review* 6 (2): 267–291. doi:10.1111/j.1740-8784.2010.00180.x.

Guo, D., K. Jiang, and C. Xu. 2017. "Institutions and Managerial Task Allocation: Evidence from Chinese Entrepreneurs." *Journal of Human Capital* 11 (3): 397–422. doi:10.1086/692844.

Hammond, D. R. 2013. "Policy Entrepreneurship in China's Response to Urban Poverty." *Policy Studies Journal* 41 (1): 119–146. doi:10.1111/psj.12005.

He, C., J. Lu, and H. Qian. 2018. "Entrepreneurship in China." *Small Business Economics*. doi:10.1007/s11187-017-9972-5.

Hessels, J., M. Van Gelderen, and R. Thurik. 2008. "Entrepreneurial Aspirations, Motivations, and Their Drivers." *Small Business Economics* 31 (3): 323–339. doi:10.1007/s11187-008-9134-x.

Huang, Q. H. 2003. "The Private Enterprises: A Main Engine to the Sustaining Growth of China's Economy." In *Sustaining Growth of the Chinese Economy the Twenty-first Century*, edited by S. Yao and X. Liu, 96–116. London: Routledge.

Huang, Y. S. 2010. "Entrepreneurship in China." Accessed 18 December 2018. http://www.worldfinancialreview.com/?p=2782

Jia, L., S. You, and Y. Du. 2012. "Chinese Context and Theoretical Contributions to Management and Organization Research: A Three-decade Review." *Management and Organization Review* 8 (1): 173–209. doi:10.1111/j.1740-8784.2011.00282.x.

Johns, G. 2006. "The Essential Impact of Context on Organizational Behavior." *Academy of Management Review* 31 (2): 386–408. doi:10.5465/amr.2006.20208687.

Lee, C. K., and S. C. Hung. 2014. "Institutional Entrepreneurship in the Informal Economy: China's Shan-zhai Mobile Phones." *Strategic Entrepreneurship Journal* 8 (1): 16–36. doi:10.1002/sej.1174.

Lehmann, J. P. 2015 "Globalization With Chinese Characteristics – What Are The Prospects?" Accessed 19 February 2018. http://www.forbes.com/sites/jplehmann/2015/06/29/globalization-with-chinese-characteristics-what-are-the-prospects/#1a1318b6f919

Li, H., Y. Zhang, Y. Li, L. A. Zhou, and W. Zhang. 2012. "Returnees versus Locals: Who Perform Better in China's Technology Entrepreneurship?." *Strategic Entrepreneurship Journal* 6 (3): 257–272. doi:10.1002/sej.1139.

Li, J., and H. Matlay. 2006. "Chinese Entrepreneurship and Small Business Development: An Overview and Research Agenda." *Journal of Small Business and Enterprise Development* Vol.13 (2): 248–262. doi:10.1108/14626000610665953.

Li, J., J. Qu, and Q. Huang. 2018. "Why are Some Graduate Entrepreneurs More Innovative than Others? the Effect of Human Capital, Psychological Factor and Entrepreneurial Rewards on Entrepreneurial Innovativeness." *Entrepreneurship & Regional Development* 30 (5–6): 479–501. doi:10.1080/08985626.2017.1406540.

Li, X. 2017. "Exploring the Spatial Heterogeneity of Entrepreneurship in Chinese Manufacturing Industries." *The Journal of Technology Transfer* 42 (5): 1077–1099. doi:10.1007/s10961-016-9474-7.

Li, X. H., and X. Liang. 2015. "A Confucian Social Model of Political Appointments among Chinese Private-firm Entrepreneurs." *Academy of Management Journal* 58 (2): 592–617. doi:10.5465/amj.2012.1067.

Li, Z., T. Ding, and J. Li. 2015. "Entrepreneurship and Economic Development in China: Evidence from a Time Varying Parameters Stochastic Volatility Vector Autoregressive (TVP-SV-VAR) Model." *Technology Analysis and Strategic Management* Vol.27 (6): 660–674. doi:10.1080/09537325.2015.1034676.

Lin, S., and S. Si. 2014. "Factors Affecting Peasant Entrepreneurs' Intention in the Chinese Context." *International Entrepreneurship and Management Journal* 10 (4): 803–825. doi:10.1007/s11365-014-0325-4.

Liou, C. S., and C. M. Tsai. 2017. "The Dual Role of Cadres and Entrepreneurs in China: The Evolution of Managerial Leadership in State-monopolized Industries." *Asian Survey* 57 (6): 1058–1085. doi:10.1525/as.2017.57.6.1058.

Liu, C. Y., L. Ye, and B. Feng. 2018a. "Migrant Entrepreneurship in China: Entrepreneurial Transition and Firm Performance." *Small Business Economics*. doi:10.1007/s11187-017-9979-y.

Liu, H., S. Shi, and M. Zhang. 2018b. "Is It Purely Instrumental? the Dual-role Model of Chinese Entrepreneurs' Political Connections in Advanced Stage of Institutional Transition." *Nankai Business Review International* 9 (4): 540–568. doi:10.1108/NBRI-01-2018-0004.

Liu, J., J. Nandhakumar, and M. Zachariadis. 2018c. "When Guanxi Meets Structural Holes: Exploring the Guanxi Networks of Chinese Entrepreneurs on Digital Platforms." *The Journal of Strategic Information Systems* 27 (4): 311–334. doi:10.1016/j.jsis.2018.10.003.

Liu, L., and Y. Zhang. 2018. "Does Non-employment Based Health Insurance Promote Entrepreneurship? Evidence from a Policy Experiment in China." *Journal of Comparative Economics* 46 (1): 270–283. doi:10.1016/j.jce.2017.04.003.

Liu, Y., and Q. H. Huang. 2018. "University Capability as Micro-foundation for Triple Helix Model: Cultivating University Capability or Attracting Talent." *Technovation*. doi:10.1016/j.technovation.2018.02.013.

Lu, J., and Z. Tao. 2010. "Determinants of Entrepreneurial Activities in China." *Journal of Business Venturing* 25 (3): 261–273. doi:10.1016/j.jbusvent.2008.10.005.

Ma, C., J. Gu, and H. Liu. 2017. "Entrepreneurs' Passion and New Venture Performance in China." *International Entrepreneurship and Management Journal* 13 (4): 1043–1068. doi:10.1007/s11365-017-0435-x.

Ma, G., O. M. Rui, and Y. Wu. 2015. "A Springboard into Politics: Do Chinese Entrepreneurs Benefit from Joining the Government-controlled Business Associations?." *China Economic Review* 36: 166–183. doi:10.1016/j.chieco.2015.09.003.

McKinsey Global Institute. 2015. "Gauging the Strength of Chinese Innovation." Accessed 18 December 2018. http://www.mckinsey.com/business-functions/strategy-and-corporate-finance/our-insights/gauging-the-strength-of-chinese-innovation

McMillan, J., and C. Woodruff. 2002. "The Central Role of Entrepreneurs in Transition Economies." *The Journal of Economic Perspectives* 16 (3): 153–170. doi:10.1257/089533002760278767.

Meyer, K. 2007. "Asian Contexts and the Search for General Theory in Management Research: A Rejoinder." *Asia Pacific Journal of Management* 24 (4): 527–534. doi:10.1007/s10490-007-9053-4.

Meyer, K. E. 2015. "Context in Management Research in Emerging Economies." *Management and Organization Review* 11 (3): 369–377. doi:10.1017/mor.2015.36.

Nambisan, S. 2017. "Digital Entrepreneurship: Toward a Digital Technology Perspective of Entrepreneurship." *Entrepreneurship Theory and Practice* 41 (6): 1029–1055. doi:10.1111/etap.12254.

Peng, H., G. Duysters, and B. Sadowski. 2016. "The Changing Role of Guanxi in Influencing the Development of Entrepreneurial Companies: A Case Study of the Emergence of Pharmaceutical Companies in China." *International Entrepreneurship and Management Journal* 12 (1): 215–258. doi:10.1007/s11365-014-0323-6.

Peng, M. W., D. Wang, and Y. Jiang. 2008. "An Institution-based View of International Business Strategy: A Focus on Emerging Economies." *J Int Bus Stud* 39: 920–936. doi:10.1057/palgrave.jibs.8400377.

Rath, J., and R Kloosterman. 2000. "Outsiders' Business: a Critical Review Of Research on Immigrant Entrepreneurship." *International Migration Review* 10: 2307/2675940. doi:10.1177/019791830003400301.

References with * are the articles included in our analysis of contextualisation in Chinese entrepreneurship research.

Shane, S. 2009. "Why Encouraging More People to Become Entrepreneurs Is Bad Public Policy." *Small Business Economics* 33 (2): 141–149. doi:10.1007/s11187-009-9215-5.

Song, L., Q. Liang, Y. Lu, and X. Li. 2016. "Why Chinese Entrepreneurial Firms Selectively Perform Corporate Social Responsibility Issues?." *Chinese Management Studies* 10 (2): 272–290. doi:10.1108/CMS-10-2015-0241.

Su, D. J., and D. W. Sohn. 2015. "Roles of Entrepreneurial Orientation and Guanxi Network with Parent University in Start-ups' Performance: Evidence from University Spin-offs in China." *Asian Journal of Technology Innovation* 23 (1): 1–19. doi:10.1080/19761597.2015.1008196.

Su, J., Q. Zhai, and H. Landström. 2015a. "Entrepreneurship Research in China: Internationalization or Contextualization?." *Entrepreneurship & Regional Development,27*, no. 1–2: 50–79. doi:10.1080/08985626.2014.999718.

Su, Z., E. Xie, and D. Wang. 2015b. "Entrepreneurial Orientation, Managerial Networking, and New Venture Performance in China." *Journal of Small Business Management* 53 (1): 228–248. doi:10.1111/jsbm.2015.53.issue-1.

Sun, P., M. Wright, and K. Mellahi. 2010. "Is Entrepreneur–Politician Alliance Sustainable during Transition? the Case of Management Buyouts in China." *Management and Organization Review* 6 (1): 101–121. doi:10.1111/j.1740-8784.2009.00157.x.

Sun, Z. 2015. "Technology Innovation and Entrepreneurial State: The Development of China's High-speed Rail Industry." *Technology Analysis & Strategic Management* 27 (6): 646–659. doi:10.1080/09537325.2015.1034267.

Talavera, O., L. Xiong, and X. Xiong. 2012. "Social Capital and Access to Bank Financing: The Case of Chinese Entrepreneurs." *Emerging Markets Finance and Trade* 48 (1): 55–69. doi:10.2753/REE1540-496X480103.

Tang, Z., and J. Tang. 2012. "Entrepreneurial Orientation and SME Performance in China's Changing Environment: The Moderating Effects of Strategies." *Asia Pacific Journal of Management* 29 (2): 409–431. doi:10.1007/s10490-010-9200-1.

Ting, S. X., L. Feng, and W. Qin. 2017. "The Effect of Entrepreneur Mentoring and Its Determinants in the Chinese Context." *Management Decision* 55 (7): 1410–1425. doi:10.1108/MD-07-2016-0477.

Tong, J., and F. Yang. 2016. "Trust at Work: A Study on Faith and Trust of Protestant Entrepreneurs in China." *Religions* 7 (12): 136. doi:10.3390/rel7120136.

Troilo, M., and J. Zhang. 2012. "Guanxi and Entrepreneurship in Urban China." *Journal of the Asia Pacific Economy* 17 (2): 315–331. doi:10.1080/13547860.2012.668280.

Tsui, A. S. 2004. "Contributing to Global Management Knowledge: A Case for High Quality Indigenous Research." *Asia Pacific Journal of Management* 21 (4): 491–513. doi:10.1023/B:APJM.0000048715.35108.a7.

Tsui, A. S. 2006. "Contextualization in Chinese Management Research." *Management and Organization Review* 2 (1): 1–13. doi:10.1111/j.1740-8784.2006.00033.x.

von Briel, F., P. Davidsson, and J. C. Recker. 2018. "Digital Technologies as External Enablers of New Venture Creation in the IT Hardware Sector." *Entrepreneurship Theory and Practice* 42 (1): 47–69. doi:10.1177/1042258717732779.

Wallis, C. 2015. "Micro-entrepreneurship, New Media Technologies, and the Reproduction and Reconfiguration of Gender in Rural China." *Chinese Journal of Communication* 8 (1): 42–58. doi:10.1080/17544750.2014.988633.

Wang, S. Y. 2012. "Credit Constraints, Job Mobility, and Entrepreneurship: Evidence from a Property Reform in China." *Review of Economics and Statistics* 94 (2): 532–551. doi:10.1162/REST_a_00160.

Wank, D. L. 1996. "The Institutional Process of Market Clientelism: Guanxi and Private Business in a South China City." *The China Quarterly* 3: 820–838. doi:10.1017/S030574100005181X.

Welter, F. 2011. "Contextualizing Entrepreneurship—Conceptual Challenges and Ways Forward." *Entrepreneurship Theory and Practice* 35 (1): 165–184. doi:10.1111/etap.2011.35.issue-1.

Whetten, DA. 1989. ""What Constitutes a Theoretical Contribution? "." *Academy Of Management Review* 14 (4): 490–495. doi:10.2307/258554.

Wright, M., I. Filatotchev, R. E. Hoskisson, and M. W. Peng. 2005. "Strategy Research in Emerging Economies: Challenging the Conventional Wisdom." *Journal of Management Studies* 42 (1): 1–33. doi:10.1111/joms.2005.42.issue-1.

Xue, D., and F. Wu. 2015. "Failing Entrepreneurial Governance: From Economic Crisis to Fiscal Crisis in the City of Dongguan, China." *Cities* 43: 10–17. doi:10.1016/j.cities.2014.11.005.

Xun, W., M. Ramesh, M. Howlett, and G. Qingyang. 2016. "Local Government Entrepreneurship and Global Competitiveness: A Case Study of Yiwu Market in China." *China: An International Journal* 14 (3): 51–66.

Yang, J. Y., and J. Li. 2008. "The Development of Entrepreneurship in China." *Asia Pacific Journal of Management* 25 (2): 335–359. doi:10.1007/s10490-007-9078-8.

Yiu, D. W., R. E. Hoskisson, G. D. Bruton, and Y. Lu. 2014a. "Dueling Institutional Logics And The Effect On Strategic Entrepreneurship In Chinese Business Groups." *Strategic Entrepreneurship Journal* 8 (3): 195–213. doi:10.1002/sej.v8.3.

Yiu, D. W., W. P. Wan, F. W. Ng, X. Chen, and J. Su. 2014b. "Sentimental Drivers of Social Entrepreneurship: A Study of China's Guangcai (glorious) Program." *Management and Organization Review* 10 (1): 55–80. doi:10.1111/more.12043.

Zahra, S. A. 2007. "Contextualizing Theory Building in Entrepreneurship Research." *Journal of Business Venturing* 22 (3): 443–452. doi:10.1016/j.jbusvent.2006.04.007.

Zahra, S. A., L. R. Newey, and Y. Li. 2014a. "On the Frontiers: The Implications of Social Entrepreneurship for International Entrepreneurship." *Entrepeneurship Theory and Practice* 38 (1): 137–158. doi:10.1111/etap.12061.

Zahra, S. A., M. Wright, and S. G. Abdelgawad. 2014b. "Contextualization and the Advancement of Entrepreneurship Research." *International Small Business Journal* 32 (5): 479–500. doi:10.1177/0266242613519807.

Zhang, C., J. Tan, and D. Tan. 2016a. "Fit by Adaptation or Fit by Founding? A Comparative Study of Existing and New Entrepreneurial Cohorts in China." *Strategic Management Journal* 37 (5): 911–931. doi:10.1002/smj.2016.37.issue-5.

Zhang, J. J. 2015a. "From Market Despotism to Managerial Hegemony: The Rise of Indigenous Chinese Management." *Management Organization Review* 11:2: 205–210. doi:10.1017/mor.2015.24.

Zhang, W., and S. White. 2016. "Overcoming the Liability of Newness: Entrepreneurial Action and the Emergence of China's Private Solar Photovoltaic Firms." *Research Policy* 45 (3): 604–617. doi:10.1016/j.respol.2015.11.005.

Zhang, X., X. Ma, Y. Wang, X. Li, and D. Huo. 2016b. "What Drives the Internationalization of Chinese SMEs? the Joint Effects of International Entrepreneurship Characteristics, Network Ties, and Firm Ownership." *International Business Review* 25 (2): 522–534. doi:10.1016/j.ibusrev.2015.09.001.

Zhang, Y. 2015b. "The Contingent Value of Social Resources: Entrepreneurs' Use of Debt-financing Sources in Western China." *Journal of Business Venturing* 30 (3): 390–406. doi:10.1016/j.jbusvent.2014.02.003.

Zhang, Z. X., Z. X. Chen, Y. R. Chen, and S. Ang. 2014. "Business Leadership in the Chinese Context: Trends, Findings and Implications." *Management and Organization Review* 10 (2): 199–221.

Zhao, Y. L., and M. E. Parry. 2012. "Mental Models and Successful First-mover Entry Decisions: Empirical Evidence from Chinese Entrepreneurs." *Journal of Product Innovation Management* 29 (4): 590–607. doi:10.1111/jpim.2012.29.issue-4.

Zheng, C., and M. C. Hu. 2018. "An Exploration of the Application of Universities as Artificial Institutional Entrepreneurs: The Case of China." *Journal of Public Affairs* 18 (1): e1697. doi:10.1002/pa.1697.

Zhou, W. 2011. "Regional Deregulation and Entrepreneurial Growth in China's Transition Economy." *Entrepreneurship & Regional Development* 23 (9–10): 853–876. doi:10.1080/08985626.2011.577816.

Zhou, W. 2013. "Political Connections and Entrepreneurial Investment: Evidence from China's Transition Economy." *Journal of Business Venturing* 28 (2): 299–315. doi:10.1016/j.jbusvent.2012.05.004.

Zhou, W. 2014. "Regional Institutional Development, Political Connections, and Entrepreneurial Performance in China's Transition Economy." *Small Business Economics* 43 (1): 161–181. doi:10.1007/s11187-013-9527-3.

Zhu, L., O. Kara, and X. Zhu. 2018. "A Comparative Study of Women Entrepreneurship in Transitional Economies: The Case of China and Vietnam." *Journal of Entrepreneurship in Emerging Economies*. 11 (1): 66–80. doi:10.1108/JEEE-04-2017-0027.

Zhu, X. 2016. "In the Name of 'citizens': Civic Activism and Policy Entrepreneurship of Chinese Public Intellectuals in the Hu–Wen Era." *Journal of Contemporary China* 25 (101): 745–759. doi:10.1080/10670564.2016.1160510.

Zhu, Y. 2013. "Policy Entrepreneurship, Institutional Constraints, and Local Policy Innovation in China." *China Review* 13 (2): 97–122.

Zhu, Y. 2015. "The Role of Qing (positive Emotions) and Li 1 (rationality) in Chinese Entrepreneurial Decision Making: A Confucian Ren-yi Wisdom Perspective." *Journal of Business Ethics* 126 (4): 613–630. doi:10.1007/s10551-013-1970-1.

Entrepreneurial ecosystems: what we know and where we move as we build an understanding of China

Juanyi Chen, Li Cai, Garry D. Bruton and Naiheng Sheng

ABSTRACT

Scholars recognize entrepreneurial ecosystems of interconnected entrepreneurial actors, organizations, institutions, context, and entrepreneurial processes are critical to new venture success. Here we examine the burgeoning academic literature on entrepreneurial ecosystems in both the West and China to build a platform for the greater understanding of ecosystems, particularly as scholars expand its understanding in China. To build this understanding, we initially examine and classify the existing research in both leading international journals and Chinese journals on entrepreneurial ecosystems into four broad themes of nature, networks, institutions, and dynamics. We then build on this review of this literature to discuss how such findings inform scholars about the future research of ecosystems in China.

Introduction

Scholars increasingly highlight that entrepreneurship does not occur as an isolated event, but rather part of a broader ecosystem, or as a set of interconnected entrepreneurial actors, organizations, institutions, and entrepreneurial processes (Isenberg 2011; Sabeti 2011; Zahra and Nambisan 2011; Feld 2012; Kanter 2012; Nambisan and Baron 2013; Spigel and Harrison 2018). Silicon Valley in the United States (US) typifies such an ecosystem with its wide range of related activities such as finance, legal, and human resources coming together into a sustainable ecosystem. While to date there has been an expanding body of research on ecosystems, this research has typically focused on mature economies (Kasabov 2015). How such literature relates to emerging economies is not well understood (Naude et al. 2008; Isenberg 2010; Amezcua et al. 2013; Dutt et al. 2016). Here we review and examine the existing literature on entrepreneurial ecosystems with the goal to understand the status of the literature today, and how this literature can be relevant to the largest emerging economy, China.

To build this understanding, we examine entrepreneurial ecosystems research in leading international journals over the years of 2000 through 2017. To identify relevant articles, we examine leading journals including the FT 50 journals (*Financial Times 50*) plus four other leading journals that publish research relevant to the topic including *Entrepreneurship & Regional Development (ERD)*, *Word Development (WD)*, *Management and Organization Review (MOR)*, and *Asia Pacific Journal of Management (APJM)*. In addition, we also examine 24 leading

Chinese journals in management and economics to ensure we have the full understanding of entrepreneurial ecosystems in China. Through our coding of the articles, we are able to identify four themes – nature, networks, institutions, and dynamics in entrepreneurial ecosystems. We discuss each of these themes and then build an agenda for future research based on these themes.

This article provides three significant contributions to the entrepreneurship literature. First, we provide a comprehensive review of the literature on entrepreneurial ecosystems. We are able in this examination to integrate articles from a wide range of disciplines beyond entrepreneurship including the literature from regional development and economics. We connect in this review both the theoretical insights from leading international journals and the phenomenon-driven research from leading Chinese journals.

Our second contribution is to build a platform for extending the theoretical understanding of ecosystems beyond the West. We specifically develop a comprehensive agenda for entrepreneurial ecosystems in China by scholars around the world. Such understanding is wildly applicable to many emerging countries. Finally, we also offer important implications for practitioners and policy-makers by answering the call for entrepreneurial ecosystems to be both rigorous and relevant to regional development. Today, the Chinese government is spending significant amounts of money aiming at developing ecosystems for entrepreneurship across China. However, the understanding of ecosystems in the country is yet to significantly develop to guide how such ecosystems should be examined, and ultimately, setting the criteria to judge if the government's spending is leading to success.

Laying the foundation

James Moore (1996) coined the term business ecosystem arguing it was 'an economic community supported by a foundation of increasing organizations and individuals – the organisms of the business world' (Moore 1996, 26), and 'characterized by a large number of loosely interconnected participants who depend on each other for their mutual effectiveness and survival' (Iansiti and Levien 2004, 8). Daniel Isenberg (2010) introduced the concept of entrepreneurial ecosystem by focusing the concept ecosystem specifically on start-up firms. An entrepreneurial ecosystem occurs when a set of start-ups, organizations, institutions, and entrepreneurship stakeholders (Spigel 2017) form a munificent environment ripe to foster entrepreneurship (Zacharakis, Shepherd, and Coombs 2003; Feld 2012; Spigel 2017).

Entrepreneurial ecosystems are typified by Silicon Valley where an agglomeration of semiconductors manufacturing companies and computer companies in San Francisco Bay Area reside (Sturgeon 2000; Feldman and Lowe 2015). These firms benefit from venture capital, human capital, universities and research institutions, and professional service infrastructure interconnected with each other (Zacharakis, Shepherd, and Coombs 2003). The interconnection of these various entities helped to support the founding of many world-leading high-technology companies including Google, Intel, Facebook, Apple, and Cisco Systems, just to name a few. It is estimated that entrepreneurs from the region generate revenues of $2.7 trillion annually and have created 5.4 million worldwide jobs (Fu and Hsia 2014).

It is not surprising that other national governments look to Silicon Valley success and seek to recreate a similar environment in their own local (Lerner 2009). For example, the idea of entrepreneurial ecosystems started in China in 1988 when the Beijing local government began to build Zhongguancun Science Park (ZGC). The goal of the science park was to house not only firms but to ensure other needed supports such as financing, accounting, and legal supports are located in one place thus creating an ecosystem for entrepreneurship. From that one science park, there are now approximately 1,600 science parks and incubators in China; officials estimate there will be 10,000 science parks in China by 2020 (The Ministry of Science and Technology of the People's Republic of China 2017).

While Silicon Valley came about organically, the Chinese ecosystems are created by the government's efforts (Qian 2000; Mueller and Jungwirth 2016). The efforts the government directed in China are that some science parks are part of broad ecosystems that include a rich range of related activities. However, many other science parks are simple collections of entities, some of which may have limited entrepreneurial connections. Thus, as we look at China there is a deep need to better understand entrepreneurial ecosystems and how they can be successfully encouraged.

To build an understanding of how to establish such ecosystems, scholars need to systematically examine the existing literature. It should not be assumed automatically that literature on ecosystems in the West is relevant to an emerging economy like China (Barney and Zhang 2009; Jack et al. 2013; Barkema et al. 2015). Therefore here, we will initially review the established literature on entrepreneurial ecosystems in the leading international journals. We will then integrate these articles with the literature in the leading Chinese journals. The leading international journals tend to be based on theory-driven research while the leading Chinese journals tend to report on phenomena (Ahlstrom, Bruton, and Yeh 2008). For example, the work by Dutt et al. (2016) employed institutional theory to examine the research question of how private, government, academic, and non-governmental organization sponsorship affect incubators. In contrast, the leading Chinese journals primarily focus on discussing how ZGC in China or Silicon Valley in the US was created and describing the 'how to' for managers, entrepreneurs, and policymakers (e.g., Mao and Zhou 2002; Qian 2000; Fu 2010).

Methods

Leading international journals

In this review, we define ecosystem as 'a set of interconnected entrepreneurial actors (both potential and existing), entrepreneurial organisations (e.g., firms, venture capitalists, business angels, banks), institutions (universities, public sector agencies, financial bodies) and entrepreneurial processes (e.g., the business birth rate, numbers of high growth firms, levels of "blockbuster entrepreneurship", number of serial entrepreneurs, degree of sellout mentality within firms and levels of entrepreneurial ambition) which formally and informally coalesce to connect, mediate and govern the performance within the local entrepreneurial environment' (Mason and Brown 2014, 5). To generate the relevant literature, we focused on the *Financial Times* (FT) list of 50 leading journals in the business schools, from the time period of 2000 to 2017. We also added another four significant journals that are relevant to our concern on entrepreneurial ecosystems including the *Entrepreneurship & Regional Development (ERD), Word Development (WD), Management Organization Review (MOR)*, and *Asia Pacific Journal of Management (APJM)*. Thus, we examined 54 leading international journals over the 18 year-period for relevant literature. We chose this time period since it represents the most intense period of academic investigation of this topic.

To retrieve relevant articles from the target journals, we first searched for articles in EBSCO host database using the terms that appear anywhere in the text including both 'entrepreneur' and 'ecosystem'. As noted previously, multiple streams of literature are relevant to the topic of entrepreneurial ecosystems. Therefore, we added to our searches the specific terms of 'entrepreneur' and 'science park', plus 'entrepreneur' and 'incubator', and finally 'entrepreneur' and 'regional entrepreneurship'. This search identified 121 articles. We then had each author carefully read and examine each article for its appropriateness focused on entrepreneurial ecosystems. This scrutiny of each article led us to eliminate 75 articles from this review because ecosystem relevant terms/concepts are not the focal element or central variables in the study, yielding a final sample of 46 articles that directly examined entrepreneurial ecosystems. To validate this review, we had three experts in entrepreneurial ecosystems systems in the international literature to review our list of articles and validate that we had not missed any major articles. These scholars identified four additional articles that we added to the review. Thus, we examined 50 international articles in this review (Bruton, Ahlstrom, and Obloj 2008; Chen, Chang, and Bruton 2017).

Leading chinese journals

To connect the leading international literature and that in China we also examined 23 leading journals in *management* cited by the National Natural Science Foundation of China as the leading business journals in the country.[1] Discussions with leading Chinese scholars led us to include one more top-tier economics journal – *Economic Research Journal* (The Chinese Academy of Social Sciences 2014) since entrepreneurial ecosystem as an effective mean to support economic development also receives increasing attention in economics domain. As a result, we examined 24 leading Chinese journals for relevant literature. We employed the leading search engine in China – National Knowledge Infrastructure (CNKI) – with the same search criteria as the international journals, and using the same terms as in the international journals that appear anywhere in the text 'entrepreneur' and 'ecosystem', 'entrepreneur' and 'science park', 'entrepreneur' and 'incubator', and finally 'entrepreneur' and 'regional entrepreneurship'. We examined the same time period as we did in the leading international journals, 2000–2017 or 18 years. In addition, we searched both the English and Chinese translated terms since keywords, abstract, and title are in English in the journals and the text may also have the terms. This research returned 1090 articles in this initial examination of Chinese journals. The method employed in the international journals was replicated to ensure those articles were relevant to the review. Unlike the leading international journals, far more articles were eliminated in this process for the Chinese journals, 1055 articles were eliminated. The articles eliminated often would simply mention the concept of an ecosystem, related term, or in passing as a future research topic. The ecosystem concept is of great interest in China but to date, the actual investigation of the topic has largely not progressed far. Specifically, we identified 35 articles that do examine ecosystems in the leading Chinese journals. Thus, a total of 85 articles from both the leading international journals and Chinese journals were included in our review.[2]

Review of extant research on entrepreneurial ecosystems

Examining the 85 articles in the sample, we find 44 employed quantitative methods, 22 qualitative methods (particularly case studies). The remaining 18 articles are conceptual articles about the ecosystem, and with only one article employing both quantitative and qualitative methods. The Chinese articles are more strongly represented in the conceptual articles, half of the Chinese articles used in this review are conceptual (specifically, out of 18 conceptual articles, there are 10 Chinese articles versus 8 international articles). These articles are not conceptual in terms of developing theory, but instead, they describe potential issues for both practice and research that related to ecosystems. Table A1 provides a brief overview of the articles in the sample.

We also reviewed the countries and locations of the samples of the 67 quantitative and qualitative articles (see Table A2). Notably, among the 42 articles in the leading international journals 34 articles employed samples from developed countries while six articles were from emerging economies; two articles use large numbers of diverse countries as their sample. US is the most frequently studied country followed by the UK and Canada. There are only two articles on China and Vietnam among the emerging economies examined in the leading international articles. All of the empirical articles in Chinese journals examine China.

Results

We employed an open code methodology to classify each of the publication by theme (Corbin and Strauss 2014). Specifically, each of the authors read the content of each article and then two authors coded the articles for a wide range of themes including definition, components, character-istics, influential factors, mechanisms of ecosystem creation, methodology, data sources, as well as theoretical framework in content, conclusions, contribution, and the implications for ecosystem and entrepreneurship. During the open coding phase, we sought to reduce the bias in analyzing the sample articles (Ahlstrom, Bruton, and Yeh 2008). In so doing, if there was a disagreement the third author's opinion was employed to evaluate the article in question. In addition, two Chinese co-authors have independently coded the leading Chinese articles. Then through several rounds of discussions among two co-authors, the discrepancies could be resolved. Thus, we were able to classify these 85 articles into four principal themes of nature, networks, institutions, and dynamics in entrepreneurial ecosystem research (see Table A3). Next, we will discuss each theme below.

Themes covered in entrepreneurial ecosystems research

As noted, we identify four themes of nature, networks, institutions, and dynamics in entrepreneur-ial ecosystems in the 85 leading international and Chinese journal articles. In the following sections, we review extant literature in each of these four topics.

Nature

The nature of entrepreneurial ecosystems stream of literature concerns articles that address the defini-tion and component parts of the entrepreneurial ecosystems. This body of literature draws on widely diverse theoretical foundations including heritage theory, social capital theory, and economic develop-ment theory. There are 32 articles in the nature theme. The research in this theme is much more focused than in the other research themes. We divide this large set of literature into three core elements: definition (e.g., Isenberg 2010; Adner 2017; Spigel 2017), components that underpin entrepreneurial ecosystems (e.g., Seidl et al. 2003; Audretsch and Keilbach 2004; Samila and Sorenson 2010), and geographic locations. The definition literature in turn impacts of what scholars see as the component parts of the ecosystem and how this definition will affect the geographic dispersion of ecosystem. Each of these three elements of the nature of entrepreneurial ecosystems we will next examine.

Definition
When examining the issue of ecosystem definition, it should be noted that a consistent definition of entrepreneurial ecosystems is still missing in the Chinese articles we examined. Specifically, most of the Chinese articles highlight the significant role of the ecosystem approach to entre-preneurship and regional economic development but they do not have a specific definition to draw on. The international articles have definitions, but there is also diversity in their definition of entrepreneurial ecosystems. However, these definitions principally draw on two competing theoretical perspectives. The first theoretical perspective is ecology theory which views 'entre-preneurial ecosystems' as an organism system that consists of 'a set of individual elements – such as leadership, culture, capital markets, and open-minded customers – that combine in complex ways to turbocharge venture creation and growth' (Isenberg 2010, 43). This definition highlights the ecosystem is composed of actors defined by networks with a focus on the 'eco' rather than 'system' (The Economist 2014) – the business network is made up of organizations and activities that are interdependent and symbiotic, and thus much of the literature highlights the number of organizations and network characteristics of a focal firm or ecosystem (Adner 2017).

The second competing theoretical perspective draws on the structural view and does not focus on network characteristics; thus, the focus is on the alignment of entrepreneurial actors, positions, and multilateral links, or the 'system' aspect of the entity. From this perspective, entities undertake interactive activities to allocate resources and develop opportunities and thus, create the joint value propositions as the general goal of entrepreneurial ecosystems (Molina-Morales and Martínez-Fernández 2009; Ansari, Garud, and Kumaraswamy 2016; Davis 2016; Adner 2017; Spigel 2017).

To date, the definition from the ecology perspective dominates the literature (Isenberg 2010; Mason and Brown 2014; Overholm 2015; Spigel 2017). However, these two different perspectives can in part explain the very diverse findings on components and geographic location we will explore below.

Components underpinning entrepreneurial ecosystem

A growing research domain examines the components of entrepreneurial ecosystem. To date, both international and Chinese articles have identified up to 12 elements necessary to sustain and support regional entrepreneurship, including government policy (e.g., policy support, tax incentives), culture, human capital, financial capital, entrepreneurship organizations, education, infrastructure, economic clusters, networks, support services, early customers, and leadership (Fu 2010; Isenberg 2010, 2011; Spigel 2017). While there is a wide acceptance of these 12 elements not all articles include all of them in their research (e.g., Qian 2000; Mao and Zhou 2002; Tang and Xi 2006; Ansari, Garud, and Kumaraswamy 2016; Motoyama and Knowlton 2016). However, the empirical evidence supporting the value of the 12 variables is also limited. For example, it is noticeable that three international articles (e.g., Huggins and Thompson 2014; Nguyen, Sullivan Mort, and D'Souza 2015; Spigel 2017) and six Chinese articles have largely highlighted the role of supportive entrepreneurial culture as the catalyst for the creation and development of entrepreneurial ecosystem. However, there is no empirical research conducted to test such role in contributing to ecosystem creation and development. Much of the literature on components has been conducted that has shown availability of capital resources (Seidl et al. 2003; Audretsch and Keilbach 2004; Naude et al. 2008), university support (Laukkanen 2000; Smith and Bagchi-Sen 2012; Feldman and Lowe 2015; Isaksen 2016), and market size (Naude et al. 2008) positively effects firm innovation and commercialize products in an entrepreneurial ecosystem. Overall, the 12 variables are more widely discussed than examined empirically.

Geographic location

Geography is examined by the nature theme articles. This focus on geography grows from a recognition in the international articles that the geographic location can determine regional entrepreneurship. The geographic location may be especially valuable as technology differences and location conditions create different environments that may make different variables valuable and different resources available in different regions of a nation (Zacharakis, Shepherd, and Coombs 2003; Cumming and Johan 2010; Huggins and Williams 2011; Li et al. 2016b; Shearmur and Doloreux 2016). Thus, the 12 variables above may not be universal in their impact and in the different regions of a nation or of the world there may be different combinations of variables that are valuable to an ecosystem (Xing, Wang, and Zhou 2015; Habersetzer 2016; Li et al. 2016a; Shearmur and Doloreux 2016). For example, evidence has demonstrated that the geographical location such as remoteness or proximity can affect a firm's speed to innovate and new market entry as the value of market-sourced technology information and the interaction frequency depend on the locations (Habersetzer 2016; Shearmur and Doloreux 2016).

However, in one respect, such view does not appear to be important in the Chinese articles (Li et al. 2016a). In part, this is because 'the government typically in some regions of China takes an active role or even a dominant role in building the ecosystem' (Bruton, Zahra, and Cai 2018). This leads to the assumption that entrepreneurial ecosystems will automatically come about by the presence of the previously noted components. In practice, the result is a proliferation of science parks, incubators, and industrial parks can be seen across China.

Networks

The second theme of entrepreneurial ecosystems literature examines the interactions within the ecosystem (e.g., Molina-Morales and Martínez-Fernández 2009; Skilton and Bernardes 2015); there must be interaction among the parts for the ecosystem to exist (Hansen et al. 2000; Bøllingtoft and Ulhøi 2005). We label this set of literature as networks since that is typically how interactions occur.

To avoid any confusion, we argue the components scholars examined in the nature theme primarily focused on the whether the component parts exit or not in an ecosystem. This body of international and Chinese literature typically draws on social network theory and social capital theory to examine interactions. There are 29 articles in the network theme. We will next examine the network literature in terms of two major domains – innovation/performance, and interaction.

Innovation/performance
International and Chinese scholars in this stream of research have both highlighted the positive relationship between the network connection and innovation/performance. A network of powerful business connections not only enables new ventures to innovate quickly by acquiring critical resources such as knowledge from internal partners and others (Fu 2010; Brekke 2015; Davis 2016), but also enables network participants to discover and exploit new business opportunities ahead of competitors (Hansen et al. 2000; Parker 2008). Additionally, network advantage from an ecosystem allows a firm to innovate faster by accessing new ideas and knowledge from external sources (del-Corte-Lora, Vallet-Bellmunt, and Molina-Morales 2015; Davis 2016) since networks allows information and resources to flow among members within or outsiders of an ecosystem (Ahuja 2000; Tang and Xi 2006; Nambisan and Baron 2013).

    To dive further in the analysis of networks in the ecosystem, international scholars have opened conversations regarding the extent that organizations depend on a network relationship to enhance performance (Molina-Morales and Martínez-Fernández 2009; Zhu, Liu, and Liu 2011; Brekke 2015; Skilton and Bernardes 2015). The evidence is that overreliance on the network can, in fact, do harm to the firm's value creation (Molina-Morales and Martínez-Fernández 2009; del-Corte-Lora, Vallet-Bellmunt, and Molina-Morales 2015; Skilton and Bernardes 2015). Thus, international scholars typically argue there is an inverted-U shape curve between the network and firm performance, the network provides increasing value while beyond a certain point where too much focus on the network leads to a decline (Molina-Morales and Martínez-Fernández 2009; del-Corte-Lora, Vallet-Bellmunt, and Molina-Morales 2015). However, our knowledge about new concepts of network across Chinese entrepreneurial ecosystems remains relatively limited as the literature in China typically discuss existing concepts (e.g., network characteristics in science park or incubator) and essentially add new mediator or moderator or test the existing theory with the Chinese samples. For example, applying some characteristics as moderator or mediator in its context, the Chinese scholarship finds that entrepreneur's entrepreneurial orientation and the capability to combine resources could affect accessing the supportive resources necessary for firm growth within the ecosystem (Hu et al. 2012; Li and Zhang 2012). Applying the existing theory to a new context might increase the 'the serious possibility of missing the truly important management or organization issues in the Chinese context' (Tsui 2006, 3).

Interaction
To avoid any confusion, the sub-theme of interaction here is different from the component aspect of the nature theme research in that consistent with our network concept we focus here on relationships developed among different participants, while in nature they focus on whether the components exit or not. This research stream has a particular interest in how participants that link to a focal actor or platform through which 'may unlock new interactions and combinations that will, in turn, increase the overall value creation of the system.' (Adner 2017, 41). Scholars examining this topic explore the role of multiple participants' interactions and their effect on ecosystems. The participants often examined include private firms, universities, government, and NGOs, just to name a few (Isenberg 2010; Amezcua et al. 2013; Dutt et al. 2016; Adner 2017; Spigel 2017) in part that these intermediates are much more developed or exit in the developed countries; the different combinations of participant interactions having a different impact on the ecosystem. For Chinese scholars, there is a particular attention to the interactions in the ecosystem with financial intermediates such as venture capital or private equity (e.g., Qu 2005; Fu 2010) since the public funding

for private firms is relatively limited in China (Armanios et al. 2017). The efforts of the firms and the funding sources are assumed to not only build and upgrade the ecosystem (Zacharakis, Shepherd, and Coombs 2003; Venkataraman 2004; Dutt et al. 2016), but to also contribute to the ecosystem creation by providing external resources such as capital funds and physical space (Kim, Kim, and Yang 2012; Dutt et al. 2016; Motoyama and Watkins 2017). To summarize, the interaction stream of research suggests a need to engage a much broader array of stakeholders, such as government, businesses, intermediaries, and institutions to ensure that ecosystem creation and development is accompanied by distributive resources.

Institutions

The third theme of articles examine institutions and their central role in shaping entrepreneurial ecosystems, drawing principally from institutional theory. The literature in the institution theme is more limited than from the two themes of nature and network, 15 articles. The core argument within this wave of institution scholarship is that entrepreneurial ecosystems and entrepreneurial activities can be beneficial from the effective formal institution as well as informal institution supportive of entrepreneurship (Armanios et al. 2017). As North (1990) and Williamson (1991) argue environments with limited institutions will exhibit voids in their ability to support entrepreneurial formation and growth, and thus inhibit the development of local ecosystems. This view leads to the focus on specific agent, government, to bridge the voids and public funds and thus, create the appropriate institutions for the ecosystem (Dutt et al. 2016). Thus, the major concern in this stream of research is the particular impact of government on relative parts in entrepreneurial ecosystems.

Role of the government

Scholars have typically argued that governments need to play a comprehensive and holistic role if they are to create a favourable environment for entrepreneurial ecosystems (Parker 2008; Huggins and Williams 2011). Thus, governments use the policy or regulation as a means can play a critical role in linking entrepreneurs with sufficient tangible resources and intangible resources (Samila and Sorenson 2010), increasing the stability of regulations, and ensuring that necessary financial supports and culture of entrepreneurship are present to enhance the sustainability of entrepreneurial ecosystems (Li et al. 2016b). The government can also provide intangible supportive resources for entrepreneurial firms to create a munificent environment for entrepreneurial ecosystem. For example, in Singapore the informal government support has helped to create such an environment (Bruton, Ahlstrom, and Singh 2002; Lerner 2009);. The evidence in mature economies supports the ability of the government to address both tangible and intangible support for an ecosystem (Heidenreich 2005; Huggins and Williams 2011; Pergelova and Angulo-Ruiz 2014; Mueller and Jungwirth 2016).

There have also been some efforts to examine institutions on the ecosystem in non-Western settings (Armanios et al. 2017). While institutional voids are common in emerging economies ecosystems (Naude et al. 2008; Dutt et al. 2016), the government typically takes an active role address such institutional failures that affect entrepreneurial ecosystems (Amezcua et al. 2013; Dutt et al. 2016). For example, most Chinese scholars typically view the government role as universally appropriately across the country in most markets such as providing tax incentives or land for incubators and science parks. The logic behind this research is the greatest barriers to new ventures in emerging countries is the absence of tangible resources such as infrastructure and forms of capital. However, the evidence is that governments in emerging economies have limited capabilities to correct such problems (Heidenreich 2005; Naude et al. 2008) such as building the networking connections and providing the needed resources (e.g., entrepreneurial training, VC funding, advice, and mentorship) necessary for ventures in entrepreneurial process (Cheng and Cui 2016; Cui and Cheng 2016; Xiang and Huang 2016). Thus, while even local

Chinese scholarship demonstrates that the government's strong intervention has a marginally positive effect that diminishes over time (e.g., Niu and Gao 2006; Liu and Zhao 2015; Xiang and Huang 2016), this recognition is yet to be widely applied in the the broader ecosystem research.

Dynamics

The fourth and final theme in the entrepreneurial ecosystem research concerns the dynamics that occur in the ecosystem with a particular focus on how structures can support and reinforce the ecosystem creation. This body of literature draws from a wide variety of theoretical perspectives including ecosystem theory, economic development theory, and inter-organizational relationships literature. There are only 9 articles in the dynamics theme. We will next explore the dynamic theme through the two major parts – structural factors and coopetition strategy.

Structural factors

In the international articles, scholars such as Spigel (2017) draw from ecosystem theory and used the cases of the ecosystems in Waterloo and Calgary, Canada to demonstrate the variety of different configurations that ecosystem can take. Similarly, Adner (2017) also draw from ecosystem theory and used the ecosystem of the firm Michelin to highlight four structural elements (activities, actors, positions, and links) that can affect the entrepreneurial ecosystem. Adner (2017) goes on to argue that changes in the configuration of the structural elements can reset the structure of an entrepreneurial ecosystem. Such a change in the configuration of these elements leads to changes in the symbiotic relationships among network members. Thus, a number of scholars argue that there is a need of more nuanced understanding of the processes through which ecosystem emerges, how the ecosystem members secure or change their role, and the influence on the actor's entrepreneurial activities (Adner 2017). For Chinese scholars, there has been a similar recognition of the need to understand the factors affect an ecosystem specifically in China (Zhang, Zhou, and Gu 2003; Hou et al. 2011), but they have not done much with this understanding.

Focusing on the dynamics of entrepreneurial ecosystems, recent research in this area has also delved into the relationship between how parties in the ecosystem change relational positions and the impact of disruptive forces. Particularly, the literature highlights that ecosystem can coevolve as the interdependent relations change result from the disruptive force. Such force will not only give rise to the change in relations with incumbent firms but also introduce changes in relation with entire interdependent entities in ecosystem (Blundel and Thatcher 2005; Tang and Xi 2006; Hou et al. 2011; Ansari, Garud, and Kumaraswamy 2016; Davis 2016) as 'ecosystem is inherently multilateral' (Adner 2017, 42). The disruptive force from technology innovations in the high-tech industry (Ansari, Garud, and Kumaraswamy 2016), global pressures on tradition industry (Blundel and Thatcher 2005) can be stemmed by entities inside or outside the ecosystem(Hou et al. 2011) who seek to transform from edge position to centralized position (Ansari, Garud, and Kumaraswamy 2016).

Coopetition strategy

A second stream of literature in this theme only from the international articles is the link between coopetition strategy and competition network; this topic has received little attention in the Chinese journals we examined. Coopetition strategy is critical for product market entry and the tensions balance between firms and their competitors (Skilton and Bernardes 2015). The logic in the research is that firms within ecosystems do not operate in isolation but an ecology of interdependent firms that and thus 'these value networks may also include ecosystem incumbents with potentially conflicting interests, especially in multisided markets' (Ansari, Garud, and Kumaraswamy 2016, 1830). This literature also suggests the coopetition strategy could lead to ecosystem co-evolution as Sarma and Sun (2017, 608) argue 'the ecosystem participants hetero-geneously specialize and evolve together, creating value through cumulative and synergistic interactions, and maintain stability of the ecosystem.' Thus, a deeper understanding of the link between coopetition strategy and competition networks and the link between the incumbent firms and focal firms is important given the coopetition strategy can balance the presence of simultaneous conflicting forces between competition and cooperation and enable the ecosystem coevolves as the relational position changes.

Moving entrepreneurial ecosystems research forward

The extant research has substantially advanced our fundamental understanding of entrepreneurial ecosystems. Yet there remain major areas that need greater research particularly since to date the extant research has been predominantly examined developed countries in the international journals. Thus, there is a need to push the research on ecosystems in emerging economies substantially forward since to date we largely do not know much about such systems in emerging economies. The existing Chinese literature typically describes the phenomenon and is not driven by theory. Building on the theory from the international journals and the phenomenon of the Chinese articles, we discuss a number of important avenues for future research on entrepreneurial ecosystems in China. Each of the topics we identify flows from one of the four major streams of research we identified above.

Four major streams of future research

Role of geographic locations
The first theme of research we identified is the nature of entrepreneurial ecosystems. A domain of future research that comes from this theme concerns geographical locations since such locations can possess different institutional settings that can be beneficial to the high rates of entrepreneur-ship (Zacharakis, Shepherd, and Coombs 2003; Spigel 2017). But geographic regions can vary in more than legal or cultural institutions. For example, scholars argue in mature economies there are ecosystems geographic location advantages from institutions including access to scarce resources, social network, infrastructure, venture capital, and entities with specialized knowledge bases (Zacharakis, Shepherd, and Coombs 2003; Feld 2012). Such an impact in China could be even higher as there is a greater dispersion of development across geographic regions in the nation. As a result, there is a need to understand how geographic regions vary in their institutions and related concerns we note above and how these effect ecosystems. Again, often the literature on ecosystem considers the previously noted 12 components as the bud for entrepreneurial ecosystems. However, the geographic location may vary in the environment settings that leads to different typologies of entrepreneurial ecosystem with distinct business models. The configuration could be the determined components across regions such as different levels of market development, technology development, entrepreneurial spirit, venture capitalism, and institutional environment unique to China. Thus, future research could also consider the typology of entrepreneurial ecosys-tems in the configuration perspective to push the understanding why some entrepreneurial ecosystems can be well interconnected and self-sustainable while others not.

Government as an ecosystem member
As previously noted, the role of government is a sub-theme in the broader area of institutions in the ecosystem. One of the key elements that become clear in examining China's entrepreneurial ecosystems is that the role of government must be considered as a major characteristic of Chinese entrepreneurial ecosystems. There is a recognized role for the government in the West in providing services for entrepreneurship such as establishing infrastructure and driving the supportive entre-preneurial culture that could encourage risk-taking within ecosystems (Spigel 2017). Nevertheless,

in China the government plays a far larger role. Scholars often see the government as a partner in the business in China, in part because the government plays a pivotal role in the economy overall (Buckley, Clegg, and Tan 2006; Dong and Glaister 2006; Lau and Bruton 2008; Ahlstrom et al. 2014). While the government does not expect direct returns from firms in China, the government will be far more active than the government in the West in shaping the entrepreneurial venture's success. Thus, rather than simply a force that provides infrastructure such as roads the government would more accurately be seen as an active force in the ecosystem such that it can determine the success or failure of a venture. Future study should take the perspective of the government playing a more central role such as being an agent to enhance interactive relationship for multiple actors into consideration as scholars examine ecosystems.

Interrelations in ecosystem processes

The third theme of research is the network since how the entrepreneurial ecosystem component part interactions are critical (Cumming and Johan 2010; Amezcua et al. 2013). However, such interactions enhance the likelihood of coordination difficulties as different participants within ecosystems often have conflicting interests and goals (Nambisan and Baron 2013). In an emerging economy such as China, such conflicting goals could be even greater due to the dysfunctional competition (Amezcua et al. 2013). The dysfunctional competition presses the firm to develop unique strategies to obtain competitive advantages (Nambisan and Baron 2013). However, the unique strategy can set the firm apart from the entrepreneurial ecosystem thus raising conflicts and limiting the interactions between a firm and its entrepreneurial ecosystem. Future research should expand the understanding of multiple interactions in a dynamic perspective to understand how such conflicting interests and goals are reconciled in a setting such as China.

This branch of suggested research has specific benefits to policymakers in a setting like China as policymakers typically act to create such ecosystems. In mature Western economies, ecosystems have typically grown organically. However, in settings where government act to build an ecosystem as the means to connect such diverse parties with different interests to support each other becomes even more critical. One example of such research would be to examine the fact that the interdependent relationships within any ecosystems are not in static but regularly evolutionary process and can be shaped by the external and internal environment (Hechavarria and Ingram 2014; Spigel 2017). Such contextualized factors could include industry variables including formal institutions such as regulatory institutions, and informal institutions such as entrepreneurial culture (Isenberg 2010; Spigel 2017). Thus, future research could also seek to better understand the different ways in which entrepreneurial ecosystems emerge and changes in response to external and internal changes by incorporating the impact of context on relationship changes.

Building the ecosystem

The final major theme of potential research we identified as dynamics in the ecosystem. In examining this domain, it is clear that future research should examine the interactions in these networks to a greater degree. Nambisan and Baron (2013, 1071) argue that 'ecosystem entrepreneurs often face the challenges associated with the need to balance the goals and priorities set by the ecosystem leader with goals and priorities of the new ventures.' In this regard, the role of lead firms and the associated relationship in ecosystems deserve more consideration (Acquier, Valiorgue, and Daudigeos 2017) as ecosystems entrepreneurs and lead firms in ecosystems might share both similar and different interests who need to reconcile the leadership to affect the technological development. However, in turn, actions of a firm in an entrepreneurial ecosystem are shaped by thick embedded relationships (Mazzanti, Montresor, and Pini 2011). Future research in China should seek to understand how different entities could develop coopetition relationship to create joint values in the entrepreneurial ecosystem.

Part of this vein of potential research should examine the role of relationship interdependence in entrepreneurial ecosystems should examine the impact of history of working together as collaborative partners (Davis 2016; Meuleman et al. 2017). Entities that work together over time build trust (Molina-Morales and Martínez-Fernández 2009). But if such trust is necessary for the ecosystem to develop then that would imply that rather than ecosystems being able to develop quickly, significant time is necessary for the development of ecosystems. Therefore, another potential vein of potential research is prior relationships among participants, the length of time of those relationships, and how those relationships affect interdependence in the entrepreneurial ecosystem.

Integration of the four themes

Integration of the four themes, there are also many other potentially valuable areas for future research and policymakers that integrate parts of these four streams of research. For example, to date the research has largely pulled on existing Western theory. Using indigenous theory to explain the associated business and management practices have been rare in China in the past 30 years (Barkema et al. 2015; Bruton, Zahra, and Cai 2018; Redding and Witt 2015). Thus, it may be that the greater understanding of ecosystems will come from indigenous theory.

Indigenous theory requires scholars to actively tap into the perceived management puzzles and problems embedded in the social environment which may lead to a rich variety of concepts, theories, and paradigms in management. Thus, it is imperative for Chinese scholars to focus on the very unique Chinese management phenomena (Barney and Zhang 2009) in terms of what, who, when, where, how, and why (Whetten 1989). Here we encourage scholars to identify unique Chinese phenomena that existing theory has not explained rather than 'the contradictions between Chinese phenomena and receive theory as new theory cannot be only applicable to a context' (Barney and Zhang 2009, 19). The indigenous approach will require scholars to develop new approaches to the study of entrepreneurial ecosystems to ensure the model is the actual Chinese model.

China has the great variety in institutions (e.g., strong government control), philosophies (e.g., Confucian, Taoism), cultures (e.g., collectivism, high power distance values), and associated management practices (returnee entrepreneurs) from the world that provides a very solid ground for scholars to identify unique phenomenon that is relatively seldom or even not observed in the Western context (Ahlstrom, Chen, and Yeh 2010; Barkema et al. 2015; Bruton, Zahra, and Cai 2018). Therefore, more indigenous research is encouraged to bring new philosophical underpinnings perhaps that can generate possible new insight to ecosystem understanding (Bruton, Zahra, and Cai 2018).

Conclusions

Entrepreneurial ecosystem is a gaining increasing acceptance as a broad core concern that impacts entrepreneurial activities significantly and in turn is a central issue to regional development (Spigel 2017). Over the past seventeen years, scholars have devoted great endeavours to make progress in the entrepreneurial ecosystems research. These studies have yielded significant insights on the understanding of entrepreneurial ecosystems. The research in entrepreneurial ecosystems is still in its infancy despite the over 85 articles we have examined here. There is a need for scholars to build on this research to deepen the understanding of entrepreneurial ecosystems. In this study, we lay the foundation of entrepreneurial ecosystems from the US and China. We then integrate and classify extant entrepreneurial ecosystems research into four topics including the role of geographic location, government as ecosystem member, interrelations in ecosystem processes, and building the ecosystems, in which scholars could explore to extend their future research beyond the West.

We especially hope to encourage Chinese scholars to use indigenous approach to develop new approaches to the study of entrepreneurial ecosystems and ensure the model is the actual Chinese model. To date, most Chinese scholars primarily adapt the existing management theory based in the West to the management practice in emerging economy (Ahlstrom, Bruton, and Zhao 2013), which fails to identify the specific value and contribution for the research on entrepreneurial ecosystems in China. This does not mean that as in all good theory that the analysis is not applicable to other settings. Instead, it is bringing fresh insights to this important domain (Barney and Zhang 2009). It is our hope that our systematic review efforts will spawn a wave of critical theoretical directions as well as practical guidance to entrepreneurs, policymakers, organizations seeking to enhance entrepreneurship and desirable regional development through entrepreneurial ecosystems.

Notes

1. The 23 leading Chinese journals include *Journal of Management Science and Engineering, Management World, System Engineering Theory and Practice, The Journal of Quantitative & Technical Economics, China Soft Science, Journal of Financial Research, Chinese Journal of Management Science, Journal of Systems Engineering, Accounting Research, Journal of Systems & Management, Business Review, Journal of Industrial Engineering and Engineering Management, Nankai Business Review, Journal of The China Society for Scientific and Technical Information Science Research Management, Journal of Public Management, Journal of Management Science, Forecasting, Operations Research and Management Science, Studies in Science of Science, China Industrial Economics,* and *Issues in Agricultural Economy.*
2. The final article list can be requested from any of the authors.

Disclosure statement

No potential conflict of interest was reported by the authors.

Funding

This work was supported by the National Natural Science Foundation of China [grant number 71620107001].

References

Acquier, A., B. Valiorgue, and T. Daudigeos. 2017. "Sharing the Shared Value: A Transaction Cost Perspective on Strategic CSR Policies in Global Value Chains." *Journal of Business Ethics* 144: 1–14. doi:10.1007/s10551-015-2820-0.

Adner, R. 2017. "Ecosystem as Structure an Actionable Construct for Strategy." *Journal of Management* 43 (1): 39–58.

Ahlstrom, D., E. Levitas, M. A. Hitt, M. T. Dacin, and H. Zhu. 2014. "The Three Faces of China: Strategic Alliance Partner Selection in Three Ethnic Chinese Economies." *Journal of World Business* 49 (4): 572–585. doi:10.1016/j.jwb.2013.12.010.

Ahlstrom, D., G. D. Bruton, and K. S. Yeh. 2008. "Private Firms in China: Building Legitimacy in an Emerging Economy." *Journal of World Business* 43 (4): 385–399. doi:10.1016/j.jwb.2008.03.001.

Ahlstrom, D., G. D. Bruton, and L. Zhao. 2013. "Turning Good Research into Good Publications." *Nankai Business Review International* 4 (2): 92–106. doi:10.1108/20408741311323317.

Ahlstrom, D., S.-J. Chen, and K. S. Yeh. 2010. "Managing in Ethnic Chinese Communities: Culture, Institutions, and Context." *Asia Pacific Journal of Management* 27 (3): 341–354. doi:10.1007/s10490-010-9218-4.

Ahuja, G. 2000. "Collaboration Networks, Structural Holes, and Innovation: A Longitudinal Study." *Administrative Science Quarterly* 45 (3): 425–455. doi:10.2307/2667105.

Amezcua, A. S., M. G. Grimes, S. W. Bradley, and J. Wiklund. 2013. "Organizational Sponsorship and Founding Environments: A Contingency View on the Survival of Business-incubated Firms, 1994–2007." *Academy of Management Journal* 56 (6): 1628–1654. doi:10.5465/amj.2011.0652.

Ansari, S. S., R. Garud, and A. Kumaraswamy. 2016. "The Disruptor's Dilemma: TiVo and the US Television Ecosystem." *Strategic Management Journal* 37 (9): 1829–1853. doi:10.1002/smj.2442.

Armanios, D. E., C. E. Eesley, J. Li, and K. M. Eisenhardt. 2017. "How Entrepreneurs Leverage Institutional Intermediaries in Emerging Economies to Acquire Public Resources." *Strategic Management Journal* 38 (7): 1373–1390. doi:10.1002/smj.2017.38.issue-7.

Audretsch, D. B., and M. Keilbach. 2004. "Does Entrepreneurship Capital Matter?" *Entrepreneurship Theory and Practice* 28 (5): 419–429. doi:10.1111/etap.2004.28.issue-5.

Barkema, H. G., X.-P. Chen, G. George, Y. Luo, and A. S. Tsui. 2015. "West Meets East: New Concepts and Theories." *Academy of Management Journal* 58 (2): 460–479. doi:10.5465/amj.2015.4021.

Barney, J. B., and S. Zhang. 2009. "The Future of Chinese Management Research: A Theory of Chinese Management versus a Chinese Theory of Management." *Management & Organization Review* 5 (1): 15–28.

Blundel, R., and M. Thatcher. 2005. "Contrasting Local Responses to Globalization: The Case of Volume Yacht Manufacturing in Europe." *Entrepreneurship & Regional Development* 17 (6): 405–429. doi:10.1080/08985620500385619.

Bøllingtoft, A., and J. P. Ulhøi. 2005. "The Networked Business Incubator—Leveraging Entrepreneurial Agency?" *Journal of Business Venturing* 20 (2): 265–290. doi:10.1016/j.jbusvent.2003.12.005.

Brekke, T. 2015. "Entrepreneurship and Path Dependency in Regional Development." *Entrepreneurship & Regional Development* 27 (3–4): 202–218. doi:10.1080/08985626.2015.1030457.

Bruton, G. D., D. Ahlstrom, and K. Obloj. 2008. "Entrepreneurship in Emerging Economies: Where are We Today and Where Should the Research Go in the Future." *Entrepreneurship Theory and Practice* 32 (1): 1–14. doi:10.1111/etap.2008.32.issue-1.

Bruton, G. D., D. Ahlstrom, and K. Singh. 2002. "The Impact of the Institutional Environment on the Venture Capital Industry in Singapore." *Venture Capital* 4 (3): 197–218. doi:10.1080/13691060213712.

Bruton, G. D., S. A. Zahra, and L. Cai. 2018. "Examining Entrepreneurship through Indigenous Theory." *Entrepreneurship Theory and Practice* 42 (3): 351–361. doi:10.1177/1042258717741129.

Buckley, P. J., J. Clegg, and H. Tan. 2006. "Cultural Awareness in Knowledge Transfer to China—The Role of Guanxi and Mianzi." *Journal of World Business* 41 (3): 275–288. doi:10.1016/j.jwb.2006.01.008.

Carree, M., E. Congregado, A. Golpe, and A. van Stel. 2015. "Self-employment and Job Generation in Metropolitan Areas, 1969–2009." *Entrepreneurship & Regional Development* 27 (3–4): 181–201. doi: 10.1080/08985626.2015.1025860.

Chen, J., A. Y. Chang, and G. D. Bruton. 2017. "Microfinance: Where are We Today and Where Should the Research Go in the Future?" *International Small Business Journal: Researching Entrepreneurship* 35 (7): 793–802. doi:10.1177/0266242617717380.

Cheng, Y., and J. Cui. 2016. "孵化器税收优惠政策的传导效应评估 [Evaluation of the conduction effect of incubator tax incentive]." *Science Research Management* 37 (3): 101–109. Chinese.

Corbin, J. M., and A. L. Strauss. 2014. *Basics of Qualitative Research: Techniques and Procedures for Developing Grounded Theory*. 4 ed. Thousand Oaks, CA: Sage Publications.

Cui, J., and Y. Cheng. 2016. "孵化器税收优惠政策对创新服务的激励效应 [The incentive effect of incubator tax preferential policy on innovation service]." *Studies in Science of Science* 34 (1): 30–39. Chinese.

Cumming, D., and S. Johan. 2010. "The Differential Impact of the Internet on Spurring Regional Entrepreneurship." *Entrepreneurship Theory and Practice* 34 (5): 857–883. doi:10.1111/j.1540-6520.2009.00348.x.

Davis, J. P. 2016. "The Group Dynamics of Interorganizational Relationships: Collaborating with Multiple Partners in Innovation Ecosystems." *Administrative Science Quarterly* 61 (4): 621–661. doi:10.1177/0001839216649350.

del-Corte-Lora, V., T. Vallet-Bellmunt, and F. X. Molina-Morales. 2015. "Be Creative but Not so Much. Decreasing Benefits of Creativity in Clustered Firms." *Entrepreneurship & Regional Development* 27 (1–2): 1–27. doi:10.1080/08985626.2014.995722.

Dong, L., and K. W. Glaister. 2006. "Motives and Partner Selection Criteria in International Strategic Alliances: Perspectives of Chinese Firms." *International Business Review* 15 (6): 577–600. doi:10.1016/j.ibusrev.2006.09.003.

Dutt, N., O. Hawn, E. Vidal, A. Chatterji, A. McGahan, and W. Mitchell. 2016. "How Open System Intermediaries Address Institutional Failures: The Case of Business Incubators in Emerging-market Countries." *Academy of Management Journal* 59 (3): 818–840. doi:10.5465/amj.2012.0463.

Farzanegan, M. R. 2014. "Can Oil-rich Countries Encourage Entrepreneurship?." *Entrepreneurship & Regional Development* 26 (9-10): 706–725. doi: 10.1080/08985626.2014.981869.

Feld, B. 2012. *Startup Communities: Building an Entrepreneurial Ecosystem in Your City*. Hoboken, NJ: Wiley.

Feldman, M., and N. Lowe. 2015. "Triangulating Regional Economies: Realizing the Promise of Digital Data." *Research Policy* 44 (9): 1785–1793. doi:10.1016/j.respol.2015.01.015.

Fini, R., R. Grimaldi, S. Santoni, and M. Sobrero. 2011. "Complements or Substitutes? The Role of Universities and Local Context in Supporting the Creation of Academic Spin-offs." *Research Policy* 40 (8): 1113–1127. doi: 10.1016/j.respol.2011.05.013.

Fu, E., and T. Hsia. 2014. "Universities and Entrepreneurial Ecosystems: Elements of the Stanford-Silicon Valley Success." *Kauffman Fellows Report*, 5: 2014. Accessed 10 December 2016. http://www.kauffmanfellows.org/journal_posts/universities-and-entrepreneurial-ecosystems-stanford-silicon-valley-success/

Fu, S. 2010. "区域创新网络与科技产业生态环境互动机制研究—以中关村海淀科技园区为例 [Research on the interaction mechanism between regional innovation network and ecological environment of sci-tech industry—A case study of Haidian Science Park in Zhongguancun]." *Manage World*, no. 6: 8–13. Chinese.

Gao, S., L. Zheng, and S. Zhang. 2006. "区域经济文化对创新模式影响的比较分析——以硅谷和温州为例 [Comparative Analyses on the Impacts of Regional Economic Culture upon Innovation Model: Case Study of Silicone Valley and Wenzhou in China]." *China Soft Science*, no. 4: 8–15. Chinese.

Habersetzer, A. 2016. "Spinoff Dynamics beyond Clusters: Pre-entry Experience and Firm Survival in Peripheral Regions." *Entrepreneurship & Regional Development* 28 (9–10): 791–812. doi:10.1080/08985626.2016.1250821.

Hansen, M. T., H. W. Chesbrough, N. Nohria, and D. N. Sull. 2000. "Networked Incubators." *Harvard Business Review* 78 (5): 74–84.

He, K., and S. Zhong. 2012. "中国企业加速器发展路径研究[The Development Path of Business Accelerators in China]." *Science Research Management* 33 (1): 112–119.

Hechavarria, D. M., and A. Ingram. 2014. "A Review of the Entrepreneurial Ecosystem and the Entrepreneurial Society in the United States: An Exploration with the Global Entrepreneurship Monitor Dataset." *Journal of Business and Entrepreneurship* 26 (1): 1–35.

Heidenreich, M. 2005. "The Renewal of Regional Capabilities: Experimental Regionalism in Germany." *Research Policy* 34 (5): 739–757. doi:10.1016/j.respol.2005.04.004.

Hou, J., Q. Lu, Y. Shi, and K. Rong. 2011. "基于组织生态学的企业成长演化：有关变异和生存因素的案例研究 [Enterprise growth and evolution based on organizational ecology: Case study of variation and survival factors]." *Manage World*, no. 12: 116–130. Chinese.

Hu, H., M. Zhang, B. Zhang, and D. Zhang. 2012. "网络交互模式与创业支持类型—基于中国孵化产业的实证分析 [Impact of network interaction on entrepreneurial assistance—Empirical analysis on Chinese incubation industry]." *Studies in Science of Science* 30 (2): 275–283. Chinese.

Huggins, R., and N. Williams. 2011. "Entrepreneurship and Regional Competitiveness: The Role and Progression of Policy." *Entrepreneurship & Regional Development* 23 (9–10): 907–932. doi:10.1080/08985626.2011.577818.

Huggins, R., and P. Thompson. 2014. "Culture, Entrepreneurship and Uneven Development: A Spatial Analysis." *Entrepreneurship & Regional Development* 26 (9–10): 726–752. doi:10.1080/08985626.2014.985740.

Iansiti, M., and R. Levien. 2004. "Strategy as Ecology." *Harvard Business Review* 82 (3): 68–81.

Isaksen, A. 2016. "Cluster Emergence: Combining Pre-existing Conditions and Triggering Factors." *Entrepreneurship & Regional Development* 28 (9–10): 704–723. doi:10.1080/08985626.2016.1239762.

Isenberg, D. 2010. "How to Start an Entrepreneurial Revolution." *Harvard Business Review* 88 (6): 40–50.

Isenberg, D. 2011. "The Entrepreneurship Ecosystem Strategy as a New Paradigm for Economic Policy: Principles for Cultivating Entrepreneurship." Accessed 12 December 2016. http://entrepreneurial-revolution.com/2011/05/11/the-entrepreneurship-ecosystem-strategy-as-a-new-paradigm-for-economic-policy-principles-for-cultivating-entrepreneurship/

Jack, G., Y. Zhu, J. Barney, M. Y. Brannen, C. Prichard, K. Singh, and D. Whetten. 2013. "Refining, Reinforcing and Reimagining Universal and Indigenous Theory Development in International Management." *Journal of Management Inquiry* 22 (2): 148–164. doi:10.1177/1056492612458453.

Kanter, R. M. 2012. "Enriching the Ecosystem." *Harvard Business Review* 90 (3): 140–149.

Kasabov, E. 2015. "Start-up Difficulties in Early-stage Peripheral Clusters: The Case of IT in an Emerging Economy." *Entrepreneurship Theory and Practice* 39 (4): 727–761. doi:10.1111/etap.2015.39.issue-4.

Kim, Y., W. Kim, and T. Yang. 2012. "The Effect of the Triple Helix System and Habitat on Regional Entrepreneurship: Empirical Evidence from the U.S." *Research Policy* 41 (1): 154–166. doi:10.1016/j.respol.2011.08.003.

Lau, C. M., and G. D. Bruton. 2008. "FDI in China: What We Know and What We Need to Study Next." *Academy of Management Proceedings* 22 (4): 30–44.

Laukkanen, M. 2000. "Exploring Alternative Approaches in High-level Entrepreneurship Education: Creating Micromechanisms for Endogenous Regional Growth." *Entrepreneurship & Regional Development* 12 (1): 25–47. doi:10.1080/089856200283072.

Lerner, J. 2009. *Boulevard of Broken Dreams: Why Public Efforts to Boost Entrepreneurship and Venture Capital Have Failed–And What to Do about It*. Princeton, NJ, USA: Princeton University Press.

Li, C. 2014. "社会文化特征对区域创业活动影响差异研究[The Difference of Social Cultural Traits Influence Rural Entrepreneurial Activity]." *Studies in Science of Science* 32 (12): 1888–1896. Chinese.

Li, M., J. Wang, Y. Wang, M. Wang, and Y. Zhao. 2016a. "大学-产业-政府三螺旋体系与区域创业—关联及区域差异 [The triple helix system of university-industry-government and regional entrepreneurship: Relevance and regional differences]." *Studies in Science of Science* 34 (8): 1211–1222. Chinese.

Li, M. H., S. J. Goetz, M. Partridge, and D. A. Fleming. 2016b. "Location Determinants of High-growth Firms." *Entrepreneurship & Regional Development* 28 (1–2): 97–125. doi:10.1080/08985626.2015.1109003.

Li, Y., and Y. Zhang. 2012. "网络资源、创业导向与在孵企业绩效研究—基于大连国家级创业孵化基地的实证分析 [Research on network resources, entrepreneurial orientation and performance of incubating enterprises based on Dalian national entrepreneurial incubator]." *China Soft Science*, no. 8: 98–110. Chinese.

Lin, S., and Y. Jiang. 2012. "创业活动为何发生:创业倾向迁移的视角[Why New Ventures Emerge: From the Angle of the Movement of Entrepreneurial Intention]." *China Industrial Economics* no. 6: 94–106. Chinese.

Liu, C., and J. Cai. 2016. "孵化网络影响高层次人才创业绩效的机理研究[Research on the Influence Mechanism of Incubator Network on the Entrepreneurship Performance of High Level Talents]." *Studies in Science of Science* 34 (11): 1672–1688. Chinese.

Liu, J., and F. Luo. 2005. "基于焦点企业成长的集群演进机理研究—以长沙工程机械集群为例[Research on Cluster Evolution Mechanism based on the Growth of Focused Enterprises —Taking Changsha Construction Machinery Cluster as an Example]." *Manage World*, no. 10: 159–161. Chinese.

Liu, R., and R. Zhao. 2015. "国家高新区推动了地区经济发展吗?—基于双重差分方法的验证 [Has the national high-tech zone promoted regional economic development? An empirical research based on the DID method]." *Manage World*, no. 8: 30–38. Chinese.

Lu, Z., and S. Liao. 2016. "农产品电商发展的区域创业效应研究 [Regional Entrepreneurship Effect from the Development of Agricultural Products E-business]." *China Soft Science*, no. 5: 67–78. Chinese.

Luo, F. 2014. "企业孵化器商业模式价值创造分析 [Business Incubator Business Model Value Creation Analysis]." *Manage World*, no. 8: 180–181. Chinese.

Lv, Y., Q. Lan, and S. Han. 2015. "开放式创新生态系统的成长基因——基于iOS、Android和Symbian的多案例研究 [Growth Genes of the Open Innovation Ecosystem—Multi-case Study Based on iOS, Android and Symbian]." *China Industrial Economics*, no. 5: 148–160. Chinese.

Mao, Y., and Y. Zhou. 2002. "硅谷机制与企业高速成长—再论企业与市场之间的关系 [Silicon Valley mechanism and rapid growth of enterprises—Discussion on the relationship between enterprises and market]." *Manage World*, no. 6: 102–108. Chinese.

Mason, C., and R. Brown. 2014. "Entrepreneurial Ecosystems and Growth Oriented Entrepreneurship." *Final Report to OECD*. Paris.

Mazzanti, M., S. Montresor, and P. Pini. 2011. "Outsourcing, Delocalization and Firm Organization: Transaction Costs versus Industrial Relations in a Local Production System of Emilia Romagna." *Entrepreneurship & Regional Development* 23 (7–8): 419–447. doi:10.1080/08985620903233986.

Meuleman, M., M. Jääskeläinen, M. V. J. Maula, and M. Wright. 2017. "Venturing into the Unknown with Strangers: Substitutes of Relational Embeddedness in Cross-border Partner Selection in Venture Capital Syndicates." *Journal of Business Venturing* 32 (2): 131–144. doi:10.1016/j.jbusvent.2017.01.001.

Molina-Morales, F. X., and M. T. Martínez-Fernández. 2009. "Too Much Love in the Neighborhood Can Hurt: How an Excess of Intensity and Trust in Relationships May Produce Negative Effects on Firms." *Strategic Management Journal* 30 (9): 1013–1023. doi:10.1002/smj.v30:9.

Moore, J. F. 1996. *The Death of Competition: Leadership and Strategy in the Age of Business Ecosystems*. New York: HarperBusiness.

Motoyama, Y., and K. Knowlton. 2016. "From Resource Munificence to Ecosystem Integration: The Case of Government Sponsorship in St. Louis." *Entrepreneurship & Regional Development* 28 (5–6): 448–470. doi:10.1080/08985626.2016.1186749.

Motoyama, Y., and K. K. Watkins. 2017. "Examining the Connections within the Startup Ecosystem: A Case Study of St. Louis." *Entrepreneurship Research Journal* 7 (1): 1–32. doi:10.1515/erj-2016-0011.

Mueller, E. F., and C. Jungwirth. 2016. "What Drives the Effectiveness of Industrial Clusters? Exploring the Impact of Contextual, Structural and Functioning Determinants." *Entrepreneurship & Regional Development* 28 (5–6): 424–447. doi:10.1080/08985626.2016.1186748.

Nambisan, S., and R. A. Baron. 2013. "Entrepreneurship in Innovation Ecosystems: Entrepreneurs' Self-regulatory Processes and Their Implications for New Venture Success." *Entrepreneurship Theory and Practice* 37 (5): 1071–1097. doi:10.1111/etap.2013.37.issue-5.

Naude, W., T. Gries, E. Wood, and A. Meintjies. 2008. "Regional Determinants of Entrepreneurial Start-ups in a Developing Country." *Entrepreneurship & Regional Development* 20 (2): 111–124. doi:10.1080/08985620701631498.

Nguyen, Q. A., G. Sullivan Mort, and C. D'Souza. 2015. "Vietnam in Transition: SMEs and the Necessitating Environment for Entrepreneurship Development." *Entrepreneurship & Regional Development* 27 (3–4): 154–180. doi:10.1080/08985626.2015.1015457.

Niu, R., and T. Gao. 2006. "科技企业孵化器制度变迁的瓶颈约束与创新途径 [Bottleneck constraints and innovative approaches to the institutional change of science and technology business incubator]." *Manage World*, no. 2: 161–162. Chinese.

North, D. C. 1990. *Institutions, Institutional Change and Economic Performance*. Cambridge, UK: Cambridge University Press.

Overholm, H. 2015. "Collectively Created Opportunities in Emerging Ecosystems: The Case of Solar Service Ventures." *Technovation* 39/40: 14–25. doi:10.1016/j.technovation.2014.01.008.

Parker, R. 2008. "Governance and the Entrepreneurial Economy: A Comparative Analysis of Three Regions." *Entrepreneurship Theory and Practice* 32 (5): 833–854. doi:10.1111/etap.2008.32.issue-5.

Pereira, A. A. 2004. "State Entrepreneurship and Regional Development: Singapore's Industrial Parks in Batam and Suzhou." *Entrepreneurship & Regional Development* 16 (2): 129–144. doi: 10.1080/08985620410001677844.

Pergelova, A., and F. Angulo-Ruiz. 2014. "The Impact of Government Financial Support on the Performance of New Firms: The Role of Competitive Advantage as an Intermediate Outcome." *Entrepreneurship & Regional Development* 26 (9–10): 663–705. doi:10.1080/08985626.2014.980757.

Qian, P. 2000. "孵化器运作的国际经验与我国孵化器产业的发展对策 [International experience of incubator operation and development countermeasures of China's incubator industry]." *Manage World*, no. 6: 78–84. Chinese.

Qu, Q. 2005. "论孵化器与风险投资融合的博弈决策 [Study the combination of business incubator and venture capital game decision-making]." *Operation Research and Management Science* 14 (6): 149–154. Chinese.

Redding, G., and M. A. Witt. 2015. "Advancing Indigenous Management Theory: Executive Rationale as an Institutional Logic." *Management & Organization Review* 11 (2): 179–203. doi:10.1017/mor.2015.23.

Sabeti, H. 2011. "The For-benefit Enterprise." *Harvard Business Review* 89 (11): 98–104.

Samila, S., and O. Sorenson. 2010. "Venture Capital as a Catalyst to Commercialization." *Research Policy* 39 (10): 1348–1360. doi:10.1016/j.respol.2010.08.006.

Sarma, S., and S. L. Sun. 2017. "The Genesis of Fabless Business Model: Institutional Entrepreneurs in an Adaptive Ecosystem." *Asia Pacific Journal of Management* 34 (3): 587–617. doi:10.1007/s10490-016-9488-6.

Seidl, I., O. Schelske, J. Joshi, and M. Jenny. 2003. "Entrepreneurship in Biodiversity Conservation and Regional Development." *Entrepreneurship & Regional Development* 15 (4): 333–350. doi:10.1080/0898562032000058914.

Shearmur, R., and D. Doloreux. 2016. "How Open Innovation Processes Vary between Urban and Remote Environments: Slow Innovators, Market-sourced Information and Frequency of Interaction." *Entrepreneurship & Regional Development* 28 (5–6): 337–357. doi:10.1080/08985626.2016.1154984.

Shen, M., and G. Sui. 2005. "高科技创业环境与区域发展循环悖论[Circumstance for Technological Entrepreneurship to Solve the Cycle Dilemma of Regional Development]." *Science Research Management* 26 (10): 46–53. Chinese.

Skilton, P. F., and E. Bernardes. 2015. "Competition Network Structure and Product Market Entry." *Strategic Management Journal* 36 (11): 1688–1696. doi:10.1002/smj.2318.

Smith, H. L., and S. Bagchi-Sen. 2012. "The Research University, Entrepreneurship and Regional Development: Research Propositions and Current Evidence." *Entrepreneurship & Regional Development* 24 (5–6): 383–404. doi:10.1080/08985626.2011.592547.

Spigel, B. 2017. "The Relational Organization of Entrepreneurial Ecosystems." *Entrepreneurship Theory and Practice* 41 (1): 49–72. doi:10.1111/etap.12167.

Spigel, B., and R. Harrison. 2018. "Toward a Process Theory of Entrepreneurial Ecosystems." *Strategic Entrepreneurship Journal* 12 (1): 151–168. doi:10.1002/sej.2018.12.issue-1.

Sturgeon, T. J. 2000. "How Silicon Valley Came to Be." In *Understanding Silicon Valley: Anatomy of an Entrepreneurial Region*, edited by M. Kenney, 15–47. California, US: Standford University Press.

Tang, F., and Y. Xi. 2006. "Exploring Dynamic Multi-level Linkages in Inter-organizational Networks." *Asia Pacific Journal of Management* 23 (2): 187–208. doi:10.1007/s10490-006-7166-9.

The Chinese Academy of Social Sciences. 2014. Accessed 10 January 2018. http://www.nsfcms.org/index.php?r=site/journalList

The Economist. 2014. "All Together Now: What Entrepreneurial Ecosystems Need to Flourish." Accessed 12 February 2017. http://www.economist.com/news/special-report/21593582-what-entrepreneurial-ecosystems-need-flourish-all-together-now

The Ministry of Science and Technology of the People's Republic of China. 2017. Accessed 10 January 2018. http://www.most.gov.cn/mostinfo/xinxifenlei/fgzc/gfxwj/gfxwj2017/201707/t20170711_133971.htm

Tsui, A. S. 2006. "Contextualization in Chinese Management Research." *Management & Organization Review* 2 (1): 1–13. doi:10.1111/j.1740-8784.2006.00033.x.

Venkataraman, S. 2004. "Regional Transformation through Technological Entrepreneurship." *Journal of Business Venturing* 19 (1): 153–167. doi:10.1016/j.jbusvent.2003.04.001.

Wang, D. 2004. "关于大学科技园的一个网络分析[A Network Analysis of The University Science Park]." *Studies in Science of Science* 22 (2): 164–169.

Whetten, D. A. 1989. "What Constitutes a Theoretical Contribution?" *Academy of Management Review* 14 (4): 490–495. doi:10.5465/amr.1989.4308371.

Williamson, O. E. 1991. "Comparative Economic Organization: The Analysis of Discrete Structural Alternatives." *Administrative Science Quarterly* 36 (2): 269–296. doi:10.2307/2393356.

Xiang, G., and W. Huang. 2016. "创业扶持方式与新创企业绩效的关系研究 [Relationship of entrepreneurial sponsorship approaches with performance of new ventures]." *Studies in Science of Science* 34 (10): 1561–1568. Chinese.

Xing, R., G. Wang, and J. Zhou. 2015. "基于GEM模型的区域创业合成能力评价研究 [The research of evaluation on business dynamic capability based on GEM model]." *Chinese Journal of Management Science*, S1: 718–725. Chinese.

Yin, P. L., J. P. Davis, and Y. Muzyrya. 2014. "Entrepreneurial Innovation: Killer Apps in the iphone Ecosystem." *American Economic Review* 104 (5): 255–59. doi: 10.1257/aer.104.5.255.

Yuan, C., and Y. Jia. 2005. "国内大学科技园区技术创业企业创新网络初步研究[A Study on the Innovation Networks of Technological Entrepreneurship Firms in the Chinese University S&t Park]." *Science Research Management* 26 (6): 26–31. Chinese.

Zacharakis, A. L., D. A. Shepherd, and J. E. Coombs. 2003. "The Development of Venture-capital-backed Internet Companies: An Ecosystem Perspective." *Journal of Business Venturing* 18 (2): 217–231. doi:10.1016/S0883-9026(02)00084-8.

Zahra, S. A., and S. Nambisan. 2011. "Entrepreneurship in Global Innovation Ecosystems." *AMS Review* 1 (1): 4–17. doi:10.1007/s13162-011-0004-3.

Zhang, L. 2012. "孵化互动、专用性人力资本和在孵企业成功毕业[Incubating Interaction, Founder's Specific Human Capital and the Survival of Tenants]." *Nankai Business Review* 15 (1): 93–101. Chinese.

Zhang, L., R. Qi, and Y. Zhou. 2014. "在孵企业成功毕业的影响因素——基于孵化互动视角的研究[Determinants of Tenants Successful Graduation: Research based on the Perspective of Co- production Theory]." *Studies in Science of Science* 32 (5): 758-766. Chinese.

Zhang, W. 2007. "中关村留学人员创业企业发展的瓶颈调研[Research on Bottlenecks in the Development of Zhongguancun overseas Students' Entrepreneurial Enterprises]." *China Soft Science*, no. 8: 116–122+130. Chinese.

Zhang, W., L. Zhou, and Q. Gu. 2003. "经济转型中的企业退出机制—关于北京市中关村科技园区的一项经验研究 [Enterprise withdrawal mechanism in economic transformation—An empirical study on Zhongguancun science and technology park in Beijing]." *Economic Research Journal*, no. 10: 3–14. Chinese.

Zhang, W., and X. Xing. 2007. "高技术企业创业孵化环境与成长绩效关系研究[An Empirical Research of the Relationship between Entrepreneurial Incubating Environment and Venture Growth in Hi-tech Enterprises]." *Studies in Science of Science* 25 (1): 74–78. Chinese.

Zhao, X., H. Li, and A. Rauch. 2012. "创业活动的国家（地区）差异：文化与国家（地区）经济发展水平的交互作用 [National (Regional) Differences in Entrepreneurial Activity: Interaction between Culture and National (Regional) Level of Economic Development]." *Manage World*, no. 8: 78–90+188. Chinese.

Zhou, F. 2013. "基于AHP-DEA方法的区域科技创业人才生态系统评价研究[Research on the Evaluation System of Regional Ecosystem for Entrepreneurial Talent of Science and Technology Based on AHP-DEA]." *Journal of Industrial Engineering and Engineering Management* 27 (1): 8–14. Chinese.

Zhu, R., Z. Liu, and Y. Liu. 2011. "架构创新、生态位优化与后发企业的跨越式赶超—基于比亚迪、联发科、华为、振华重工创新实践的理论探索 [Structure innovation, niche optimization and leapfrog of the post-development enterprises–Based on the theoretical exploration of the innovation practice of BYD, MediaTek, Huawei and Zhenhua heavy industry]." *Manage World*, no. 7: 69–97. Chinese.

Appendix

Table A1. Methodologies used in reviewed articles.

Method	Totals by Method in Chinese Journals and International Journals		Method
Quantitative	46	International: 26 Chinese: 20	Regression Analysis: OLS, the largest log-likelihood estimation, content analysis, parsimonious analysis, hierarchical regression analysis, multivariate analysis, Poisson multi-level model, three-stage least squares, structural equation modeling, binary logistic regression, DID, combination weighting method, REM, and AHP.
Qualitative	22	International: 17 Chinese: 5	Case studies
Conceptual	18	International: 8 Chinese: 10	Theory-driven papers Phenomenon-driven papers with practical implications, only two are theory-driven papers
Both Quantitative and Qualitative	1	Chinese: 1	Semi-structured interviews and multivariate analysis
Total by Method	85		

Table A2. Number of countries and locations of quantitative articles in sample.

Sample	Sample locations	Totals by Sample
International Journals:		
Emerging economies	China (2), South Africa (1), Vietnam (2), multiple (1)	6
Mature economies	US (14), UK (3), Canada (3), Germany (2), Switzerland (2), Australia (2), Denmark (1), France (1), Ireland (1), Italy (1), Norway (1), Spain (1), Swiss (1), Sweden (1)	34
Mixed countries	Singapore (1), China (1), and Indonesia (1), multiple (1)	2
Chinese Journals:		
China	City: Beijing, Dalian, Shanghai, Xi'an, Wuhan, Ningbo, Suzhou, Wuxi, Nanjing, Guangzhou, Zhuhai, Shenzhen, Shenyang, Dezhou, 283 cities, 15 cities, Province: Zhejiang, Hunan, Guangxi, Yunnan, Guangdong, Hubei, Fujian, Gansu, Hubei, Hunan, Jiangsu, Qinghai, 13 provinces, 31 provinces, Taiwan	25
Totals		67

Table A3. Themes covered in entrepreneurial ecosystems research.

Theme	Method	Examples
Nature	Conceptual	Laukkanen 2000; Smith and Bagchi-Sen 2012; Sabeti 2011; Kanter 2012; Isenberg 2010; Shen and Sui 2005; Lin and Jiang 2012; Gao, Zheng, and Zhang 2006; Qian 2000; Mao and Zhou 2002
	Case study	Seidl et al. 2003; Isaksen 2016; Kasabov 2015; Feldman and Lowe 2015; Spigel 2017; Adner 2017
	Quantitative	Naude et al. 2008; Huggins and Thompson 2014; Farzanegan 2014; Carree, Congregado, Golpe, and van Stel 2015; Li et al. 2016b; Shearmur and Doloreux 2016; Habersetzer 2016; Audretsch and Keilbach 2004; Cumming and Johan 2010; Samila and Sorenson 2010; Zhang 2007; Zhou 2013; Li 2014; Lu and Liao 2016; Xing, Wang, and Zhou 2015; Zhao, Li, and Rauch 2012
Networks	Conceptual	Hansen et al. 2000; Venkataraman 2004; Nambisan and Baron 2013; Qu 2005; Wang 2004
	Case study	Davis 2016; Brekke 2015; Motoyama and Knowlton 2016; Bøllingtoft and Ulhøi 2005; Parker 2008; Fu 2010
	Quantitative	Yin, Davis, and Muzyrya 2014; Amezcua et al. 2013; Dutt, Hawn, Vidal,Chatterji, McGahan,& Mitchell, 2016; Mazzanti, Montresor,& Pini, 2011; del-Corte-Lora, Vallet-Bellmunt, and Molina-Morales 2015; Zacharakis, Shepherd, and Coombs 2003; Molina-Morales and Martínez-Fernández 2009; Skilton and Bernardes 2015; Fini, Grimaldi, Santoni, and Sobrero 2011; Kim, Kim, and Yang 2012; Li and Zhang 2012; Zhang 2012; Zhang, Qi, and Zhou 2014; Hu et al. 2012; Liu and Cai 2016; Yuan and Jia 2005; Li et al. 2016a
	Mixed	Zhang and Xing 2007
Institutions	Conceptual	Niu and Gao 2006; Luo 2014
	Case study	Heidenreich 2005; Huggins and Williams 2011; Pereira 2004; Zhu, Liu, and Liu 2011
	Quantitative	Pergelova and Angulo-Ruiz 2014; Nguyen, Sullivan Mort, and D'Souza 2015; Mueller and Jungwirth 2016; Armanios et al. 2017; Cheng and Cui 2016; Cui and Cheng 2016; Xiang and Huang 2016; Liu and Zhao 2015
Dynamics	Conceptual	Liu and Luo 2005
	Case study	Tang and Xi 2006; Blundel and Thatcher 2005; Ansari, Garud, and Kumaraswamy 2016; Lv, Lan, and Han 2015; He and Zhong 2012; Hou et al. 2011
	Quantitative	Sarma and Sun 2017; Zhang, Zhou, and Gu 2003

Martínez-Fernández.

The impact of sub-national institutions on SMEs' diversification into new businesses: evidence from China

Dong Chen ⓘ, Donghong Li and Yongsun Paik

ABSTRACT

This study explores how sub-national institutions affect the diversification of small and medium-sized enterprises (SMEs) into new businesses. Using a sample of 3240 SMEs in China, we found that the dominance of state-owned enterprises (SOEs) and the development of market systems in a province were related to local SMEs' diversification. Specifically, in provinces dominated by SOEs, SMEs were less likely to diversify into new businesses. The development of market systems tended to reduce the odds of diversification for SMEs that primarily served local markets, and lower the likelihood of unrelated diversification. As a rare attempt to examine the impact of sub-national institutions on SMEs' diversification, this study contributes to the research on diversification, institutions, and SME management.

Introduction

Corporate diversification is a major research topic in the field of strategic management (Nippa, Pidun, and Rubner 2011). In recent years, a number of studies, especially those focused on emerging and transitional economies, have examined this issue from an institutional perspective, (e.g., Wan and Hoskisson 2003; Chakrabarti, Singh, and Mahmood 2007; Delios, Xu, and Beamish 2008; Lee, Peng, and Lee 2008). Scholars in this stream of research have largely viewed institutions as moderating factors and argued that diversification is more likely to offer resource benefits and enhance performance in underdeveloped institutional settings (Wan et al. 2011). For instance, Wan and Hoskisson (2003) showed that diversification negatively impacts performance in more munificent home country environments while improving performance in less munificent environments, while Lee, Peng, and Lee (2008) found that there is a diversification premium in emerging economies and this premium tends to dissipate during institutional transitions.

In this stream of research, there are still several knowledge gaps. First of all, as institutions are often treated as contingency factors, only a limited number of studies have explicitly examined institutional factors as antecedents of corporate diversification (Wan et al. 2011). However, since strategic decisions are endogenous to performance (Hamilton and Nickerson 2003), firms may choose to diversify in response to external institutional factors (Miller 2004). More research is needed to understand how institutions drive firms' diversification. Secondly, previous studies have mainly examined cross-country institutional differences and paid limited attention to subnational institutions. While national institutions are critical to business decision-making, the institutional environment is not necessarily coherent throughout a country (Lenartowicz and Roth 2001).

Significant sub-national, cross-region differences may exist, especially in those large emerging markets (Peng, Wang, and Jiang 2008). A small number of studies have addressed the impact of sub-national institutions on foreign investment (Meyer and Nguyen 2005), joint venture partner selection (Shi, Sun, and Peng 2012), foreign firm performance (Li and Sun 2017), and local firm performance (Nguyen, Le, and Bryant 2013). However, to the best of our knowledge, few studies have examined the direct impact of sub-national institutions on corporate diversification. Wang and Luo's (2018) recent paper is an exception, which suggests that Chinese provincial governors' emphasis on social stability positively affects the diversification of publicly listed firms. Thirdly, prior diversification research has mainly focused on large multi-business firms, such as Chaebols in South Korea and business groups in India and China (Guillén 2000; Nachum 2004), and largely neglected small and medium-sized enterprises (SMEs). Compared to large companies, SMEs typically have fewer resources and capabilities but are more sensitive to external environments (Hessels and Parker 2013). Regardless of their resource constraints, however, it is common for SMEs to diversify into new businesses (Robson, Gallagher, and Daly 1993). More research is needed to better understand how external institutions influence SMEs' diversification (Cardoza et al. 2015).

Given the above considerations, our study examines how sub-national institutions affect SMEs' diversification into new businesses in China. According to the institution-based view in the management literature, firms' strategic choices are influenced by institutional settings, especially in economies undergoing institutional transitions (Peng 2002, 2003). Meanwhile, the incumbent firms of an area may collectively lobby local authorities and form new traditions, thus creating pressures on institutions (Hall and Soskice 2001). To assess the business climate of an area, firms need to examine both the composition of local organizations and the development of market-supporting institutions (Meyer and Nguyen 2005). Specifically, in their study on the impact of sub-national institutions on foreign investors' entry decisions, Meyer and Nguyen (2005) examined the dominance of state-owned enterprises (SOEs) and the accessibility of scarce resources. Similarly, in a study on the impact of sub-national institutions on private firm performance, Nguyen, Le, and Bryant (2013) investigated SOE dominance and the accessibility of information. Nevertheless, resource and information accessibility may not adequately reflect the sub-national institutional constraints faced by SMEs (Zhou 2011). There is a need to examine the overall development of market systems in a region, i.e., to what extent market mechanisms facilitate resource allocation in capital, labor, technology, and product transactions (Khanna and Palepu 2010). Therefore, in this study, we focus on two aspects of sub-national institutions – SOE dominance and the development of market systems. While the former reflects the composition of local firms, the latter provides a general view of market-supporting institutions.

Following the institution-based view, we argue that SOE dominance and the development of market systems in a region tend to affect local SMEs' diversification, and such relationships are moderated by SMEs' geographic market scope. A large sample of SMEs in China was used to test our hypotheses. China presented an ideal setting for this research. During its economic reform, the Chinese government implemented various regional experimentation and deregulation, resulting in drastic regional institutional variances (Zhou 2011; Wang, Fan, and Yu 2016). As regional governments have become regulators of local economies, China to some extent has functioned like a market-preserving federalist state (Blanchard and Shleifer 2001). This study also expands our understanding of Chinese SMEs by focusing on their diversification. Since China's economic reform, SMEs have undergone drastic development. According to the Yearbook of China's small and medium enterprises (2014), SMEs contribute about 60% of the country's GDP and 80% of employment, and their development exhibits significant cross-region differences; traditionally concentrated on labor-intense manufacturing and trading, nowadays many Chinese SMEs have diversified into other businesses. Given SMEs' growing importance for the Chinese economy, it would be worthwhile to examine the impact of sub-national institutions on SMEs' diversification strategy.

With this study, we aim to make three contributions to the literature. First, this study increases our understanding of how institutions are linked to firms' diversification (Wan et al. 2011). We argue that sub-national institutions directly affect SMEs' likelihood of diversification, and this relationship is moderated by SMEs' geographic market scope. Second, this study provides new evidence regarding the importance of sub-national institutions. Not only do regional institutional differences influence foreign investors' entry decisions (Meyer and Nguyen 2005; Shi, Sun, and Peng 2012), but they also drive local firms' strategic choices. Third, this study expands our knowledge regarding SMEs' strategic moves. While prior diversification research has mainly focused on large firms (Wan 2005), our research explores whether SMEs demonstrate unique behavioral patterns when facing institutional constraints.

In the following text, we first briefly review the relevant theories on corporate diversification, and then develop hypotheses regarding the relationships between sub-national institutions and SMEs' diversification into new businesses. In the method section, we describe how the hypotheses were tested using a sample of 3,240 SMEs in China. After reporting the empirical results, we discuss the theoretical contributions and practical implications of our findings. Limitations and future research directions are also discussed.

Theory and hypothesis development

Over decades of research on corporate diversification, scholars have investigated multi-business firms from different theoretical perspectives and generated various findings (see reviews by Nippa, Pidun, and Rubner 2011; Benito-Osorio, Guerras-Martín, and Ángel Zuñiga-Vicente 2012). Drawing upon market power, transaction cost, and portfolio theory, some studies have stressed the positive impact of diversification as it allows multi-business firms to leverage market power advantages across different businesses, efficiently allocate capital and other resources through internal markets, reduce financial risks, and gain taxation advantages (Palich, Cardinal, and Miller 2000; Gomes and Livdan 2004). Focusing on internal transaction costs and principal-agent relationships, some other scholars have highlighted the downside of diversification such as the bureaucracy and coordination costs of multi-business firms, and the agency costs caused by interest conflicts between managers and shareholders (Palich, Cardinal, and Miller 2000). The resource-based view argues that a firm can achieve economies of scope by sharing its resources and capabilities among multiple related business units; thus related diversification tends to outperform unrelated diversification and single-business strategy (Wan et al. 2011). This view suggests that a moderate level of diversification offers an optimal trade-off between the benefits and costs of diversification. In summary, the views mentioned above mainly focus on the internal drivers of diversification.

To develop a clear understanding of corporate diversification, we also need to investigate the external drivers. As Benito-Osorio, Guerras-Martín, and Ángel Zuñiga-Vicente (2012) have highlighted, there is a lack of explicit consideration of home country institutions in corporate diversification literature. In recent years, studies from the institution-based view have shed some light on this issue. As 'the humanly devised constraints that structure human interactions' (North 1990, 3), institutions set the 'rules of the game' for firm strategy and behavior. There are two main streams of research that concentrate on the role of institutions within society (Peng 2002). The first has its roots in new institutional economics, which focuses on how institutions affect transaction costs and the choice of governance structure (North 1990; Williamson 1994, 1998). The second is derived from institution theory in sociology, which suggests organizations conform to institutional pressures to obtain legitimacy (DiMaggio and Powell 1983; Scott 1995). Both streams emphasize that institutions matter and presume that organizations make rational choices to cope with institutional constraints (Gronow 2008). More detailed reviews on these two streams of research can be found in Peng (2002), Gronow (2008), and Garrido et al. (2014). Proponents of the institution-based view believe that the two streams of research offer complementary perspectives and propose an integrative approach to examining the relationship between institutional conditions and firm behavior (Peng 2002).

According to the institution-based view, strategic choices are driven not only by industry and firm conditions but also institutional constraints (Peng, Wang, and Jiang 2008). The interaction between institutions and organizations becomes a more critical issue when the institutions are underdeveloped (Peng 2003). In emerging economies, it is particularly important to understand how different institutions influence firm behavior (Wright et al. 2005; Peng, Wang, and Jiang 2008). The institution-based view has been increasingly used in strategic management research, as the role of institutions is incorporated into understanding why firms differ in strategy and performance (Peng et al. 2009; Garrido et al. 2014). Specifically, local institutions may significantly affect corporate diversification. In less developed institutional settings, firms are likely to incur higher transaction costs because of imperceptions in external capital, labor, and product markets. Therefore, they may use diversification to replace external markets with internal transactions (Wan and Hoskisson 2003). The empirical findings suggest that multi-business firms are prevalent and tend to outperform single-business firms in countries with weak institutional development, such as China (Li and Wong 2003; Yiu, Bruton, and Lu 2005), India (Khanna and Palepu 2000; Ramaswamy, Li, and Petitt 2004), and other emerging or transitional economies (Guillén 2000; Nachum 2004; Lee, Peng, and Lee 2008). In a comparative study, Shackman (2007) found that weak capital markets, commonly found in developing countries, are more likely to increase the value of diversification than developed capital markets.

The notion of institution typically covers a wide range of issues that affect economic outcomes, such as contract enforcement, property rights, investor protection, the severity of corruption, the predictability of policy-making, and so on (Kaufmann, Kraay, and Mastruzzi 2011). A number of indicators of national institutions have been used in academic research (Kuncic 2014). For instance, the World Bank's *ease of doing business index* is a composite index measuring deregulation, property rights, and contract rights protection. The *index of economic freedom*, created by the Heritage Foundation, includes various measures of business freedom, legal protection, and governance effectiveness. Such indicators mainly focus on the national level and hardly address subnational institutions. Nevertheless, substantial cross-region differences exist in many emerging economies (Peng, Wang, and Jiang 2008). In China, the decentralization of power by the top authorities began at the provincial level, and the provincial governments play a primary role in economic reform, fiscal arrangements, and regional protectionism (Montinola, Qian, and Weingast 1995). For instance, in the 1990s, while Jiangsu Province emphasized the development of collectively-owned town and village enterprises, Zhejiang province adopted a different model that mainly promoted private firms (Zhou 2011).

From the institution-based view, this study examines how provincial institutions influence SMEs' diversification in China. In other words, we explore under what province-level institutional conditions Chinese SMEs are more likely to diversify into new businesses. While most previous studies have adopted aggregated measures of regional institutions (e.g., Gao et al. 2010; Li and Sun 2017), only a few studies have addressed specific aspects (Meyer and Nguyen 2005; Nguyen, Le, and Bryant 2013). Following Meyer and Nguyen (2005), we examine two aspects of provincial institutions: the dominance of SOEs and the development of market systems. Provincial differences in these aspects have been noted in the prior literature (Zhou 2011). SME research has also shown that SMEs pay attention to regulatory constraints and market system development when planning for business development (Storey 1994). In China, large SOEs usually have a superior status and still control some key industries. Due to government favoritism toward large SOEs, SMEs are often subject to regulatory discrimination. They may not be allowed to enter certain industries or gain access to state-controlled assets. Meanwhile, well-developed market systems are essential for SMEs' growth, as SMEs typically lack internal resources relative to large firms. They are probably more dependent on market intermediaries and the external supply of labor, capital, and other crucial factors.

The dominance of SOEs

SOEs have a strong presence in emerging economies such as China (Peng, Tan, and Tong 2004). Before its economic reform, the Chinese economy was dominated by SOEs. The Chinese government then began to restructure them and develop non-state-owned sectors. Through measures like reorganization, merger and acquisition, joint partnership, and sell-off, the Chinese government gradually reduced the number of small SOEs and concentrated on growing large ones. Meanwhile, thanks to various incentive and promotional policies, private, foreign, and other ownership types experienced rapid growth. This transition exhibited considerable sub-national variations, as Chinese provincial governments employed different approaches and paces for economic reform (Zhou 2011).

Compared to SMEs, large SOEs are more likely to have superior status and obtain preferential treatment. Their presence in a province may significantly affect the external conditions of SMEs. First, large SOEs typically enjoy resource slacks provided by governments (Nolan 2001). They get favorable treatment in obtaining business licenses, being listed on stock markets, and acquiring international trading permits, and they have better access to strategic resources such as land, capital, bank loans, technology, and information. Therefore, key resources that are critical to implementing diversification may not be readily available to SMEs. Moreover, large SOEs are more likely to diversify into new businesses (Lu and Yao 2006). Not only can they get the required resources, but they also have incentives to do so. Given their inherent ownership nature, SOEs are likely to incorporate political and social considerations in their strategies (Daniels, Krug, and Nigh 1986). They may use diversification to reduce local unemployment and increase social stability rather than seek profitability and efficiency (Wang and Luo 2018). Additionally, large SOEs often have long-standing connections with authorities and business networks. They may use their connections to lobby local governments and influence informal institutions (Meyer and Nguyen 2005), thus creating a business environment that favors large SOEs over other types of firms. In China, large SOEs have gained monopolistic positions in a number of industries. Non-state-owned firms are either not allowed or required to partner with SOEs, and they have to meet specific scale, technological, and operational requirements (Zhou 2011). Therefore, in provinces dominated by SOEs, SMEs lack resources and opportunities to pursue diversification.

Conversely, the weak presence of SOEs suggests that government-controlled resources and diversification opportunities are more likely to be available to SMEs. As governments removed restrictions on non-state-owned sectors, SOEs gradually lost their dominance over private enterprises in some Chinese provinces (Naughton 2007). With fewer SOEs, there may be more room for the development of SMEs. On the one hand, they are able to access strategic resources that used to be reserved for large SOEs; they may even enjoy government support and incentives in provinces that emphasize economic growth. On the other hand, as SOEs no longer have monopolistic positions, local markets embrace a higher degree of competition, which, in turn, push SMEs to seek growth opportunities. This may result in SMEs' diversification into other industries. In addition, the prevalence of private firms in various industries signals potential opportunities to SMEs. Institutional theory has long argued the mimetic phenomenon, whereby organizations respond to uncertainty by mimicking actions of other organizations (DiMaggio and Powell 1983). Venturing into a new business brings numerous uncertainties. If there are successful private firms in that business, SMEs may be more likely to follow those firms' steps. Based on the above discussion, we hypothesize the following:

Hypothesis 1: The greater the dominance of SOEs in a province, the less likely SMEs in that province are to diversify into new businesses.

The development of market systems

Emerging economies often lack institutions that facilitate business transactions, such as information exchange, contract enforcement, and credit screening systems (Peng and Delios 2006). Such market imperfections, commonly found in capital, labor, technology, and product markets (Khanna and Palepu 2010), are especially challenging for SMEs. For instance, underdeveloped capital markets offer limited means for SME financing; commercial banks are reluctant to provide loans to SMEs, which tend to have a high debt/equity ratio; compared to large firms, SMEs are also less likely to attract skilled workers and obtain advanced technologies.

Over the decades of economic reform, the development of Chinese market systems has shown considerable variations across provinces (Fan, Wang, and Zhu 2007, 2011). China took a decentralization approach and allowed provincial governments authorities to carry out different regulations, determine local expenditures, and coordinate regional development. Since their career development was linked to local economic growth, government officials were incentivized to promote market development (Naughton 2007). For instance, in Zhejiang province, local governments developed a number of special marketplaces (ranging from shoes and lighters to electronics and auto parts) to facilitate business transactions, and helped establish institutions such as credit unions and private banks to provide capital and other production factors. They were willing to experiment with new policies that might be suitable for local conditions or imitate successful policies that had worked for other regions. Consequently, SMEs in different provinces face different levels of market development.

Lacking the bargaining power to influence governments and other external forces, SMEs may modify their own strategies to adapt to local institutions. Prior literature suggests that when facing underdeveloped markets, firms generally find it beneficial to pursue diversification (Wan and Hoskisson 2003; Wan 2005). In provinces with underdeveloped market systems, market imperfections increase the costs of business operations and may even obstruct market transactions. By diversifying into new businesses, SMEs may circumvent unfavorable market conditions (Hill and Hoskisson 1987). For instance, by spreading default risks into different product lines, a diversified SME may increase its attractiveness to potential lenders. By efficiently allocating funds among internal business units, it may compensate for inadequate external capital markets. By spreading costs across business units, the SME may be able to acquire assets that would be uneconomical for single businesses. It may leverage its reputation and knowledge efficiently across different types of businesses, and carry its existing connections with governments and business networks into new businesses. In summary, a multi-business firm can generate value through its internal capital market and talent pool, as well as shared assets, expertise, and reputation (Khanna and Palepu 2010). Therefore, SMEs in provinces with underdeveloped markets are incentivized to diversify into new businesses.

In comparison, in provinces with relatively developed market systems, diversification is less likely to accrue resource benefits and improve performance. SMEs can gain access to various resources in external markets, directly or via market intermediaries. Since firms are able to conduct transactions in existing businesses efficiently, they do not necessarily favor diversification over concentrating on a single business. According to Lee, Peng, and Lee (2008), as market institutions improve, diversification premiums may turn into diversification discounts. In other words, while the benefits associated with diversification diminish with institutional development, its drawbacks become more noticeable. Without sufficient information processing capacities to monitor a wide range of business activities, a diversified firm encounters difficulties in coordination and control (Hill and Hoskisson 1987). Meanwhile, as developed markets bring about intense competition, firms are compelled to stay focused and increase specialized product competitiveness (Wan and Hoskisson 2003). Given these considerations, we argue that SMEs in underdeveloped market systems are more likely to enter a new business than SMEs in relatively developed market systems. We hypothesize the following:

Hypothesis 2: The greater the development of market systems in a province, the less likely SMEs in that province are to diversify into new businesses.

The moderating role of SMEs' geographic market

Although SMEs are physically located in a province, their products and services may reach markets beyond provincial borders. Naturally, the SMEs that focus on local markets are mainly involved with local business communities and exposed to local institutional settings. One may wonder to what extent those SMEs with a broader geographic market scope are still subject to the influence of provincial institutions. Prior research has suggested that export-oriented firms are less likely to be affected by local institutions (Nguyen, Le, and Bryant 2013; Li and Sun 2017). By engaging overseas business connections and institutions, exporting firms may be able to mitigate or bypass certain local constraints. Moreover, exporting firms generally have more resources and capabilities than local-market oriented firms, and thus are more likely to subdue the impact of local institutions. Following a similar logic, we argue that the impact of provincial institutions is weaker for the firms that primarily focus on outside-the-region, national, or international markets.

In provinces dominated by large SOEs, SMEs may evade discrimination and competition from SOEs by entering other markets (Nguyen, Le, and Bryant 2013). Despite being blocked from accessing government-controlled resources and industries in their home provinces, firms with a broader market area may be able to obtain resources and opportunities for diversification outside provincial borders, especially in provinces with a lower degree of SOE dominance. Conversely, local-market oriented firms' pursuit of diversification is more likely to be restricted, as they have limited access to resources both in and out of the province. In provinces with a relatively weak presence of SOEs, there are more opportunities for SMEs to diversify. However, those SMEs with a broader market also have additional opportunities to fully utilize their specialized competitive advantages. They may commit to expanding and penetrating outside-the-region markets rather than diversifying into new businesses.

Similarly, a broader geographic market enables SMEs to escape underdeveloped market systems in their home provinces (Witt and Lewin 2007). Not only can they access factors and institutions in other provinces, but they can also transfer and share assets across provinces. In a way, the values of market expansion are a substitute for the benefits provided by product diversification. Therefore, in provinces with underdeveloped market systems, local-market oriented SMEs are more likely to diversify into new business than those SMEs with a broader market, because the former do not have geographic market expansion as an alternative option to circumvent local market inadequacies. Conversely, when home-province market systems are relatively developed, SMEs are less likely to diversify. This relationship tends to be weaker for those SOEs with a broader market because they may encounter underdeveloped markets in other provinces.

In summary, SMEs with a broader market area have a greater latitude to pursue their desired strategies. To those SMEs, SOEs' dominance and market underdevelopment become less of an issue for their diversification. Therefore, we suggest the following hypotheses:

Hypothesis 3: The impact of provincial SOE dominance on diversification is weaker for SMEs with a broader geographic market scope.

Hypothesis 4: The impact of provincial market development on diversification is weaker for SMEs with a broader geographic market scope.

Method

Data and sample

To test our hypotheses, we used data from a government survey on SMEs and the NERI (National Economic Research Institute) Index of Marketization on China's provinces. China's National Development and Reform Commission conducted a large-scale national survey on SME management practices in 2005–2006.[1] Then thousand SMEs were randomly selected from a government-compiled directory of SMEs, which followed the SME criteria set by the National Bureau of Statistics (2003).[2] A self-administered questionnaire about firm strategy was distributed to the 10,000 SMEs via provincial small business administration offices throughout the country. After several rounds of reminders, 3339 responses were received. We then dropped those responses with incomplete answers and obtained a sample of 3240 SMEs for our study. The corresponding response rate was 32.40%. Kolmogorov-Smirnov tests on firm age and registered capital showed no significant differences between respondents and non-respondents.

Among the sample SMEs, 1361 (42.01%) were categorized as medium-sized enterprises, and the remaining 1879 (57.99%) were small enterprises. In terms of location, 52.62% were located in relatively developed eastern provinces, 28.03% in central China, and 19.35% in western provinces. Those SMEs were from thirteen industries, including agriculture, mining, manufacturing, utility, construction, transportation, information technology, wholesaling and retailing, hotel and restaurants, financial services, real estate, professional services, and others. In terms of ownership, 55.05% were privately owned, 12.44% state-owned, 5.81% collectively owned, 5.99% foreign-owned, and 20.71% had mixed ownership.

Data on provincial institutions were obtained from a report on the marketization of China's provinces conducted by NERI (i.e., the NERI Index Report, Fan, Wang, and Zhu 2007). Based on survey and secondary data, the report provided ratings on multiple items about institutional development in each province, covering the role of government and the development of non-state-owned sectors, product and factor markets, as well as market intermediaries and legal rights protection. The NERI Index has been commonly used in prior economics and management literature to quantify China's provincial institutions (e.g., Gao et al. 2010; Markóczy et al. 2013; Shi, Sun, and Peng 2012; Shi et al. 2014). The minimum and the maximum values of the index items in 2001 (the base year) were set to 1 and 10 respectively. Those ratings were updated every few years. In later years, some provinces scored higher than 10 on certain items as their ratings surpassed the maximum values in the base year. For this study, we used the ratings of 2005, the year of the SME survey. Those ratings were included in the 2006 NERI Index Report and later published in 2007 (Fan, Wang, and Zhu 2007). Three items were selected to indicate SOE dominance, and four were used to measure market development (please see details in the following section).

Measurement

In the questionnaire, the respondents were asked to identify the firm's corporate strategy for the next three years. A dummy variable was created to indicate if the firm would concentrate on a single business (coded as 0) or diversify into a new business (coded as 1). If a respondent chose the latter answer, he or she would be asked to further classify the new business as related or unrelated to the existing business. We acknowledge that there are more complicated continuous measures of corporate diversification, but those measures are often difficult to interpret and inapplicable to non-manufacturing industries (Robins and Wiersema 2003). In a recent article, Mackey, Barney, and Dotson (2017, 329) used a dummy measure of diversification and noted that 'continuous measures of diversification are good at measuring differences in the degree of diversification, but are less effective at comparing diversified firms with focused firms.' Given these considerations, we believe our measures adequately indicate whether an SME would diversify into a new business.

In order to properly measure the extent of SOE dominance and the development of market systems in a province, we conducted a factor analysis on select items in the NERI index. We first dropped items that were not closely relevant to our theory, such as tax burden for farmers and consumer rights protection. To obtain distinct factors and avoid multicollinearity problems, we then removed cross-loading items (i.e., items with equivalent loadings on more than one factors).

For instance, the item about financial market development was measured by the proportion of deposits and loans held by non-state-owned financial institutions, and thus related to both SOE dominance and market development.

Eventually, we obtained three items that reflected non-state-owned firms' shares in total industrial output, total capital investment, and total employment in a province. Those ratings concerned non-state-owned sectors, and some of them were above 10 (the maximum value based on the 2001 base ratings) but no more than 12. Therefore, we reversely coded the three items by subtracting their values from 12, and used their average to indicate SOE dominance (Cronbach's Alpha = 0.899). In Meyer and Nguyen's (2005) study on sub-national institutions, SOE dominance was proxied by SOEs' share in total output. However, this proxy does not necessarily reflect how many resources SOEs have occupied (Nguyen, Le, and Bryant 2013). By adding SOEs' shares in investment and employment, our measure may better reflect the role of SOEs in the province.

Meanwhile, the development of market systems was measured with four items in the NERI Index – the significance of market mechanisms in resource allocation, the extent to which prices are determined by market mechanisms rather than government commands, the reduction of regional protectionism, and the development of factor markets. While the first item was calculated based on the percentage of government spending in GDP, the remaining three were composite indexes based on secondary and survey data (Fan, Wang, and Zhu 2007). The average of the four items was used in our study (Cronbach's Alpha = 0.774). While Meyer and Nguyen (2005) only examined the accessibility of scarce resources (proxied by real estate made available in industrial zones), this measure provides a broader view of the development of market systems.

Data on the SMEs' geographic market scope were obtained from the survey. The respondents were asked to identify their major geographic markets. Given our research focus on provincial institutions, we used a dummy variable to separate SMEs primarily concentrated on within-the-province markets (coded as 0) and those focused on outside-the-province markets (coded as 1). In an extended analysis, we further separated outside-the-province markets into domestic and international markets, and obtained similar findings. For ease of interpretation, we only used the dummy variable here to indicate the SMEs' geographic market scope.

In addition, several firm-level control variables were included in our study. Firm age may influence organizational experience, and consequently strategic choices. As firms last longer, they are more likely to seek opportunities in new industries (Campa and Kedia 2002). We measured firm age with the difference between the year of data collection and the starting year of each sample firm. Meanwhile, firm size may indicate the abundance of resources and capabilities, and thus is often considered a determinant of diversification (Dass 2000). In this study, we controlled for firm size using the logarithm values of the number of employees. Since firms' technological capabilities may be linked to corporate diversification (Hoskisson and Johnson 1992), we included the percentage of technical personnel among all employees. Additionally, the diversification literature has demonstrated the impact of firms' prior performance on their diversification decision (Park 2002). Due to practical reasons, we were not able to obtain specific financial data from the sample SMEs. Instead, the respondents were asked to report their average sales growth over the last two years in three categories – no or low growth (below 10%), moderate growth (10–30%), and high growth (above 30%). We believed this simple categorical measure, although not ideal, would help increase the response rate and encourage truthful answers. This variable was included in our analyses as a proxy for firm performance. Ownership type was controlled with dummy variables, indicating private, state-owned, collectively owned, foreign firms, and those with mixed ownership. In addition, as the sample SMEs were from thirteen different industries, industry dummies were used to control for industry effects.

Analysis

To test our hypotheses, we employed multilevel modeling for categorical outcomes (Heck, Thomas, and Tabata 2013). The dependent variable of this study was a dichotomous variable that separated two types of strategy – concentrating on a single business or diversifying into a new business. Since it follows a binomial probability distribution, we applied logit link function in the modeling. The hypothesized model was hierarchical, with the dependent variables at the firm level, and the independent variables being province-level constructs. In addition, our data were hierarchical, as SMEs were nested in different provinces. Therefore, we adopted binomial multilevel modeling in this study.

Results

The descriptive statistics and correlations of the main variables are reported in Table 1. The sample consisted of 3240 SMEs with an average of nine years in operation and 166 employees. Among the sample SMEs, 51.2% intended to pursue diversification. While 15.5% experienced high sales growth in the last two years, 49.2% had moderate sales growth. On average, technical personnel accounted for 8.6% of all employees. About one-third of the SMEs made the majority of sales within their provinces, and the remaining two-thirds had a significant presence beyond provincial borders.

SMEs' diversification was significantly correlated with firm size, sales growth, the percentage of technical personnel, geographic market scope, and SOE dominance at the province level. The two provincial institutional variables were correlated at −0.131. To check potential multicollinearity problems, we calculated the variance inflation factor (VIF) of each predictor variable. The VIF values ranged from 1.137 to 1.823, below the commonly used threshold of 4 or 10 (O'brien 2007), suggesting that multi-collinearity was not a concern. In order to improve the interpretation of the intercept term in multilevel analysis, the grand mean-centered values of the province-level variables were used in subsequent analyses (Enders and Tofighi 2007).

Due to space limitations, industry and ownership type dummies are not reported in Table 1. Chi-squared tests showed that SMEs' diversification had some degrees of association with industry (Chi-square = 22.944, Phi = 0.084, p < .05) and ownership type (Chi-square = 12.223, Phi = 0.061, p < .05).

Table 1. Descriptive Statistics and Correlations.

	1	2	3	4	5	6	7	8	9
Mean	0.512	9.104	5.115	0.155	0.492	0.086	0.670	2.252	9.977
s.d.	0.499	6.059	1.010	0.362	0.500	0.060	0.472	2.548	1.036
1. Diversification[a]	1								
2. Firm age	0.013	1							
3. Firm size	0.125***	0.306***	1						
4. Sales growth – high[b]	0.083***	−0.044**	0.119***	1					
5. Sales growth – moderate[b]	0.019	0.023	0.088***	−.435***	1				
6. The percentage of technical personnel	0.088***	0.042*	0.121***	0.174***	0.027	1			
7. Geographic market scope[b]	0.102***	0.043*	0.230***	0.128***	0.089***	0.126***	1		
8. The extent of SOE dominance	−0.107***	−0.052**	−0.167***	−0.089***	−0.089***	−0.071***	−0.098***	1	
9. The extent of market development	0.022	−0.016	−0.009	−0.003	−0.058**	0.056**	−0.024	−0.131***	1

N = 3240
Note: industry and ownership type dummies are not reported for space considerations.
*p < .05; ** p < .01; *** p < .001
[a]New business entry coded as 1; otherwise 0
[b]These variables were coded as dummies (yes = 1, no = 0).

Table 2 presents the results of the binomial multilevel modeling for the dichotomous outcome – focusing on the existing business or diversifying into a new business. Following the approach suggested by Heck, Thomas, and Tabata (2013), we tested our theory in three steps. First, we estimated a null model with intercept only and allowed random effect variation across provinces. The variance of intercept was 0.110 (s.e. 0.044, $p < 0.05$), indicating significant differences among provinces in terms of the probability of SMEs' diversification. This result suggests that multilevel modeling can be used to analyze the data.

In the second step, we added control and firm-level variables to our analysis (see Model 1 in Table 2). Firm age had no significant relationship with SMEs' diversification, suggesting that older SMEs are not necessarily more inclined to diversify. It is possible that long-standing SMEs have developed unique competitiveness in their niche markets, and thus have little desire to enter other industries. Firm size was positively related to SMEs' diversification with an odds ratio of 1.255 (exp(0.227) = 1.255; 95% confidence interval (CI) 1.160 to 1.357). The coefficient of the percentage of technical personnel was also positive. We calculated the odds ratio and found that for every one percentage point increase, the probability of diversification increased by about 1.4%. In addition, SMEs' geographic market scope had a positive relationship with their diversification (odds ratio 1.290, 95% CI 1.094 to 1.522), suggesting SMEs with a broader geographic market scope were 29% more likely to diversify. These findings are largely consistent with prior literature that highlights the importance of resources in corporate diversification (Wan et al. 2011). Meanwhile, both high and moderate sales growth had negative relationships with SMEs' diversification, suggesting that SMEs are less likely to diversify when they experience strong growth in existing businesses. It should be noted that even after including these firm-level variables and industry and ownership dummies, the variance of intercept remained significant, indicating the need to examine province-level factors.

In the third step, we added the two province-level predictors of interest (see Model 2 in Table 2). Compared to Model 1, the intercept variance of Model 2 was no longer significant, and the accuracy rate (i.e., the percentage of cases correctly predicted) increased from 57.6% to 59.4%, suggesting that the province-level variables helped explain the cross-province variance. Specifically, the extent of SOE dominance had a negative relationship with SMEs' diversification. The odds ratio was 0.941 (95% CI 0.898 to 0.986). In other words, for one unit increase of the value of SOE dominance, the probability of SMEs' diversification decreased by 5.9%. This result supports Hypothesis 1, which suggests that the dominance of SOEs in a province reduces the odds of SMEs' diversification in that province. However, Hypothesis 2, which predicts that the development of market systems decreases the likelihood of SMEs' diversification, is not supported. As shown in Model 2, the effect of market development was negative but not significant. To verify these findings, we examined the two province-level variables individually and obtained similar results.

Hypotheses 3 and 4 focus on the moderating effect of SMEs' geographic market scope. Since geographic market scope was coded as a dummy variable, its moderating effect can be tested using interaction terms (Heck, Thomas, and Tabata 2013). In Model 3, the interaction term of SOE dominance and geographic market scope was insignificant, not supporting Hypothesis 3. In Model 4, the interaction term of market development and geographic market scope was positive and significant. When both interaction terms were included in Model 5, similar results were obtained. To validate the moderating effect, we also examined two subsamples: one included SMEs concentrated on within-the-province markets (see Model 6), and the other included SMEs focused on outside-the-province markets (see Model 7). The effect of SOE dominance showed no significant difference between the two subsamples. The extent of market development significantly reduced the odds of SMEs' diversification (odds ratio 0.828, 95% CI 0.701 to 0.978) in Model 6, but had no significant effect in Model 7, suggesting that the impact of market development on diversification was weaker for those SMEs with a broader geographic market scope. Therefore, Hypothesis 4 is supported.

Additionally, in an extended analysis, we tested the impact of provincial institutions on SMEs' choice between related and unrelated diversification. Excluding those concentrating on a single business, we examined the SMEs intending to diversify (N = 1660), among which 15.7% aimed at

Table 2. Binomial multilevel modeling for SMEs' diversification.

Variables	Model 1	Model 2	Model 3	Model 4	Model 5	Model 6 (narrow market scope)	Model 7 (broad market scope)
Level 1							
Intercept	-0.850**	-0.800**	-0.815**	-0.801**	-0.810**	-0.442	-0.828*
	(0.304)	(0.303)	(0.304)	(0.304)	(0.304)	(0.553)	(0.367)
Firm age	-0.004	-0.005	-0.005	-0.005	-0.005	-0.005	-0.006
	(0.006)	(0.006)	(0.006)	(0.006)	(0.006)	(0.010)	(0.007)
Firm size	0.227***	0.223***	0.224***	0.224***	0.225***	0.104	0.280***
	(0.040)	(0.040)	(0.040)	(0.040)	(0.040)	(0.076)	(0.047)
The percentage of technical personnel	1.400*	1.389*	1.401*	1.374*	1.383*	1.223	1.612*
	(0.636)	(0.637)	(0.637)	(0.637)	(0.638)	(1.121)	(0.784)
Sales growth							
High growth	-0.388**	-0.374**	-0.374**	-0.376**	-0.375**	-0.198	-0.371**
	(0.118)	(0.118)	(0.118)	(0.118)	(0.118)	(0.240)	(0.139)
Moderate growth	-0.246*	-0.240*	-0.239*	-0.240*	-0.240*	-0.174	-0.361**
	(0.108)	(0.108)	(0.108)	(0.108)	(0.108)	(0.232)	(0.124)
Low or no growth (reference)							
Geographic market scope	0.255**	0.250**	0.259**	0.255**	0.260**		
	(0.084)	(0.084)	(0.084)	(0.084)	(0.084)		
Industry dummies [a]	—	—	—	—	—	—	—
Ownership dummies [a]	—	—	—	—	—	—	—
Level 2							
The extent of SOE dominance		-0.061**	-0.029	-0.060**	-0.041	-0.044†	-0.067**
		(0.023)	(0.031)	(0.023)	(0.032)	(0.023)	(0.033)
The extent of market development		-0.067	-0.069	-0.187*	-0.176*	-0.189*	-0.003
		(0.059)	(0.059)	(0.075)	(0.077)	(0.084)	(0.077)
Interactions							
The extent of SOE dominance * Geographic market scope			-0.049		-0.029		
			(0.031)		(0.032)		
The extent of market development * Geographic market scope				0.185*	0.166*		
				(0.073)	(0.076)		
Random effect							
Variance (Intercept)	0.066*	0.045	0.046	0.043	0.044	0.065	0.024
	(.033)	(0.029)	(0.028)	(0.028)	(0.028)	(0.053)	(0.025)
N	3240	3240	3240	3240	3240	1085	2155
Accuracy	57.6%	59.4%	59.6%	61.0%	61.0%	61.4%	60.9%
-2 log likelihood	13,946.076	13,937.742	13,943.286	13,927.816	13,934.811	4696.273	9282.596

N = 3240. † $p < .10$ * $p < .05$; ** $p < .01$; *** $p < .001$ (two-tailed)
[a] These dummies were included in the analysis, but not reported here for space considerations.

Table 3. Binomial multilevel modeling for SMEs' entry into unrelated (vs. related) businesses.

Variables	Model 1	Model 2
Level 1		
Intercept	−4.040***	−4.098***
	(0.580)	(0.581)
Firm age	0.021[†]	0.023[†]
	(0.012)	(0.012)
Firm size	0.238***	0.246***
	(0.071)	(0.072)
The percentage of technical personnel	1.064	1.055
	(1.224)	(1.225)
Sales growth		
High growth	0.402[†]	0.383[†]
	(0.219)	(0.221)
Moderate growth	−0.007	−0.023
	(0.198)	(0.199)
Low or no growth (*reference*)		
Geographic market scope	−0.107	−0.104
	(0.170)	(0.170)
Industry dummies [a]	−	−
Ownership dummies [a]	−	−
Level 2		
The extent of SOE dominance		−0.055
		(0.053)
The extent of market development		−0.338*
		(0.172)
Random effect		
Variance (Intercept)	0.155*	0.133
	(0.082)	(0.086)
Accuracy	84.5%	85.5%
−2 log likelihood	8391.311	8381.842

N = 1660. [†]p < .10 * p < .05; ** p < .01; *** p < .001 (two-tailed)
[a]These dummies were included in the analysis, but not reported here for space considerations.

unrelated diversification. The dependent variable was coded 1 for unrelated and 0 for related diversification. The analysis results are reported in Table 3. Among the firm-level controls, firm size was positively related to unrelated diversification, and firm age and high sales growth had marginal effects. With the inclusion of the provincial factors, the variance of intercept became insignificant, suggesting that provincial institutions help explain cross-province differences in SMEs' unrelated diversification. Interestingly, the impact of provincial intuitions on the related-or-unrelated choice was somewhat different from their impact on the diversify-or-not decision. The extent of SOE dominance showed no significant relationship with SMEs' unrelated diversification. Hence, SOE dominance negatively affected SME's diversification in general but did not necessarily favor unrelated over related or *vice versa*. The development of market systems was negatively linked to unrelated diversification (odds ratio 0.713, 95% CI 0.508 to 0.999). It seems that better-developed market systems reduce the odds of SMEs' unrelated diversification, but not so for related diversification.

Discussion

The above results demonstrate that province-level institutional factors have significant relationships with SMEs' diversification in China. Specifically, the dominance of SOEs in a province tends to reduce the odds of local SMEs' entry into new businesses. This finding suggests that SOE dominance imposes restrictions on SMEs' strategic choices. A high level of SOE dominance implies that SMEs not only face regulative constraints but are also challenged on normative and cognitive aspects (Scott 1995). When the level of SOE dominance is low, market competition tends to push SMEs to seek new opportunities, and the development of non-state-owned sectors establishes legitimacy for SMEs' business development. Such a relationship was largely consistent for SMEs focused on within-the-province markets and those with a broader market area. In other words, SMEs' geographic market scope did not seem to interact with the impact of SOE dominance on SMEs' diversification. As we have argued, a broader market may help SMEs obtain resources to mitigate restrictions imposed by SOE dominance. Nevertheless, such resource benefits still exist when SOE dominance is low, and may even become greater in munificent institutional environments (Wan and Hoskisson 2003). This probably explains why the interaction term of geographic market scope and SOE dominance was insignificant.

Moreover, in our study, while the SMEs facing less SOE dominance were more inclined to diversify, they did not show a preference towards either related or unrelated diversification. Related businesses allow the sharing of resources and capabilities but are subject to similar market risks; in contrast, unrelated businesses may allow firms to diversify risks but are not likely to generate synergies (Hitt, Ireland, and Hoskisson 2014). While firms with resource surplus usually benefit more from related diversification (Wan et al. 2011), SMEs tend to have limited resources and may value risk aversion more than resource sharing. Consequently, the extent of SOE dominance may not influence SMEs' preference between related and unrelated diversification.

The effect of market development on SMEs' diversification was different from that of SOE dominance. It was negative for SMEs focused on within-the-province markets but insignificant for those with a broader market area. This finding suggests that when facing underdeveloped home-province market systems, SMEs confined to their home provinces are more likely to pursue diversification, as it can create internal mechanisms to overcome certain market inadequacies (Wan 2005). However, their diversification is less likely to be influenced when they have a significant market presence outside their home provinces. This result implies that SMEs may escape from underdeveloped market systems in their home provinces by reaching markets beyond provincial borders. While previous research has shown that firms may pursue internationalization to escape home-country institutional constraints (Witt and Lewin 2007), our study provides compelling evidence that such an escape mechanism also exists at the sub-national level. This finding is especially meaningful for SMEs, many of which do not have adequate resources and capabilities to expand internationally.

In addition, our extended analysis on the choice of unrelated versus related diversification demonstrates that the extent of market development is negatively related to unrelated diversification. In other words, underdeveloped market systems tend to increase the likelihood of SMEs' entry into unrelated businesses. This result is generally consistent with prior research that views highly diversified business groups as an effective organization form to succeed in emerging markets (Khanna and Palepu 2000, 2010). In underdeveloped markets, unrelated businesses may help SMEs circumvent market inadequacies that affect their existing businesses. However, as market systems improve, the costs of unrelated diversification may surpass its benefits (Lee, Peng, and Lee 2008), at which point SMEs will concentrate on a single business or turn to related diversification.

This study contributes to the literature in three ways. First, our findings offer new insights into the intricate relationship between institutions and corporate diversification. While institutions are often viewed as contingency factors for the diversification-performance relationship in prior literature (Wan et al. 2011), our results suggest that sub-national institutions directly influence SMEs' decision of diversification, and different types of institutions exert influence in different ways. Specifically, SOE dominance has a restrictive effect. In regions dominated by SOEs, SMEs tend to reduce their efforts of diversification. In a different manner, underdeveloped market systems push SMEs to develop certain coping mechanisms. The moderating effect of SMEs' geographic market scope suggests that SMEs confined to their home provinces tend to use diversification to cope with underdeveloped markets, while those with a broader market scope are able to escape home-province markets and are thus less likely to pursue diversification.

Second, this study complements existing institutional research by presenting new evidence on the significance of sub-national institutions. While their influences on foreign investors' entry strategies and performance have been addressed in a few studies (Meyer and Nguyen 2005; Shi,

Sun, and Peng 2012; Li and Sun 2017), this research is a rare attempt to examine the impact of sub-national institutions on local firms' strategic choices. At the national level, firms in underdeveloped markets tend to benefit more from diversification than those in developed countries (Khanna and Palepu 2010), and they may expand internationally to escape home-country constraints (Witt and Lewin 2007). Our findings suggest that a similar pattern exists at the province level in China – SMEs confined to a province with underdeveloped markets are more likely to diversify than those with a broader market scope. However, the impact of SOE dominance reveals a different pattern – SMEs confined to a province dominated by SOEs are restricted from diversification while those with a broader market are not necessarily incentivized to diversify.

Third, this study helps enhance our understating of SMEs' strategic decisions. By examining sub-national institutions as antecedents of SMEs' diversification, we shed light on why and how SMEs follow different strategies when facing different institutional conditions. With limited resources and capabilities, they are likely to comply, circumvent, or escape institutional constraints (Wan 2005). Our results suggest that SMEs tend to comply with restrictions imposed by SOE dominance; nevertheless, despite resource limitations, they may respond to underdeveloped market systems by diversifying into other businesses or expanding beyond their home provinces.

After decades of economic reform, Chinese provinces still demonstrate significant institutional differences (Wang, Fan, and Yu 2016). It is essential for SME managers and government officials to understand the impact of sub-national institutions. Several practical implications can be inferred from the findings of our study. First, SME managers should be aware of the different effects of specific provincial institutions. In provinces dominated by large SOEs, SMEs' efforts of diversification could be constrained. In provinces with underdeveloped markets, they may expand their geo-graphic markets to escape market inadequacies. Furthermore, SMEs need to carefully balance the risks of institutional constraints and the risks of diversification. For instance, our findings suggest that the appeal of unrelated diversification is greater when the extent of market development is relatively low; however, as market conditions improve, such appeal is likely to decline and disappear. Meanwhile, provincial governments should understand their roles in local institutions and consequent effects on SME development. Since the dominance of SOEs tends to restrict SMEs' strategic choices, the reduction of favoritism toward SOEs may help the development of local SMEs. Underdeveloped market systems tend to push local SMEs to diversify, but they may escape such a push by expanding geographic markets. In contrast, better-developed market systems tend to help SMEs concentrate on growing their existing businesses and local markets.

Several limitations and future research directions should be noted. First, due to the importance of provinces in China's government system, we focused on province-level institutional conditions in this study. However, there may exist substantive variances within a province, and city- and municipal-level institutions can have significant influences on SMEs. Because of the lack of available data on city and municipal level institutions, we were unable to examine within-province institu-tional differences. Future research could try to collect information on cities and municipalities and test within-province institutional differences. Second, while both external and internal factors drive SMEs' strategic decisions, our study primarily focused on external institutional conditions. Although we controlled for industry and firm-level variables, we were unable to capture specific resource types and managerial characteristics, which may influence corporate diversification (Wan et al. 2011). It is possible that SMEs' characteristics interact with institutional constraints to affect their strategic choices. For instance, when facing strong institutional constraints, the choice between staying in the same business and entering a new business may be contingent on top managers' risk attitude. Future studies could incorporate additional firm-level variables and examine their interactions with institutional factors. Third, due to data limitations, we used categorical variables to indicate SMEs' diversification. While those variables can signal critical strategic shifts, they may not fully reflect the nuanced differences of new business development. Future research could explore the specific dimensions of SME's diversification. For instance, SMEs may use different approaches, such as partnership, acquisition, or greenfield investment, to enter a new business;

the new business entry may involve different organizational arrangements – creating an independent unit or embedding it in existing structures. Fourth, given the cross-sectional nature of this study, we did not trace the co-evolution of SMEs and institutional conditions over time. A central feature of the Chinese economy is its continuous transition. Firms need to adjust their activities in line with the progression of institutional factors. It would be interesting to study the dynamics of SME development and institutional transition from a co-evolutionary perspective.

Conclusion

Overall, this study examined whether and how sub-national institutions affect SMEs' diversification in China. Our results show that SOE dominance in a province was negatively linked to local SMEs' diversification. The development of market systems tended to reduce the odds of diversification for SMEs that primarily served local markets, but had no significant impact on those with a broader geographic market scope. Underdeveloped markets also seemed to increase the likelihood of unrelated diversification, but this is not so for related diversification. These results suggest that sub-national institutions affect not only firm performance but also strategic choices, and thus the findings provide important implications for SME management and regional development.

Notes

1. According to the Chinese National Survey Data Archive (as of 2018), there were no other national surveys on SME management since 2006. Also, information on Chinese SMEs' strategic choices is not reported in financial reports, and thus not readily available in most archival datasets.
2. China's National Statistics Bureau set specific definitions for SMEs in different industries in 2003, and then revised the definitions in 2011 (see National Bureau of Statistics 2003, 2011 for details). In line with the time of data collection, the 2003 definitions were used here. For example, for manufacturing sectors, firms with less than 300 employees and less than 30 million RMB annual sales were categorized as small enterprises, and firms with 300 to 2000 employees and 30 to 300 million RMB annual sales were categorized as medium enterprises. For retail businesses, firms with less than 100 employees and less than 10 million RMB annual sales were categorized as small enterprises, while firms with 100 to 500 employees and 10 to 150 million RMB annual sales were categorized as medium enterprises.

Acknowledgments

This work was supported by the National Natural Science Foundation of China under Grant No. 71872100.

Disclosure statement

No potential conflict of interest was reported by the authors.

ORCID

Dong Chen 🆔 http://orcid.org/0000-0003-0941-312X

References

Benito-Osorio, D. L., A. Guerras-Martín, and J. Ángel Zuñiga-Vicente. 2012. "Four Decades of Research on Product Diversification: A Literature Review." *Manage Decis* 50 (2): 325–344. doi:10.1108/00251741211203597.
Blanchard, O., and A. Shleifer. 2001. "Federalism with and without Political Centralization: China versus Russia." *Imf Staff Papers* 48 (1): 171–179.
Campa, J. M., and S. Kedia. 2002. "Explaining the Diversification Discount." *J Financ* 57: 1731–1762. doi:10.1111/1540-6261.00476.

Cardoza, G., G. Fornes, P. Li, N. Xu, and S. Xu. 2015. "China Goes Global: Public Policies' Influence on Small- and Medium-sized Enterprises' International Expansion." *Asia Pac Bus Rev* 21 (2): 188–210. doi:10.1080/13602381.2013.876183.

Chakrabarti, A., K. Singh, and I. Mahmood. 2007. "Diversification and Performance: Evidence from East Asian Firms." *Strateg Manage J* 28 (2): 101–120. doi:10.1002/smj.572.

Daniels, J., J. Krug, and D. Nigh. 1986. "US Joint Ventures in China: Motivation and Management of Political Risk." *Calif Manage Rev* 27 (4): 46–58. doi:10.2307/41165155.

Dass, P. 2000. "Relationship of Firm Size, Initial Diversification, and Internationalization with Strategic Change." *J Bus Res* 48 (2): 135–146. doi:10.1016/S0148-2963(98)00097-6.

Delios, A., D. Xu, and P. W. Beamish. 2008. "Within-country Product Diversification and Foreign Subsidiary Performance." *J Int Bus Stud* 39 (4): 706–724. doi:10.1057/palgrave.jibs.8400378.

DiMaggio, P., and W. W. Powell. 1983. "The Iron Cage Revisited: Collective Rationality and Institutional Isomorphism in Organizational Fields." *Am Sociol Rev* 48 (2): 147–160. doi:10.2307/2095101.

Enders, C. K., and D. Tofighi. 2007. "Centering Predictor Variables in Cross-sectional Multilevel Models: A New Look at an Old Issue." *Psychol Methods* 12 (2): 121–138. doi:10.1037/1082-989X.12.2.121.

Fan, G., X. Wang, and H. Zhu 2007. *NERI index of marketization of China's provinces 2006 report*. Beijing: Economic Science Press. Chinese. DOI: 10.1094/PDIS-91-4-0467B.

Fan, G., X. Wang, and H. Zhu 2011. *NERI index of marketization of China's provinces 2011 report*. Beijing: Economic Science Press. Chinese.

Gao, G. Y., J. Y. Murray, M. Kotabe, and J. Lu. 2010. "A 'strategy Tripod' Perspective on Export Behaviors: Evidence from Domestic and Foreign Firms Based in an Emerging Economy." *J Int Bus Stud* 41 (3): 377–396. doi:10.1057/jibs.2009.27.

Garrido, E., J. Gomez, J. P. Maicas, and R. Orcos. 2014. "The Institution-based View of Strategy: How to Measure It." *Bus Res Q* 17 (2): 82–101. doi:10.1016/j.brq.2013.11.001.

Gomes, J., and D. Livdan. 2004. "Optimal Diversification: Reconciling Theory and Evidence." *J Financ* 59 (2): 507–535. doi:10.1111/j.1540-6261.2004.00641.x.

Gronow, A. 2008. "Not by Rules or Choice Alone: A Pragmatist Critique of Institution Theories in Economics and Sociology." *J Inst Econ* 4 (3): 351–373.

Guillén, M. F. 2000. "Business Groups in Emerging Economies: A Resource-based View." *Acad Manage J* 43 (3): 362–380.

Hall, P. A., and D. Soskice. 2001. *Varieties of Capitalism: The Institutional Foundations of Comparative Advantage*. Oxford (UK): Oxford University Press.

Hamilton, B. H., and J. A. Nickerson. 2003. "Correcting for Endogeneity in Strategic Management Research." *Strateg Organ* 1 (1): 51–78. doi:10.1177/1476127003001001218.

Heck, R. H., S. Thomas, and L. Tabata. 2013. *Multilevel Modeling of Categorical Outcomes Using IBM SPSS*. New York (NY): Routledge.

Hessels, J., and S. C. Parker. 2013. "Constraints, Internationalization and Growth: A Cross-country Analysis of European SMEs." *J World Bus* 48 (1): 137–148. doi:10.1016/j.jwb.2012.06.014.

Hill, C., and R. E. Hoskisson. 1987. "Strategy and Structure in the Multiproduct Firm." *Acad Manage Rev* 12 (2): 331–341. doi:10.5465/amr.1987.4307949.

Hitt, M. A., R. D. Ireland, and R. E. Hoskisson. 2014. *Strategic Management Concepts: Competitiveness and Globalization*. 11th ed. Cincinnati (OH): South-Western College Pub.

Hoskisson, R. O., and R. A. Johnson. 1992. "Corporate Restructuring and Strategic Change: The Effect on Diversification Strategy and R&D Intensity." *Strateg Manage J* 13 (8): 625–634. doi:10.1002/smj.4250130805.

Kaufmann, D., A. Kraay, and M. Mastruzzi. 2011. "The Worldwide Governance Indicators: Methodology and Analytical Issues." *Hague J Rule Law* 3 (2): 220–246. doi:10.1017/S1876404511200046.

Khanna, T., and K. Palepu. 2000. "Is Group Affiliation Profitable in Emerging Markets? an Analysis of Diversified Indian Business Groups." *J Financ* 55 (2): 867–891. doi:10.1111/0022-1082.00229.

Khanna, T., and K. Palepu. 2010. *Winning in Emerging Markets: A Road Map for Strategy and Execution*. Boston (MA): Harvard Business Press.

Kuncic, A. 2014. "Institutional Quality Dataset." *J Inst Econ* 10 (1): 135–161.

Lee, K., M. W. Peng, and K. Lee. 2008. "From Diversification Premium to Diversification Discount during Institutional Transitions." *J World Bus* 43 (1): 47–65. doi:10.1016/j.jwb.2007.10.010.

Lenartowicz, T., and K. Roth. 2001. "Does Subculture within a Country Matter? a Cross-cultural Study of Motivational Domains and Business Performance in Brazil." *J Int Bus Stud* 32 (2): 305–326. doi:10.1057/palgrave.jibs.8490954.

Li, M., and Y. Y. Wong. 2003. "Diversification and Economic Performance: An Empirical Assessment of Chinese Firms." *Asia Pac J Manag* 20 (2): 243–265. doi:10.1023/A:1023804904383.

Li, X., and L. Sun. 2017. "How Do Sub-national Institutional Constraints Impact Foreign Firm Performance?" *Int Bus Rev* 26 (3): 555–565. doi:10.1016/j.ibusrev.2016.11.004.

Lu, Y., and J. Yao. 2006. "Impact of State Ownership and Control Mechanisms on the Performance of Group Affiliated Companies in China." *Asia Pac J Manag* 23 (4): 485–503. doi:10.1007/s10490-006-9017-0.

Mackey, T. B., J. B. Barney, and J. P. Dotson. 2017. "Corporate Diversification and the Value of Individual Firms: A Bayesian Approach." *Strateg Manage J* 38 (2): 322–341. doi:10.1002/smj.2480.

Markóczy, L., S. Li, M. W. Peng, and B. Ren. 2013. "Social Network Contingency, Symbolic Management, and Boundary Stretching." *Strateg Manage J* 34 (11): 1367–1387. doi:10.1002/smj.2072.

Meyer, K., and H. V. Nguyen. 2005. "Foreign Investment Strategies and Sub-national Institutions in Emerging Market: Evidence from Vietnam." *J Manage Stud* 42 (1): 63–93. doi:10.1111/j.1467-6486.2005.00489.x.

Miller, D. J. 2004. "Firms' Technological Resources and the Performance Effects of Diversification: A Longitudinal Study." *Strateg Manage J* 25: 1097–1119. doi:10.1002/smj.411.

Montinola, G., Y. Qian, and B. R. Weingast. 1995. "Federalism, Chinese Style: The Political Basis for Economic Success in China." *World Polit* 48 (1): 50–81. doi:10.1353/wp.1995.0003.

Nachum, L. 2004. "Geographic and Industrial Diversification of Developing Country Firms." *J Manage Stud* 41 (2): 273–294. doi:10.1111/j.1467-6486.2004.00432.x.

National Bureau of Statistics. 2003. "The Categorization of Large, Medium, and Small Enterprises." Accessed 18 June 2016. http://www.stats.gov.cn/ztjc/zdtjgz/zgjjpc/pcfa/200411/t20041101_52398.htm

National Bureau of Statistics. 2011. "The Categorization of Large, Medium, Small, and Micro- Enterprises." Accessed 6 May 2018. http://www.stats.gov.cn/statsinfo/auto2073/201310/t20131031_450691.html

Naughton, B. 2007. *The Chinese Economy: Transitions and Growth*. Boston (MA): MIT Press.

Nguyen, T. V., N. T. Le, and S. E. Bryant. 2013. "Sub-national Institutions, Firm Strategies and Firm Performance: A Multi-level Study of Private Manufacturing Firms in Vietnam." *J World Bus* 48 (1): 68–76. doi:10.1016/j.jwb.2012.06.008.

Nippa, M., U. Pidun, and H. Rubner. 2011. "Corporate Portfolio Management: Appraising Four Decades of Academic Research." *Acad Manage Perspect* 25 (4): 50–66. doi:10.5465/amp.2010.0164.

Nolan, P. 2001. *China and the Global Business Revolution*. New York (NY): Palgrave.

North, D. C. 1990. *Institutions, Institutional Change, and Economic Performance*. Cambridge (UK): Cambridge University Press.

O'brien, R. M. 2007. "A Caution regarding Rules of Thumb for Variance Inflation Factors." *QUAL QUANT* 41 (5): 673–690. doi:10.1007/s11135-006-9018-6.

Palich, L. E., L. B. Cardinal, and C. C. Miller. 2000. "Curvilinearity in the Diversification-performance Linkage: An Examination of over Three Decades of Research." *Strateg Manage J* 21 (2): 155–174. doi:10.1002/(SICI)1097-0266-(200002)21:2<155::AID-SMJ82>3.0.CO;2-2.

Park, C. 2002. "The Effects of Prior Performance on the Choice between Related and Unrelated Acquisitions: Implications for the Performance Consequences of Diversification Strategy." *J Manage Stud* 39 (7): 1003–1019. doi:10.1111/1467-6486.00321.

Peng, M. W. 2002. "Towards an Institution-based View of Business Strategy." *Asia Pac J Manag* 19 (2–3): 251–267. doi:10.1023/A:1016291702714.

Peng, M. W. 2003. "Institutional Transitions and Strategic Choices." *Acad Manage Rev* 28 (2): 275–296. doi:10.5465/amr.2003.9416341.

Peng, M. W., and A. Delios. 2006. "What Determines the Scope of the Firm over Time and around the World? an Asia Pacific Perspective." *Asia Pac J Manag* 23 (4): 385–405. doi:10.1007/s10490-006-9021-4.

Peng, M. W., S. L. Sun, B. Pinkham, and H. Chen. 2009. "The Institution-based View as a Third Leg for a Strategy Tripod." *Acad Manage Perspect* 23 (3): 63–81. doi:10.5465/amp.2009.43479264.

Peng, M. W., J. Tan, and T. W. Tong. 2004. "Ownership Types and Strategic Groups in an Emerging Economy." *J Manage Stud* 41 (7): 1105–1129. doi:10.1111/j.1467-6486.2004.00468.x.

Peng, M. W., D. Wang, and Y. Jiang. 2008. "An Institution-based View of International Business Strategy: A Focus on Emerging Economies." *J Int Bus Stud* 39: 920–936. doi:10.1057/palgrave.jibs.8400377.

Ramaswamy, K., M. Li, and B. Petitt. 2004. "Who Drives Unrelated Diversification? a Study of Indian Manufacturing Firms." *Asia Pac J Manag* 21 (4): 403–423. doi:10.1023/B:APJM.0000048711.41701.f3.

Robins, J. A., and M. F. Wiersema. 2003. "The Measurement of Corporate Portfolio Strategy: Analysis of the Content Validity of Related Diversification Indexes." *Strateg Manage J* 24 (1): 39–59. doi:10.1002/smj.282.

Robson, G., C. Gallagher, and M. Daly. 1993. "Diversification Strategy and Practice in Small Firms." *Int Small Bus J* 11 (2): 37–53. doi:10.1177/026624269301100204.

Scott, W. R. 1995. *Institutions and Organizations*. Thousand Oaks, CA: Sage.

Shackman, J. D. 2007. "Corporate Diversification, Vertical Integration, and Internal Capital Markets: A Cross-country Study." *Manage Int Rev* 47 (4): 479–504. doi:10.1007/s11575-007-0027-z.

Shi, W. S., S. L. Sun, and M. W. Peng. 2012. "Sub-national Institutional Contingencies, Network Positions, and IJV Partner Selection." *J Manage Stud* 49 (7): 1221–1245. doi:10.1111/j.1467-6486.2012.01058.x.

Shi, W. S., S. L. Sun, B. C. Pinkham, and M. W. Peng. 2014. "Domestic Alliance Network to Attract Foreign Partners: Evidence from International Joint Ventures in China." *J Int Bus Stud* 45 (3): 338–362. doi:10.1057/jibs.2013.71.

Storey, D. J. 1994. *Understanding the Small Business Sector*. London and New York: Routledge.

Wan, W. P. 2005. "Country Resource Environments, Firm Capabilities, and Corporate Diversification Strategies." *J Manage Stud* 42 (1): 161–182. doi:10.1111/j.1467-6486.2005.00492.x.

Wan, W. P., and R. E. Hoskisson. 2003. "Home Country Environments, Corporate Diversification Strategies, and Firm Performance." *Acad Manage J* 46 (1): 27–45.

Wan, W. P., R. E. Hoskisson, J. C. Short, and D. W. Yiu. 2011. "Resource-based Theory and Corporate Diversification: Accomplishments and Opportunities." *J Manage* 37 (5): 1335–1368.

Wang, D., and X. R. Luo. 2018. "Retire in Peace: Government Officials' Political Incentives and Corporate Diversification in an Emerging Economy." *Admin Sci Quart*. accessed 15 Sep 2018. doi:10.1177/0001839218786263.

Wang, X., G. Fan, and J. Yu 2016. *Marketization of China's provinces: NERI report 2016*. Beijing: Social Science Academic Press. Chinese.

Williamson, O. 1994. "Transaction Costs Economics and Organization Theory." In *The Handbook of Economic Sociology*, edited by N. J. Smelser and R. Swedberg, 77–107. Princeton (NJ): Princeton University Press.

Williamson, O. 1998. "The Institutions of Governance." *Am Econ Rev* 88 (2): 75–79.

Witt, M. A., and A. Y. Lewin. 2007. "Outward Foreign Direct Investment as Escape Response to Home Country Institutional Constraints." *J Int Bus Stud* 38 (4): 579–594. doi:10.1057/palgrave.jibs.8400285.

Wright, M., I. Filatotchev, R. E. Hoskisson, and M. W. Peng. 2005. "Strategy Research in Emerging Economies: Challenging the Conventional Wisdom." *J Manage Stud* 42 (1): 1–33. doi:10.1111/j.1467-6486.2005.00487.x.

Yearbook of China's small and medium enterprises. 2014. Beijing: Enterprise Management Publishing House.

Yiu, D., G. D. Bruton, and Y. Lu. 2005. "Understanding Business Group Performance in an Emerging Economy: Acquiring Resources and Capabilities in order to Prosper." *J Manage Stud* 42 (1): 183–206. doi:10.1111/j.1467-6486.2005.00493.x.

Zhou, W. 2011. "Regional Deregulation and Entrepreneurial Growth in China's Transition Economy." *Entrep Region Dev* 23 (9–10): 853–876. doi:10.1080/08985626.2011.577816.

Hear it straight from the horse's mouth: recognizing policy-induced opportunities

Weiqi Dai, Felix Arndt and Mingqing Liao

ABSTRACT

What types of entrepreneurs are more likely to 'stay tuned' to government policies and does it pay? Integrating work on opportunity recognition and the institution-based view, this study examines the link between the pursuit of policy-induced opportunities and firm performance. Based on data analysis of 3284 Chinese privately owned firms in 31 regions/provinces in China, we find that entrepreneurs who have past working experience within the government are more likely to stay alert to government policies involving entrepreneurial opportunities, which leads to entrepreneurial activities and ultimately firm performance. This study enriches our understanding of opportunity recognition and development by expanding it to political markets. We assess the role of institutional variation as an important factor in emerging economies. We unravel the pivotal role of entrepreneurial alertness to government policies on enhancing firm performance by strengthening entrepreneurial activities.

Introduction

Entrepreneurial opportunities are core to the field of entrepreneurship (Venkataraman 1997; Shane and Venkataraman 2000; Sarasvathy et al. 2003). Scholars distinguish between two opportunity theories, namely, discovery theory and creation theory (Alvarez and Barney 2007). Previous research on 'discovered' opportunities suggests that opportunities objectively exist and primarily concern the opportunities identified in the 'commercial' market. In the opportunity recognition and development literature, however, there is little consideration of opportunities arising in the political market (Short et al. 2010), which we label as *'policy-induced opportunities'* in this paper. Although Drucker (1985) suggests that one source of opportunities is the emergence of significant changes in political forces, 'policy-induced opportunities' have not been explicitly articulated, let alone comprehensively investigated (Jacquemin and Janssen 2015; Short et al. 2010).

The omission of policy-induced opportunities is problematic as this kind of opportunities is ubiquitous in emerging markets. They may help to shed light on the puzzle of the rapid growth of the private sector in emerging markets such as China. Over the past 40 years, Chinese privately owned firms have risen from a starting point with almost nothing to achieving a prominent position in the Chinese economy. According to the China National Bureau of Statistics, there are 2,859,000 privately owned firms in China, accounting for 78.3% of the total number of firms (China National Bureau of Statistics 2018a). Privately owned firms create more than 80% of the nation's industrial value added and employ more than 80% of the working population (China National

Bureau of Statistics 2018b), despite the unfavourable institutional environment facing the private sector (Zhou 2011; Su, Zhai, and Landström 2015; Dai and Liao 2018).

Two streams of research strive to explain this phenomenon. One stream of research highlights the role of informal institutions such as 'guanxi' or personal connections as substitutions for formal institutions in regulating the economic exchanges and supporting the development of private firms in China (e.g. Armanios et al. 2017; Zhou 2013; Peng and Luo 2000). The other stream, however, emphasizes the role of positive changes in the formal institutional framework especially the policies enacted by the Chinese governments that offered ample opportunities for private firms (e.g. Zhou 2011, 2013). Although the former offers intriguing insights with explanatory power, the latter has recently captured increasing scholarly attention (e.g. Ge et al. 2017; Dai and Liao 2018). To move this line of research forward, there is a need for researchers to explicate how changes in the formal institutional frameworks and, in particular, the promulgation of new government policies (e.g. deregulations) motivates private firms to grow and prosper in China. Indeed, a range of privately owned firms in China were growing out of 'relying upon government policies' (Dai and Liao 2018). Both existing research and managerial practice motivated us to posit that a comprehensive understanding of policy-induced opportunities is the key to further explain the growth miracle of Chinese private firms. As a point of departure, this paper thus aims to explore policy-induced opportunities by examining the following two questions: (1) How are 'policy-induced' opportunities identified and developed? (2) Does it pay for entrepreneurs to engage with government policies and exploit 'policy-induced opportunities'?

We address the research questions by assessing the factors fostering entrepreneurial alertness towards government policies, subsequent entrepreneurial actions, and resulting financial performance. Specifically, we combine insights from the entrepreneurial opportunity recognition literature and the institution-based view with special attention to the context of emerging markets. We build on Ardichvili, Cardozo, and Ray (2003) and Tang, Kacmar, and Busenitz's (2012) conception of entrepreneurial alertness, and integrate Peng, Wang, and Jiang's (2008) institution-based view of emerging market business into our framework to account for the Chinese context and understand the underlying nature of Ardichvili and his colleagues' (2003) opportunity recognition and development framework for emerging economies.

The Chinese context is a perfect 'laboratory' for this study. First, policy-induced opportunities have been pervasive in China (Zhou 2011). Ever since the reform and opening up, the Chinese government has deregulated and implemented a range of pro-market reforms, giving rise to a proliferation of policies that encourage individuals and/or incumbent firms to engage in entrepreneurial activities (Dai and Liao 2018). The exemplary policies that have been implemented by *the central government of China* are listed in Table 1. These policies, especially those regarding deregulations, constitute the main sources of policy-induced opportunities (Dai et al. 2018; Dai and Liao 2018).

Second, some Chinese entrepreneurs are enthusiastic about policy-induced opportunities. Due to a lack of formal institutions supporting private businesses (Ahlstrom and Ding 2014; Huang 2008), entrepreneurs from privately owned firms in China often establish personal ties with government officials in the hope that these political ties may protect their private property and lead to favourable treatment fromofficials (Dai et al. 2018). Importantly, such political ties not only enable entrepreneurs to capture the essence of newly promulgated government policies, but also facilitate the identification and development of actionable opportunities by discussing with or consulting government officials (Jacquemin and Janssen 2015). Occasionally, entrepreneurs from privately owned firms may be involved in shaping government policies. Indeed, Xing, Liu, and Cooper's (2018) qualitative research shows that in emerging markets, entrepreneurs may be involved in making rules at the local or regional level rather than just following them.

Based on a sample of 3284 private firms in China, we find that entrepreneurs with prior work experience in the government are more likely to be alert to government policies and translate policy-induced opportunities into firm performance via entrepreneurial activities. In doing so, we contribute to the entrepreneurship literature in significant ways. First, we introduce the concept of 'policy-induced

Table 1. Exemplary policies encouraging entrepreneurship in China.

	Year	Policy	Key messages	Interpretation of the policy
1	2003	'The 2003 Small and Medium Enterprises (SME) Promotion Law'	The government treats the development of small and medium-sized enterprises as a long-term strategy, ensuring equal rights and equal opportunities for all small and medium-sized enterprises through creating a favorable environment	For the first time, the government is required to develop support systems that provide SME with resources and inputs needed to start and grow their venture
2	2005	'Thirty-six Principles on the Non-public Economy'	This policy allows non-public capital to enter industries and areas not prohibited by laws and regulations. Non-public capital are entitled to enter industries and sectors that allow foreign capital to enter	The State Council promulgated this policy to seriously tackle the problems of government predation of and discrimination against private firms
3	2010	'Opinions on encouraging and guiding the healthy development of private investment'	Private firms are encouraged to invest in such industries as infrastructure, public utilities, policy-oriented housing construction, defense and military industries, etc.	The State Council issued this policy to expand the scope of investments by private firms
4	2012	'Opinions on further supporting the healthy development of small and micro-sized enterprises'	Small and micro businesses will receive assistance in terms of tax relief, financing, technological innovation and market entry from the government.	The State Council promulgated this policy to help small and micro businesses boost confidence, operate stably, improve profitability and sustainability, and enhance their sustainable developments.
5	2014	'Guiding Opinions on Innovating Investment and Financing Mechanisms in Key Areas and Encouraging Social Investment'	Private firms are encouraged to participate in investments in key areas such as public service, resources and environment protection, ecological development and infrastructure	The state council promulgated to unleash the potential of private capital and increase the investments in several key industries
6	2015	'Guidelines on Developing Maker Space for Mass Entrepreneurship and Innovation'	This policy aims to accelerate the development of new entrepreneurial service platforms such as the Maker Spaces	The general office of the State Council issued this policy to develop a better environment for mass entrepreneurship and innovation
7	2016	'Opinions on promoting venture capital investment'	This policy issued by the State Council provides guidance on the development of venture capital industry from the aspects of investment subject, capital source, exit mechanism, etc.	This policy is an overarching institutional design for the venture capital industry in China
8	2017	'Opinions on further motivate investments to the social sector'	Investors in the social service industry will receive a range of supports from the government in terms of tax relief, financing, recruitment, etc.	The general office of the State Council issued this policy to encourage all kinds of investors to engage in social service such as elderly care

opportunities' to signify the special nature of opportunities that are presented outside of the regular marketplace. In echoing the call from Eckhardt and Shane (2003), Short et al. (2010) as well as Jacquemin and Janssen (2015), we examine these unique opportunities in emerging economies in a comprehensive manner, answering how they are recognized, by whom, and with what consequences (Venkataraman 1997). Second, we not only build upon but also enrich Ardichvili and his colleagues' (2003) framework of opportunity recognition and development by extending it to emerging economies. Specifically, we show that there is heterogeneity between entrepreneurs in being alert to policy-induced opportunities and demonstrate subsequent implications for firm performance. Such an extension is meaningful, as emerging economies follow a different rulebook and play an increasingly important role for the world economy.

Theoretical framework

Monitoring the environment, identifying opportunities, developing actions, and deciding to act upon the opportunities are key to the entrepreneurial process (Venkataraman 1997; Shane and Venkataraman 2000). The literature on opportunity recognition and development has discussed a large range of different models, often concentrating on a particular part of the process or offering a perspective from a particular lens (e.g. Ardichvili, Cardozo, and Ray 2003; Baron and Ensley 2006; Ozgen and Baron 2007). In this paper, we argue that particularly in economies that rely on state interventions or where investments are guided by actors close to the state (as especially in parts of Asia, the Middle East, and Africa), institutions – here, the state – and entrepreneurial actions are at times intertwined. Thus, we may benefit from an embeddedness perspective to understand the entrepreneurial process in these contexts.

The traditional understanding of opportunities relates to creating or addressing market dis-equilibria (Schumpeter 1934; Kirzner 1973), often through a recombination of resources and capabilities to address (latent) demands. As such, opportunities created through changing institutional frameworks or opportunities designed through state interventions have not been at the forefront of the research agenda as they do not reflect the traditional understanding of the markets in equilibrium theory but have rather been systems discussions with ideological flair (Hayek 1945). Nevertheless, these kinds of opportunities have gained importance in a changing world order driven through the institutional settings of emerging economies and particularly the specific ways these economies have been developing. In our sample, we can see that some entrepreneurs seem to 'make a living' from following policies closely.

Opportunity recognition consists of at least three processes. First, it incorporates the sensing of opportunities. Sensing may be directed towards resources that may be better deployed and market needs that may be addressed. In our case, sensing includes the scanning of opportunities involved in government policies that may be actionable for the entrepreneur. The second process we label as seizing of opportunities. This process includes the matching of the opportunity with the resources available to the entrepreneur. This process, for example, may entail an action plan including resource allocation of the entrepreneur to address, make use of, or even shape government policies. Indeed, we need to take into account that in emerging economies, entrepreneurs often shape institutions to their own interests (Xing, Liu, and Cooper 2018). The third process encompasses action to exploit the opportunity, for example, the development of a product to fulfil market needs or entrepreneurial activities that result from favourable policies.

Ardichvili, Cardozo, and Ray (2003) stress four factors next to the characteristics of the entrepreneur that affect opportunity recognition. First, entrepreneurial alertness describes the openness and sensitivity of the entrepreneur to a certain kind of information. Second, information asymmetry and prior knowledge make entrepreneurs more likely to recognize opportunities. Third, search describes the active and conscious search for new opportunities in a certain space. Fourth, strong and weak ties or generally social networks enhance the chance of opportunity recognition.

In our setting of emerging markets and with special interest to the exploitation of government policies, the above four factors propose that entrepreneurs that are close to the government, be it through active lobbying, prior exposure, privileged access, etc., may be more prone to recognize opportunities than entrepreneurs without these characteristics (Jacquemin and Janssen 2015).

We address at least one point that has attracted little attention in prior research. That is, little is known about the factors that trigger incumbent firms to engage in entrepreneurial activities that are based on policy-induced opportunities. This gap results from understanding markets as well-developed. However, policy-induced opportunities are a reality in many emerging markets and may play an important role in these markets (Dai et al. 2018).

As 'insightful as the industry- and resource-based views are, they can be criticized for largely ignoring the formal and informal institutional underpinning that provides the context of competition among industries and firms studied with these lenses' (Peng, Wang, and Jiang 2008). According to this idea, strategic choices can be driven through institutional frameworks such as government policies. As such, institutions may be directly responsible for strategic decisions (Ingram and Silverman 2002). These effects seem to be particularly visible in emerging/transition economies with direct implications for firm performance (Makino, Isobe, and Chan 2004).

Peng, Wang, and Jiang (2008) stress the Chinese growth miracle that occurs despite relatively weakly developed formal institutions. As such, understanding some of the mechanisms behind how Chinese entrepreneurs make decisions within their institutional context and based on government policy is an important aspect of merging an institutions-based view of strategy and the literature on opportunity recognition. Here, the contextual nature of the four factors outlined by Ardichvili, Cardozo, and Ray (2003) is particularly important. Outlining the driving nature of the strategic decisions of entrepreneurs based on government policies and considering specific contexts of institutional developments may be a first step towards closing this gap.

Hypotheses

Experience and entrepreneurial alertness

Entrepreneurial alertness is a concept that goes back to Kirzner's (1973) work. While the idea of profit generation is traditionally understood as the purpose and outcome of entrepreneurial alertness (Hitt and Ireland 2000), there is no consensus about the definition, antecedents or drivers of entrepreneurial alertness (Valliere 2013). There has been a lively debate regarding the inclusiveness of the concept (Tang, Kacmar, and Busenitz 2012). Discussions incorporate the question of the nature of opportunities, the processes associated with opportunities, and their underpinnings. In this study, we take a broad view in the adoption of Tang, Kacmar, and Busenitz (2012) encompassing the sensing and seizing of opportunities as well as evaluating and judging the opportunities for potential action.

In our context of emerging markets and policy-induced opportunities, the four factors identified by Ardichvili, Cardozo, and Ray (2003) are applicable to increase the propensity for entrepreneurs to be alert. First, the openness of entrepreneurs to collaborate and be involved with the government is a predisposition for being alert to government-induced opportunities. There is a divide between entrepreneurs with close connections to the government and those with no ties and some resistance toward working with the government, possibly due to the involved practices and financial implications (Shi, Markóczy, and Stan 2015; Sun and Wright 2012). Often, the openness to and closeness with government related activities is related to prior experience and involvement.

Second, informal ties to government officials and long-term affiliation with government departments may provide preferential access to information regarding new policies. For example, entrepreneurs with work experience in government functions are likely to have lasting bonds beyond the formal communication channels.

Third, in the process of sensing new opportunities, the entrepreneur engages in conscious, sometimes passive, sometimes active efforts to search for relevant information that may confirm, change, or lead to new beliefs of the world (Valliere 2013). Information scanning is carried out with existing mental frames and schemas that have been shaped through prior experiences (Gaglio and Katz 2001). In our context, we expect entrepreneurs that have had prior exposure to government activities to be alert to government-induced or policy-induced opportunities.

Fourth, receiving relevant information is often tied to an entrepreneur's social networks (Ozgen and Baron 2007; Rong and Shenkar 2011). Extensive research shows the role of strong and weak ties for sensing opportunities, seizing them, and taking subsequent actions (e.g. Sarasvathy 2001). While networks erode, are rebuilt, and can be redirected, prior experiences shape many of the strong and weak ties of the entrepreneur. As such, entrepreneurs with prior exposure to government related activities are likely to be more alert to policy-induced opportunities through their networks and political involvement (Liu and Huang 2018; Jacquemin and Janssen 2015).

In summary, sensing and seizing policy-induced opportunities benefits from prior exposure and experience to government-related activities. We formulate these insights into a hypothesis as follows:

Hypothesis 1: Prior working experience of the entrepreneur within the government is positively associated with entrepreneurial alertness towards government policies.

Experience, institutional development and entrepreneurial alertness towards government policies

Institutions shape the 'rules of the game' in a society (North 1990; Scott 2008). China shows significant institutional differences across regions due to its size and degree of marketisation. Recent research further shows that there are significant differences in terms of formal institutions between adjacent cities in the same region in China (Liu and Huang 2018). Such differences between subnational institutions have increasingly attracted scholarly attention (e.g. Nguyen, Le, and Bryant 2013; Shi, Sun, and Peng 2012; Chan, Makino, and Isobe 2010; Meyer and Nguyen 2005). For instance, Kafouros et al. (2015) showed that variations in subnational institution development had effects on innovative, collaborative and financial performance.

We expect that regional institutional development shapes the association of entrepreneur working experience in the government and entrepreneurial alertness towards government policies. Specifically, in regions with lower levels of institutional development, entrepreneurial opportunities are more likely to stem from changes in government policies because the governments in these regions participate more actively in economic affairs. In such settings, entrepreneurs pay constant attention to government policies and seek to increase their entrepreneurial alertness towards government policies by leveraging their prior working experience in the government (e.g. activate their ties to former colleagues in governments). Accordingly, in regions with lower levels of institutional development, the strength of the link between working experience within the government and entrepreneurial alertness towards government policies is enhanced.

In contrast, for firms situated in regions with higher levels of institutional development, the market may play a larger role than government activities (Child, Lu, and Tsai 2007). More importantly, the governments in these developed areas avoid intervening in economic development by controlling the policies or regulations that involve entrepreneurial activities (Dai et al. 2018; Dai and Liao 2018). Accordingly, entrepreneurs in such settings locate valuable entrepreneurial opportunities primarily in response to the market instead of responding to government action. Under such circumstances, the working experience within the government is less likely to be translated into entrepreneurial alertness towards government policies. We posit the following:

Hypothesis 2: The relationship between the entrepreneur's prior working experience within the government and entrepreneurial alertness toward government policies is negatively moderated by regional institutions.

Entrepreneurial alertness and entrepreneurial activity

Corporate entrepreneurship refers to a company's strategic actions to take risks, innovate, and be proactive (Zahra and Covin 1995; Sharma and Chrisman 1999). It is about the idea of continuous renewal and is often ingrained into the 'DNA' of companies (Minola et al. 2016). Generally, firms undertake actions related to corporate entrepreneurship and particular corporate venturing with a mid- and long-term horizon. External corporate venturing is a form of corporate entrepreneurship that incorporates 'investments that facilitate the founding and/or growth of external businesses'

(Covin and Miles 2007, 183). External corporate venturing is particularly relevant for the case of pursuing policy-induced opportunities due to the market facilitating character of policies. In our case, this idea is reflected by prior experiences of entrepreneurs in the political arena that become part of their natural habitat. Policy-induced opportunities generally target market-based activities that may enhance the market or are protective to it. They will be changes in the institutional frame for mid- and long-range activities. Following and exploiting the development of policies enables entrepreneurs to take calculated risks in proactively addressing these opportunities and recalibrate their business activities accordingly.

Entrepreneurs with close attachment to the government do not only benefit from potentially better, more accurate, and timely information, but they also may be more agile to adapt and reconfigure their companies for grasping opportunities (Dai and Liu 2015). As such, we expect entrepreneurs with alertness to government movements to benefit from policy-induced opportunities in terms of corporate venturing activities (Keil 2004; Kuratko, Hornsby, and Hayton 2015; Vanacker, Collewaert, and Zahra 2017). Thus, we propose the following hypothesis:

Hypothesis 3: Entrepreneurial alertness towards government policies is positively associated with corporate venturing activities.

Entrepreneurial alertness, entrepreneurial activities, and firm performance

Entrepreneurial alertness directly affects strategic decision making and financial performance (Roundy et al. 2017). Alert entrepreneurs are more likely to understand and act on opportunities as they may see a first-mover advantage that is pertinent for policy-induced opportunities that may not be as transparently communicated and not be as competitively followed by other entrepreneurs. The alertness also may reduce perceived uncertainty as government policies and discussion around changes may be ongoing and do not catch alert entrepreneurs unprepared. As such, entrepreneurs who constantly update their beliefs about the environment and stay tuned into news may make better use of policy-induced opportunities, adapt, and benefit from them. Thus, we hypothesize the following:

Hypothesis 4: Increased entrepreneurial alertness towards government policies is positively associated with firm performance.

Entrepreneurial activities may empower a firm by enhancing its profitability (Simsek and Heavey 2011), by realizing strategic renewal (Guth and Ginsberg 1990), by pursuing innovation (Baden-Fuller 1995), by helping it to gain knowledge to develop future revenue streams (Simsek and Heavey 2011), by achieving international success (Zahra and Garvis 2000) or by reconfiguring resources to develop competitive advantages (Kuratko, Ireland, and Hornsby 2001).

Through such entrepreneurial activities, firms are enabled to successfully expand their business portfolios and increase their sales (Yiu and Lau 2008; Antoncic and Prodan 2008; Kemelgor 2002; Zahra and Garvis 2000). In addition, policy-induced opportunities may often be highly rewarding, as they allow access to formerly exclusive opportunities for state-owned firms. Competition in this opportunity space may be less crowded as not all firms closely follow government policies. Privately owned firms that engage in entrepreneurial activities by pursuing policy-induced opportunities are thus able to reap considerable benefits and increase their return on investments (Zahra and Hayton 2008; Antoncic and Hisrich 2001; Covin and Slevin 1989). Thus, we hypothesize the following:

Hypothesis 5: Increased entrepreneurial actions as a result of entrepreneurial alertness towards government policies are positively associated with firm performance.

Figure 1 presents the theoretical framework for the aforementioned hypotheses.

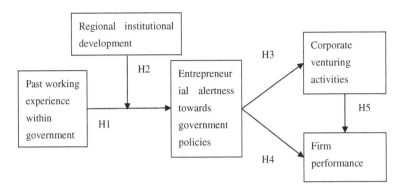

Figure 1. The theoretical framework.

Methods

Data and sample

To validate our hypotheses, we gathered data from two sources. The first data source was from the 2012 China National Privately Owned Firms Survey conducted jointly by researchers from four institutions, namely, the Academy of Social Science, the All China Industry and Commerce Federation and the United Front Work Department of the Central Committee of the Communist Party. The survey intended to collect information from Chinese entrepreneurs in the private sector and to assist the central government to fine tune policies regarding to private owned firms (Zhao and Lu 2016). To ensure that the sample firms were representative of Chinese privately owned firms, the researchers generated a nationwide random sample of such firms, using a multistage stratified sampling technique across all provinces and industries (for the detailed sampling scheme, see Jia and Mayer 2017). The researchers interviewed entrepreneurs (or founders) of each private firm represented in the sample. These procedures gave rise to reliable datasets for high-quality studies in the literature (e.g. Dai and Liao 2018; Jia and Mayer 2017; Zhao and Lu 2016; Gao and Hafsi 2015; Du 2014).

The data collected through this national survey of Chinese privately owned firms are suitable for this study for three reasons. First, they provide relevant information on representative Chinese privately owned firms. Second, the initial aim of the survey was not to explicate policy-induced opportunities but to collect information on the performance of Chinese privately owned firms. As a result, it is unlikely to introduce any threats from interviewer induced bias in using this dataset. Third, the sample firms are exactly the kind of entrepreneur-controlled privately owned firms (Zhao and Lu 2016) in which entrepreneurs dominated the decision-making process. As such, this sample is appropriate for our purpose of examining how the entrepreneurial alertness to government policies (which is a seemingly individual-level construct) is shaped by entrepreneurs' prior working experience and how such alertness instigates entrepreneurial activities and stimulate firm performance.

The second data source for our study is the Index of Marketisation of Chinese Provinces, which was developed by the National Economic Research Institute (NERI) for China (Fan, Wang, and Zhu 2009; Wang, Fan, and Yu 2017). This index follows the methodology of the Economic Freedom of the World Index and ranks Chinese provinces according to their levels of market/regulatory/legal development (Zhou 2011). This dataset was widely employed for indicating regional institutional development in China (e.g. Zhao and Lu 2016; Shi, Sun, and Peng 2012; Chen and Kim 2010).

The final dataset for our study consists of firm-province observations. These observations are included for two reasons. First, each firm's location can only be identified at the provincial level. Second, the level of regional institutional development is also measured at the provincial level. Following Barnett and Lewis (1994), we winsorize the sample at the 1% level to exclude

Table 2. Study sample distribution by region, age, and employee number.

Region	Number	Percentage	Firm age (HIS)	Number	Percentage
Beijing	126	3.84	<10	2243	68.30
Tianjing	83	2.53	10–20	1006	30.63
Shanghai	182	5.54	>20	35	1.07
Chongqing	113	3.44	Total	3284	100
North China	343	10.44			
Northeast China	387	11.78	Employee number	Number	Percentage
East China	878	26.74	<100	2093	63.73
Central China	345	10.51	100–1000	1063	32.37
South China	365	11.11	>1000	128	3.90
Southwest China	220	6.70	Total	3284	100
Northwest China	242	7.37			
Total	3284	100			

extreme values. Our final sample contains 3284 observations. Table 2 reports the descriptive information regarding our sample.

Measures

Firm performance (ROS/ROE)
To capture the economic outcome from entrepreneurial alertness towards government policies, we follow Yiu and Lau (2008), Antoncic and Prodan (2008), Kemelgor (2002), and Zahra and Garvis (2000) by using return on sales (ROS) as the dependant variable. To test the robustness of the regression analyses, we follow Zahra and Hayton (2008), Antoncic and Hisrich (2001) and Covin and Slevin (1989) to employ return on equity (ROE) as the dependant variable. Both of these variables have been widely used in previous entrepreneurship studies involving firm performance.

Entrepreneurial alertness towards government policies (ALERTNESS)
Entrepreneurial alertness towards government policies represents the extent to which entrepreneurs pay attention to and are aware of the policies enacted by government agencies. In transition economies such as China, the governments constantly promulgate policies or regulations affecting the private sector as initiatives to foster economic growth (Zhou 2011). We thus gauge entrepreneurial alertness towards government policies by determining the extent to which entrepreneurs are familiar with the latest government policies regarding the private sector, with '3' indicating detailed familiarity, '2' indicating general awareness and '1' indicating a lack of awareness.

In the 2012 China National Privately Owned Firms Survey, the respondents were asked to rate the degree to which they were familiar with the following five national policies in relation to the private sector: (1) Several Guidelines on Further Promoting the Development of Small and Medium-sized Enterprises, issued by the State Council; (2) Several Guidelines on Encouraging and Guiding the Healthy Development of Private Investment, issued by the State Council; (3) Several Guidelines on Further Enhancing the Financial Service to SMEs, jointly issued by the People's Bank of China, the banking regulatory commission of the CSRC, and the insurance regulatory commission of China; (4) SME Growth Planning in the 12th Five-Year Planning Period, issued by the Ministry of Industry and Information Technology; and (5) Nine Initiatives of Supporting Small and Micro Businesses, issued by the State Council., we aggregated the respondents' scores for these items to derive a continuous variable of entrepreneurial alertness towards government policy.

Corporate venturing (CV)
Corporate venturing represents firm-level entrepreneurial activities that occur outside of the incumbent firms (Narayanan, Yang, and Zahra 2009). Corporate venturing is a dynamic concept whose dimensions change overtime (Keil 2004; Kuratko, Hornsby, and Hayton 2015). Corporate venturing consists of investments in new businesses that involve setting up new external entities, investments

for mergers with other firms or acquisitions of existing external firms (Burgelman 1983; Narayanan, Yang, and Zahra 2009). We thus measured corporate venturing by aggregating a focal firm's investments in these aspects reported in the 2012 China National Privately Owned Firms Survey.

Past working experience within government (EXPR_GOV)

The government is a critical component of the Danwei system in China. During the era of the planned economy, the Danwei system included not only government departments and institutions but also state-owned and collective enterprises (Bjorklund 1986). This system had a pervasive influence on almost every aspect of the employees' and their families' lives (Whyte 1999; Dai et al. 2018). We measure entrepreneurs' past working experience within the government by asking whether an entrepreneur had worked for a government department or institution *before* starting his or her own business (1 = yes, 0 = no).

Institutional development (INSTITUTION)

Institutional development is measured annually at the provincial level according to the NERI's marketisation indices (for details, see Wang, Fan, and Yu 2017). The NERI index provides an overall assessment of each province's institutional development from the following five perspectives: the government-market relations (i.e. governmental intervention in markets), the share of non-state-owned enterprises, the level of development for product (and service) markets, the level of development for factor markets and the level of development for market intermediaries and the legal system (Shi, Sun, and Peng 2012). As mentioned earlier, the NERI index is widely used in the management literature (e.g. Zhao and Lu 2016; Chen and Kim 2010; Shi, Sun, and Peng 2012).

Controls

To account for alternative explanations, we also include sets of individual-and firm-level variables as controls. At the individual level, we control for the entrepreneurs' social class (SOCLSS) and the entrepreneurs' education level (EDU). The entrepreneurs' social class indicates the social capital of all surveyed business leaders, as social class may have an influence on their strategic decisions (Roussanov 2010). We measure social class (SOCLSS) using a 10-point scale (1 = lowest, 10 = highest). As the entrepreneurs' education levels may also affect their decision-making processes (Wiersema and Bantel 1992), we control for entrepreneurs' education (EDU) by using a dummy variable that indicates whether an entrepreneur has a university degree (1 = yes, 0 = no).

At the firm level, we include the controls of firm age (HIS), firm size (LnEMPLOY, SIZE), family ownership (FAMOWN), formal structure (FORMALSTC), firm leverage (LEV), firm exports (EXPORT) and firm OFDI (outward foreign direct investment, or FRINVST). Firm age (HIS) is related to a firm's strategic behaviour (Hamilton 2012). Thus, we control for the number of years since the firm's foundation. Firm size also has important effects on a firm's strategic behaviour and outcomes (Acs and Audretsch 1988). We therefore add the natural logarithm of the number of employees (LnEMPLOY) and the natural logarithm of assets (SIZE) as controls. Following Garcés-Galdeano et al. (2016), family ownership (FAMOWN), which is measured by the ratio of equity owned by the founder and his or her family, is also controlled for. Formal structure (FORMALSTC) indicates the extent to which a firm has sound corporate governance (Dai and Si 2018). This factor is measured by whether a firm has its own board of shareholders, board of directors or board of supervisors. We also include financial leverage (LEV), which is measured as the total of a firm's bank loans, scaled by its sales revenue in the surveyed year (Du 2014). Following Zhang and Li (2010), firm exports (EXPORT) (measured as the ratio of annual export sales to annual total sales) and OFDI (or FRINVST) (measured by the ratio of outward foreign direct investment to revenue) are also controlled for. To rule out the possible threats posed by industrial heterogeneity, we included industry dummies in all regression models.

Statistical modelling

The unit of analysis in this study is the firm. We apply the OLS regression, the Tobit regression and multi-level hierarchical linear modelling (HLM) to estimate all of the models, according to the types of dependent variables and the research levels of independent variables included in each specific model. Specifically, we use the OLS regression to estimate related models whose dependent variables are either ROS or ROE because these dependent variables (i.e. ROS, ROE) are continuous and normally distributed. We employ the Tobit regression when the dependant variable of the model is corporate venturing since it is non-negative (Wooldridge 2010). Since the regional institutional development is measured at the regional level, while other variables are measured at the firm level, we use multi-level hierarchical liner models (HLM) to test the moderating role of regional institutional development on the link of entrepreneurs' past working experience in government and entrepreneurial alertness towards government policies (Bliese 2000; Hofmann 1997; Raudenbush 1988).

Findings

Table 3 presents the descriptive statistics concerning all of the variables, and Table 4 presents the correlations of the main variables.

Table 5–6 present the results of the regression analysis. In Hypothesis 1, we propose that the past working experience within governments (EXPR_GOV) is positively related to entrepreneurial alertness towards government policies (ALERTNESS). To test Hypothesis 1, model 1 in Table 5 uses the Tobit regression, showing that past working experience within government (EXPR_GOV) is positively and significantly related to entrepreneurial alertness towards government policies (ALERTNESS) (b = 1.492, p < 0.01). Thus, Hypothesis 1 is supported.

Hypothesis 2 suggests that regional institutional development (INSTITUTION) moderates the relationship between past working experience in government (EXPR_GOV) and entrepreneurial alertness towards government policies (ALERTNESS). To test this hypothesis, we include the interaction term of past working experience in government and institutional development (EXPR_GOV×INSTITUTION). The factors are mean-centred before the creation of the interaction term, to reduce the potential problem of multicollinearity (Aiken and West 1991). Since the regional institutional development is measured at the provincial level, while other variables are measured at the firm level, we thus employ multi-level hierarchical linear modelling (HLM) to examine the role of regional institutions. The results shown in model 4 of Table 5 indicate that the interaction term is

Table 3. Descriptive statistics.

	count	mean	s.d.	min	p25	p50	p75	max
ROS	3284	0.09	0.22	−0.72	0.01	0.04	0.12	1.00
ROE	3284	0.25	0.71	−0.34	0.00	0.03	0.18	4.15
CV	3284	0.12	0.36	0.00	0.00	0.00	0.07	2.53
ALERTNESS	3284	5.04	3.28	0.00	3.00	5.00	7.00	10.00
INSTITUTION	3284	7.18	1.83	0.00	6.10	6.89	8.67	9.95
EXPR_GOV	3284	0.54	0.50	0.00	0.00	1.00	1.00	1.00
SOCLSS	3284	5.50	1.77	1.00	4.33	5.67	6.67	10.00
EDU	3284	0.31	0.46	0.00	0.00	0.00	1.00	1.00
FAMOWN	3284	0.67	0.36	0.00	0.45	0.80	1.00	1.00
FORMALSTC	3284	0.50	0.32	0.00	0.33	0.33	0.67	1.00
LnEMPLOY	3284	4.24	1.30	2.30	3.14	4.09	5.14	7.75
HIS	3284	8.02	5.42	0.00	3.00	8.00	12.00	22.00
SIZE	3284	6.97	2.43	0.69	5.30	7.21	8.70	12.01
LEV	3284	0.48	1.39	0.00	0.00	0.00	0.33	10.12
EXPORT	3284	0.01	0.03	0.00	0.00	0.00	0.00	0.17
FRINVST	3284	0.05	0.21	0.00	0.00	0.00	0.00	1.00

Table 4. Pearson correlation matrix.

	1	2	3	4	5	6	7	8	9	10	11	12	13	14	15	16
1.ROS	1															
2.ROE	0.201***	1														
3.CV	0.161***	0.233***	1													
4.ALERTNESS	0.120***	0.260***	0.279***	1												
5.INSTITUTION	−0.024	0.038**	−0.039**	0.064***	1											
6.EXPR_GOV	−0.024	0.022	0.032*	0.088***	0.051***	1										
7.SOCLSS	0.019	0.091***	0.069***	0.237***	0.106***	0.128***	1									
8.EDU	0.003	0.025	0.01	0.077***	0.017	0.109***	0.073***	1								
9.FAMOWN	0.024	0.045***	0.027	−0.003	0.095***	−0.044**	0.030*	−0.074***	1							
10.FORMALSTC	−0.073***	0.006	0.024	0.065***	−0.041**	0.058***	0.100***	0.070***	−0.147***	1						
11.LnEMPLOY	−0.009	0.111***	0.065***	0.216***	0.137***	0.133***	0.224***	0.115***	−0.035**	0.193***	1					
12.HIS	−0.01	0.045***	−0.009	0.178***	0.187***	0.163***	0.212***	0.02	0.042**	−0.005	0.253***	1				
13.SIZE	−0.111***	0.066***	−0.065***	0.293***	0.216***	0.154***	0.229***	0.144***	−0.039**	0.200***	0.239***	0.278***	1			
14.LEV	−0.033*	0.258***	0.065***	0.101***	0.067***	0.040**	0.091***	−0.026	0.036**	0.026	0.153***	0.095***	0.179***	1		
15.EXPORT	0.024	0.033*	0.028	0.059***	0.180***	0.011	0.112***	−0.024	−0.016	0.008	0.204***	0.100***	0.151***	0.097***	1	
16.FRINVST	0.035**	0.043**	0.030*	0.034**	−0.009	0.017	0.067***	0.012	−0.047***	0.02	0.108***	0.056***	0.067***	0.015	0.108***	1

*p < 0.10, **p < 0.05, ***p < 0.01

Table 5. Working experience in governments, regional institutions and entrepreneurial alertness towards government policies.

	(1)	(2)	(3)	(4)
	ALERTNESS	ALERTNESS	ALERTNESS	ALERTNESS
EXPR_GOV	1.492***		0.867***	3.203***
	(11.68)		(8.32)	(8.83)
INSTITUTION		−0.750***	−0.655***	−0.260**
		(−4.93)	(−8.45)	(−2.56)
EXPR_GOV * INSTITUTION				−0.375***
				(−6.83)
SOCLSS	0.191***	0.198***	0.176***	0.162***
	(4.80)	(6.27)	(5.61)	(5.38)
EDU	0.179	0.249**	0.191*	0.207**
	(1.36)	(2.26)	(1.74)	(1.96)
FAMOWN	0.007	−0.027	0.039	0.123
	(0.04)	(−0.20)	(0.28)	(0.92)
FORMALSTC	−0.128	−0.020	−0.045	0.058
	(−0.65)	(−0.12)	(−0.28)	(0.37)
LnEMPLOY	0.515***	0.427***	0.426***	0.429***
	(7.12)	(7.24)	(7.30)	(7.64)
HIS	0.027**	0.028***	0.020**	0.025**
	(2.28)	(2.77)	(2.01)	(2.56)
SIZE	0.121***	0.093***	0.076**	0.050
	(2.88)	(2.85)	(2.34)	(1.61)
LEV	0.085	0.092**	0.089**	0.080**
	(1.60)	(2.57)	(2.51)	(2.35)
EXPORT	−0.946	0.285	0.195	0.511
	(−0.47)	(0.16)	(0.11)	(0.29)
FRINVST	0.078	0.101	0.086	−0.024
	(0.27)	(0.45)	(0.39)	(−0.11)
$\sum$-0.11)YC	Included	Included	Included	Included
_cons	−0.360	5.982***	5.148***	2.635***
	(−1.26)	(11.11)	(8.39)	(3.86)
pseudo R^2	0.04	N.A.	N.A.	N.A.
F	55.81***	N.A.	N.A.	N.A.
LR test (chi2)	N.A.	331.03***	279.16***	117.76***
N	3284	3284	3284	3284
Number of groups	N.A.	5	5	31
Obs per group: min	N.A.	108.1	108.1	5
Avg	N.A.	420	420	108.1
Max	N.A.	5	5	420
chi2	N.A.	672.33	587.22	866.89
Log restricted-likelihood	−8112.53	−8297.12	−8263.38	−8131.85

Model (1) presents the result of the Tobit regression.
Model (2), Model (3) and Model (4) present the results of the multi-level hierarchical linear modelling (HLM).
t statistics in parentheses
*$p < 0.10$, **$p < 0.05$, ***$p < 0.01$

significantly and negatively related to economic performance ($b = -0.375$, $p < 0.01$). Thus, Hypothesis 2 is supported.

In Hypothesis 3, we propose that entrepreneurial alertness towards government policies drives entrepreneurial activities. The results shown in model 2 of Table 6 show that entrepreneurial alertness towards government policies (ALERTNESS) is significantly and positively related to corporate venturing (CV) ($b = 0.065$, $p < 0.01$). Thus, Hypothesis 3 is supported.

In Hypothesis 4, we posit that entrepreneurial alertness towards government policies tends to enhance private firms' economic performance. The results shown in model 5 of Table 6 show that entrepreneurial alertness towards government policies (ALERTNESS) is significantly and positively related to firm performance (ROS) ($b = 0.010$, $p < 0.01$). Thus, Hypothesis 4 is supported.

In Hypothesis 5, we propose that corporate venturing is conducive to firm performance. The results shown in model 4 of Table 6 show that corporate venturing (CV) is significantly and

Table 6. Entrepreneurial alertness towards government policies, corporate venturing and firm performance (ROS).

	(1)	(2)	(3)	(4)	(5)	(6)
	CV	CV	ROS	ROS	ROS	ROS
ALERTNESS		0.065***			0.010***	0.008***
		(12.40)			(7.37)	(6.09)
CV				0.084***		0.065***
				(4.25)		(3.24)
INSTITUTION	0.001	0.001	−0.001	−0.000	−0.001	−0.001
	(0.11)	(0.19)	(−0.45)	(−0.23)	(−0.43)	(−0.27)
EXPR_GOV	0.053**	0.043*	−0.006	−0.008	−0.008	−0.009
	(2.22)	(1.94)	(−0.82)	(−1.10)	(−1.04)	(−1.21)
SOCLSS	0.039***	0.024***	0.007***	0.006**	0.005**	0.005*
	(4.77)	(3.21)	(2.89)	(2.36)	(2.14)	(1.89)
EDU	0.010	−0.009	0.010	0.009	0.008	0.008
	(0.37)	(−0.38)	(1.25)	(1.12)	(0.97)	(0.93)
FAMOWN	0.077**	0.074**	0.008	0.005	0.008	0.006
	(2.29)	(2.32)	(0.71)	(0.50)	(0.69)	(0.53)
FORMALSTC	0.045	0.045	−0.039***	−0.042***	−0.039***	−0.041***
	(1.22)	(1.27)	(−3.51)	(−3.83)	(−3.53)	(−3.78)
LnEMPLOY	0.149***	0.120***	0.023***	0.018***	0.019***	0.016***
	(9.28)	(8.44)	(5.46)	(4.33)	(4.31)	(3.68)
HIS	−0.000	−0.002	0.001	0.001	0.000	0.000
	(−0.10)	(−1.04)	(0.87)	(0.95)	(0.46)	(0.60)
SIZE	−0.046***	−0.054***	−0.021***	−0.017***	−0.022***	−0.019***
	(−4.83)	(−5.98)	(−6.12)	(−5.12)	(−6.46)	(−5.65)
LEV	0.030***	0.021**	−0.003	−0.005**	−0.004*	−0.005**
	(3.17)	(2.34)	(−1.31)	(−2.09)	(−1.87)	(−2.38)
EXPORT	0.484	0.556	0.184	0.168	0.196	0.182
	(1.24)	(1.52)	(1.33)	(1.26)	(1.44)	(1.37)
FRINVST	0.077	0.083*	0.031*	0.028*	0.031*	0.029*
	(1.51)	(1.73)	(1.77)	(1.73)	(1.84)	(1.79)
Σ1.79)TYC	Included	Included	Included	Included	Included	Included
_cons	−0.836***	−0.874***	0.115***	0.112***	0.107***	0.106***
	(−10.84)	(−11.62)	(5.07)	(4.96)	(4.77)	(4.75)
adj. R^2 (pseudo R^2)	0.05	0.12	0.03	0.05	0.05	0.06
F	15.02***	18.56***	5.95***	6.52***	10.16***	9.45***
N	3284	3284	3284	3284	3284	3284

Model (1) and Model (2) present the result of the Tobit regression.
Model (3) to Model (6) present the result of the OLS regression.
t statistics in parentheses
*p < 0.10, **p < 0.05, ***p < 0.01

positively related to firm performance (ROS) (b = 0.084, p < 0.01). Thus, Hypothesis 5 is supported.

To test the robustness of the above findings, we use ROE to represent firm performance and investigate the relationships between entrepreneurial alertness towards government policies, corporate venturing and firm performance. The findings, which are listed in Table 7, show that the results remain largely unchanged, thereby supporting the above hypotheses we examine.

Discussion

Theoretical contributions

To shed new lights on the puzzle of rapid growth of Chinese private firms in the past four decades, this study explores the idea of policy-induced opportunities. We show how prior working experience leads entrepreneurs to be aware of opportunities resulting from policy changes and how this affects their actions. In emerging economies, governments play more of a vitalizing role for entrepreneurial firms than we would expect in entirely market-governed economies.

Table 7. Entrepreneurial alertness towards government policies, corporate venturing and firm performance (ROE).

	(1)	(2)	(3)	(4)	(5)	(6)
	CV	CV	ROE	ROE	ROE	ROE
ALERTNESS		0.065***			0.076***	0.039***
		(12.40)			(14.37)	(10.39)
CV				1.232***		1.135***
				(4.03)		(2.80)
INSTITUTION	0.001	0.001	0.007	0.013**	0.007	0.013**
	(0.11)	(0.19)	(1.01)	(2.53)	(1.10)	(2.50)
EXPR_GOV	0.053**	0.043*	0.003	−0.026	−0.009	−0.030
	(2.22)	(1.94)	(0.13)	(−1.36)	(−0.39)	(−1.61)
SOCLSS	0.039***	0.024***	0.022**	0.000	0.006	−0.006
	(4.77)	(3.21)	(2.56)	(0.07)	(0.81)	(−0.93)
EDU	0.010	−0.009	0.046*	0.029	0.028	0.021
	(0.37)	(−0.38)	(1.66)	(1.38)	(1.07)	(1.02)
FAMOWN	0.077**	0.074**	0.070**	0.035	0.068**	0.037
	(2.29)	(2.32)	(2.18)	(1.47)	(2.24)	(1.57)
FORMALSTC	0.045	0.045	−0.013	−0.051*	−0.013	−0.048
	(1.22)	(1.27)	(−0.34)	(−1.68)	(−0.34)	(−1.61)
LnEMPLOY	0.149***	0.120***	0.062***	−0.013	0.026*	−0.025**
	(9.28)	(8.44)	(3.99)	(−1.06)	(1.86)	(−2.11)
HIS	−0.000	−0.002	−0.000	0.000	−0.003	−0.001
	(−0.10)	(−1.04)	(−0.09)	(0.20)	(−1.04)	(−0.43)
SIZE	−0.046***	−0.054***	−0.027***	0.025***	−0.035***	0.017***
	(−4.83)	(−5.98)	(−2.99)	(4.34)	(−4.07)	(3.01)
LEV	0.030***	0.021**	0.128***	0.105***	0.120***	0.102***
	(3.17)	(2.34)	(6.79)	(6.01)	(7.15)	(6.24)
EXPORT	0.484	0.556	−0.285	−0.506	−0.188	−0.439
	(1.24)	(1.52)	(−0.57)	(−1.37)	(−0.40)	(−1.21)
FRINVST	0.077	0.083*	0.108	0.071	0.109	0.075
	(1.51)	(1.73)	(1.46)	(1.14)	(1.58)	(1.23)
$\sum 1.23$)TYC	Included	Included	Included	Included	Included	Included
_cons	−0.836***	−0.874***	−0.110*	−0.163*	−0.173***	−0.190***
	(−10.84)	(−11.62)	(−1.68)	(−3.13)	(−2.76)	(−3.71)
adj. R^2 (pseudo R^2)	0.05	0.12	0.08	0.45	0.19	0.48
F	15.02***	18.56***	8.55***	61.48***	22.97***	59.78***
N	3284	3284	3284	3284	3284	3284

Model (1) and Model (2) present the result of the Tobit regression.
Model (3) to Model (6) present the result of the OLS regression.
t statistics in parentheses
* $p < 0.10$, ** $p < 0.05$, *** $p < 0.01$

Entrepreneurs may see opportunities through the policy making process and gain advantages from their involvement (Xing, Liu, and Cooper 2018). Our study makes three contributions.

First, we use the concept of 'policy-induced opportunities' to note the special nature of opportunities that are presented outside of the regular marketplace. Most of our insights are based on market settings in developed economies. In emerging economies, market settings may be more ambiguous than traditionally assumed. We provide evidence of the transitional nature and the importance for policy-induced opportunities in countries that are developing their economies. We show that past working experience in governments and thus closeness to the government are beneficial to understanding policy-induced opportunities with direct implications for corporate venturing activities and firm performance. As a result, we explicate the phenomena of 'policy-induced opportunities' in a comprehensive manner, answering how they are recognized, by whom, and with what consequences (Venkataraman 1997).

Second, we not only build upon but also enrich Ardichvili and his colleagues' (2003) framework of opportunity recognition and development by extending it to emerging markets in which a considerable portion of entrepreneurial opportunities stem from government policies. Such an extension is meaningful as emerging economies play an increasingly important role in the world economy. Ardichvili and his colleagues (2003) focus on two types of entrepreneurial opportunities in their theoretical framework, namely, unmet market demand (i.e. value sought) and under-utilized valuable resources (i.e. value creation capability). These types of opportunities are prevalent in developed market system settings. We add a third type of opportunities that we label as 'policy-induced opportunities' that account for the transitional nature of these economies.

Third, we combine and extend the concept of entrepreneurial alertness (Ardichvili, Cardozo, and Ray 2003; Tang, Kacmar, and Busenitz 2012) with the institution-based view that expands over a) policy-induced opportunities and b) considering the development stage of the regional institutions. By doing this, we extend the literature on entrepreneurial alertness perspective with an emerging market perspective. Some researchers suggest that as time goes by, a clear-cut economic boundary between government and market activities will emerge, and the market system will take on the role of governments for distributing crucial resources and opportunities. Other scholars argue that the government will continue to play a pivotal role in economic development. In this view, entrepreneurial alertness to shifting government policies will remain important for entrepreneurs as long as the political system of state intervention exists (Haveman et al. 2017). There is evidence that shows that political co-creation plays an increasingly significant role in promoting the performance of privately owned firms (Xing, Liu, and Cooper 2018; Haveman et al. 2017). If the latter fraction of researchers is right, our study offers much potential for future research endeavours that further examine entrepreneurial activities and development from the entrepreneurial alertness perspective.

Managerial implications

Our findings also have several practical implications. First, entrepreneurs should be aware that a significant portion of entrepreneurial opportunities in emerging economies are tied to government-related activities. As Shane and Eckhardt (2003) and Ge et al. (2017) suggest, entrepreneurial opportunities emerge not only in the commercial market but also in the political market (Peng and Luo 2000; Wang et al. 2011; Yiu and Lau 2008). Just as Yang's (2002, 2004) 'double entrepreneurship' concept indicates, entrepreneurs in China should be politicians in addition to businessmen, staying alert to new movements in the government and effectively making use of institutional rules (Yang 2007). Entrepreneurs in transition economies need to become experts in not only doing their business but also reading the signals and interpreting the shifts of government policy (Bruton, Ahlstrom, and Obloj 2008). Developing this kind of 'non-business' capability is a challenge that entrepreneurs in transition economies need to face (Yang 2007; Bruton, Ahlstrom, and Obloj 2008).

Second, our findings indicate that entrepreneurial alertness is one of the most valuable corporate resources, as evidenced by our findings that the allocation of entrepreneurial alertness is directly linked to entrepreneurial activity and firm performance. As a result, it is highly critical for entrepreneurs to steer their alertness in a way that facilitates the discovery of potential opportunities and enhances firm performance. We also find that working experience dictates entrepreneurial prior knowledge, forming 'corridors of knowledge' for screening entrepreneurial opportunities and shaping entrepreneurial alertness (Kirzner 1985). In this sense, entrepreneurs need to enrich their experience to create more 'knowledge corridors' that recognize a variety of entrepreneurial opportunities.

Limitations and future directions

Although this study presents a number of important theoretical and practical implications, it inevitably has its limitations that open up opportunities for future researchers. First, as presented by Ardichvili, Cardozo, and Ray (2003), a host of variables are able to shape entrepreneurial alertness, including entrepreneurs' personality traits and their social networks. Accordingly, future research may focus its attention on these factors in addition to entrepreneurial working experience and prior knowledge. Beyond that, we encourage future research to look at other factors including the background (e.g. local entrepreneurs vs. returnees) or their approaches (e.g. bricoleurs, entre-preneurs using causation, effectuation etc.) (Liu 2018; Liu and Almor 2016). Second, although China is the largest emerging/transition economy in the world, and although it bears similarities to other transition countries, this nation has distinctive characteristics resulting from its long history, unique culture and distinctive traditions. Thus, future research should replicate our model in other emer-ging/transition economies to test its generalizability. Finally, subject to the dataset used, we apply a cross-sectional research design, which hinders the establishment of causal relationships between various variables. Future research should further investigate these relationships by using a longitudinal dataset and research design.

Conclusion

Focusing on the questions of how policy-induced opportunities, which take on unique roles in the context of emerging/transition economies, are recognized, by whom, and with what consequences, we delineate and substantiate a unique pattern of opportunity identification and development that has been practiced by Chinese privately owned firms during the country's transition from a planned economy to a market economy. We thus enrich the theoretical framework of opportu-nity recognition and development by Ardichvili, Cardozo, and Ray (2003) and lay the foundations for future research to explicate policy-induced opportunities in a deeper and wider manner.

Acknowledgments

The authors are grateful to Qihai Huang, Xueyuan (Adrian) Liu and Jun Li, the guest editors of the special issue entitled "Entrepreneurship in China", for their guidance in the review process. The authors thank two anonymous reviewers for their insightful comments and developmental suggestions. The study is partially supported by the Nation Natural Science Foundation of China (Grant # 71672168; # 71402056), the Humanity and Social Science Youth foundation of Ministry of Education (Grant # 18YJC630085) as well as the Fundamental Research Funds for the Central Universities (Grant # XMS02). All views expressed are those of the authors and not of the sponsoring organizations.

Disclosure statement

No potential conflict of interest was reported by the authors.

References

Acs, Z. J., and D. B. Audretsch. 1988. "Innovation and Firm Size in Manufacturing." *Technovation* 7 (3): 197–210. doi:10.1016/0166-4972(88)90020-X.

Ahlstrom, D., and Z. Ding. 2014. "Entrepreneurship in China: An Overview." *International Small Business Journal* 32 (6): 610–618. doi:10.1177/0266242613517913.

Aiken, L. S., and S. G. West. 1991. *Multiple Regression: Testing and Interpreting Interactions.* Thousand Oaks, CA: Sage Publications.

Alvarez, S. A., and J. B. Barney. 2007. "Discovery and Creation: Alternative Theories of Entrepreneurial Action." *Strategic Entrepreneurship Journal* 1 (1–2): 11–26. doi:10.1002/(ISSN)1932-443X.

Antoncic, B., and R. D. Hisrich. 2001. "Intrapreneurship: Construct Refinement and Cross-cultural Validation." *Journal of Business Venturing* 16 (5): 495–527. doi:10.1016/S0883-9026(99)00054-3.

Antoncic, B., and I. Prodan. 2008. "Alliances, Corporate Technological Entrepreneurship and Firm Performance: Testing a Model on Manufacturing Firms." *Technovation* 28 (5): 257–265. doi:10.1016/j.technovation.2007.07.005.

Ardichvili, A., R. Cardozo, and S. Ray. 2003. "A Theory of Entrepreneurial Opportunity Identification and Development." *Journal of Business Venturing* 18 (1): 105–123. doi:10.1016/S0883-9026(01)00068-4.

Armanios, D. E., C. E. Eesley, J. Li, and K. M. Eisenhardt. 2017. "How Entrepreneurs Leverage Institutional Intermediaries in Emerging Economies to Acquire Public Resources." *Strategic Management Journal* 38 (7): 1373–1390. doi:10.1002/smj.2017.38.issue-7.

Baden-Fuller, C. 1995. "Strategic Innovation, Corporate Entrepreneurship and Matching Outside-in to Inside-out Approaches to Strategy Research." *British Journal of Management* 6: S3–S16. doi:10.1111/bjom.1995.6.issue-s1.

Barnett, V., and T. Lewis. 1994. *Outliers in Statistical Data.* Chichester, UK: John Wiley & Sons.

Baron, R. A., and M. D. Ensley. 2006. "Opportunity Recognition as the Detection of Meaningful Patterns: Evidence from Comparisons of Novice and Experienced Entrepreneurs." *Management Science* 52 (9): 1331–1344. doi:10.1287/mnsc.1060.0538.

Bjorklund, E. M. 1986. "The Danwei: Socio-spatial Characteristics of Work Units in China's Urban Society." *Economic Geography* 62 (1): 19–29. doi:10.2307/143493.

Bliese, P. D. 2000. "Within-group Agreement, Non-independence, and Reliability: Implications for Data Aggregation and Analysis." In *Multilevel Theory, Research, and Methods in Organizations: Foundations, Extensions, and New Directions*, edited by K. J. Klein and S. W. J. Kozlowski, 349–381. San Francisco, CA: Jossey-Bass.

Bruton, G. D., D. Ahlstrom, and K. Obloj. 2008. "Entrepreneurship in Emerging Economies: Where are We Today and Where Should the Research Go in the Future." *Entrepreneurship Theory and Practice* 32 (1): 1–14. doi:10.1111/j.1540-6520.2007.00213.x.

Burgelman, R. A. 1983. "A Process Model of Internal Corporate Venturing in the Diversified Major Firm." *Administrative Science Quarterly* 28 (2): 223–244. doi:10.2307/2392619.

Chan, C. M., S. Makino, and T. Isobe. 2010. "Does Subnational Region Matter? Foreign Affiliate Performance in the United States and China." *Strategic Management Journal* 31 (11): 1226–1243. doi:10.1002/smj.v31:11.

Chen, C. J., and C. Kim. 2010. "High-level Politically Connected Firms, Corruption, and Analyst Forecast Accuracy around the World." *Journal of International Business Studies* 41 (9): 1505–1524. doi:10.1057/jibs.2010.27.

Child, J., Y. Lu, and T. Tsai. 2007. "Institutional Entrepreneurship in Building an Environmental Protection System for the People's Republic of China." *Organization Studies* 28 (7): 1013–1034. doi:10.1177/0170840607078112.

China National Bureau of Statistics. 2018a. "Various Types of Market Entities Jointly Promote the Development of China's Industrial Economy." http://www.stats.gov.cn/tjsj/sjjd/201804/t20180414_1593926.html

China National Bureau of Statistics. 2018b. "Statistical Communiqué of the People's Republic of China on National Economic and Social Development in 2017." http://www.stats.gov.cn/tjsj/zxfb/201802/t20180228_1585631.html

Covin, J. G., and M. P. Miles. 2007. "Strategic Use of Corporate Venturing." *Entrepreneurship Theory and Practice* 31 (2): 183–207. doi:10.1111/etap.2007.31.issue-2.

Covin, J. G., and D. P. Slevin. 1989. "Strategic Management of Small Firms in Hostile and Benign Environments." *Strategic Management Journal* 10 (1): 75–87. doi:10.1002/(ISSN)1097-0266.

Dai, W., and M. Liao. 2018. "Entrepreneurial Attention to Deregulations and Reinvestments by Private Firms: Evidence from China." *Asia Pacific Journal of Management*. doi:10.1007/s10490-018-9574-z.

Dai, W., and Y. Liu. 2015. "Local Vs. Non-local Institutional Embeddedness, Corporate Entrepreneurship, and Firm Performance in a Transitional Economy." *Asian Journal of Technology Innovation* 23 (2): 255–270. doi:10.1080/19761597.2015.1074516.

Dai, W., Y. Liu, M. Liao, and Q. Lin. 2018. "How Does Entrepreneurs' Socialist Imprinting Shape Their Opportunity Selection in Transition Economies? Evidence from China's Privately Owned Enterprises." *International Entrepreneurship and Management Journal* 14 (4): 823–856. doi:10.1007/s11365-017-0485-0.

Dai, W., and S. Si. 2018. "Government Policies and Firms' Entrepreneurial Orientation: Strategic Choice and Institutional Perspectives." *Journal of Business Research* 93: 23–36. doi:10.1016/j.jbusres.2018.08.026.

Drucker, P. F. 1985. *Innovation and Entrepreneurship*. New York: Harper and Row.

Du, X. 2014. "Is Corporate Philanthropy Used as Environmental Misconduct Dressing? Evidence from Chinese Family-owned Firms." *Journal of Business Ethics* 129 (2): 341–361. doi:10.1007/s10551-014-2163-2.

Eckhardt, J. T., and S. A. Shane. 2003. "Opportunities and Entrepreneurship." *Journal of Management* 29 (3): 333–349. doi:10.1177/014920630302900304.

Fan, G., X. Wang, and H. Zhu. 2009. *NERI Index of Marketization of China's Provinces*. Beijing China: Economics Science Press.

Gaglio, C. M., and J. A. Katz. 2001. "The Psychological Basis of Opportunity Identification: Entrepreneurial Alertness." *Small Business Economics* 16 (2): 95–111. doi:10.1023/A:1011132102464.

Gao, Y., and T. Hafsi. 2015. "Government Intervention, Peers' Giving and Corporate Philanthropy: Evidence from Chinese Private SMEs." *Journal of Business Ethics* 132 (2): 433–447. doi:10.1007/s10551-014-2329-y.

Garcés-Galdeano, L., M. Larraza-Kintana, C. García-Olaverri, and M. Makri. 2016. "Entrepreneurial Orientation in Family Firms: The Moderating Role of Technological Intensity and Performance." *International Entrepreneurship and Management Journal* 12 (1): 27–45. doi:10.1007/s11365-014-0335-2.

Ge, J., L. J. Stanley, K. Eddleston, and F. W. Kellermanns. 2017. "Institutional Deterioration and Entrepreneurial Investment: The Role of Political Connections." *Journal of Business Venturing* 32 (4): 405–419. doi:10.1016/j.jbusvent.2017.04.002.

Guth, W. D., and A. Ginsberg. 1990. "Guest Editors' Introduction: Corporate Entrepreneurship." *Strategic Management Journal* 11 (special issue): 5–15.

Hamilton, R. T. 2012. "How Firms Grow and the Influence of Size and Age." *International Small Business Journal* 30 (6): 611–621. doi:10.1177/0266242610383446.

Haveman, H. A., N. Jia, J. Shi, and Y. Wang. 2017. "The Dynamics of Political Embeddedness in China." *Administrative Science Quarterly* 62 (1): 67–104. doi:10.1177/0001839216657311.

Hayek, F. A. 1945. "The Use of Knowledge in Society." *American Economic Review* 35 (4): 519–530.

Hitt, M. A., and R. D. Ireland. 2000. "The Intersection of Entrepreneurship and Strategic Management Research." In *The Blackwell Handbook of Entrepreneurship*, edited by D. Sexton and H. Landstrom, 45-63. Oxford, UK: Blackwell.

Hofmann, D. A. 1997. "An Overview of the Logic and Rationale of Hierarchical Linear Models." *Journal of Management* 23: 723–744. doi:10.1177/014920639702300602.

Huang, Y. 2008. *Capitalism with Chinese Characteristics: Entrepreneurs and the State*. Cambridge, UK: Cambridge University Press.

Ingram, P., and B. S. Silverman. 2002. "Introduction: The New Institutionalism in Strategic Management." *Advances in Strategic Management* 19: 1–30.

Jacquemin, A., and F. Janssen. 2015. "Studying Regulation as a Source of Opportunity Rather than as a Constraint for Entrepreneurs: Conceptual Map and Research Propositions." *Environment and Planning C: Government and Policy* 33 (4): 846–862. doi:10.1068/c11180b.

Jia, N., and K. J. Mayer. 2017. "Political Hazards and Firms' Geographic Concentration." *Strategic Management Journal* 38 (2): 203–231. doi:10.1002/smj.2474.

Kafouros, M., C. Wang, P. Piperopoulos, and M. Zhang. 2015. "Academic Collaborations and Firm Innovation Performance in China: The Role of Region-specific Institutions." *Research Policy* 44 (3): 803–817. doi:10.1016/j.respol.2014.11.002.

Keil, T. 2004. "Building External Corporate Venturing Capability." *Journal of Management Studies* 41 (5): 799–825. doi:10.1111/j.1467-6486.2004.00454.x.

Kemelgor, B. H. 2002. "A Comparative Analysis of Corporate Entrepreneurial Orientation between Selected Firms in the Netherlands and the USA." *Entrepreneurship & Regional Development* 14 (1): 67–87. doi:10.1080/08985620110087023.

Kirzner, I. M. 1973. *Competition and Entrepreneurship*. Chicago, IL: University of Chicago Press.

Kirzner, I. M. 1985. *Discovery and the Capitalist Process*. Chicago, IL: University of Chicago Press.

Kuratko, D. F., J. S. Hornsby, and J. Hayton. 2015. "Corporate Entrepreneurship: The Innovative Challenge for a New Global Economic Reality." *Small Business Economics* 45 (2): 245–253. doi:10.1007/s11187-015-9630-8.

Kuratko, D. F., R. D. Ireland, and J. S. Hornsby. 2001. "Improving Firm Performance through Entrepreneurial Actions: Acordia's Corporate Entrepreneurship Strategy." *Academy of Management Executive (1993–2005)* 15 (4): 60–71.

Liu, Y. 2018. "Contextualizing Risk while Building Resilience: Returnee Vs. Local Entrepreneurs in China." *Applied Psychology: An International Review*. doi:10.1111/apps.12177.

Liu, Y., and T. Almor. 2016. "How Culture Influences the Way Entrepreneurs Deal with Uncertainty in Inter-organizational Relationships: Returnee Vs. Local Entrepreneurs in China." *International Business Review* 25 (1): 4–14. doi:10.1016/j.ibusrev.2014.11.002.

Liu, Y., and Q. Huang. 2018. "University Capability as a Micro-foundation for the Triple Helix Model: The Case of China." *Technovation*. doi:10.1016/j.technovation.2018.02.013.

Makino, S., T. Isobe, and C. M. Chan. 2004. "Does Country Matter?" *Strategic Management Journal* 25 (10): 1027–1043. doi:10.1002/(ISSN)1097-0266.

Meyer, K. E., and H. V. Nguyen. 2005. "Foreign Investment Strategies and Sub-national Institutions in Emerging Markets: Evidence from Vietnam." *Journal of Management Studies* 42 (1): 63–93. doi:10.1111/joms.2005.42.issue-1.

Minola, T., M. Brumana, G. Campopiano, R. P. Garrett, and L. Cassia. 2016. "Corporate Venturing in Family Business: A Developmental Approach of the Enterprising Family." *Strategic Entrepreneurship Journal* 10 (4): 395–412. doi:10.1002/sej.v10.4.

Narayanan, V. K., Y. Yang, and S. A. Zahra. 2009. "Corporate Venturing and Value Creation: A Review and Proposed Framework." *Research Policy* 38 (1): 58–76. doi:10.1016/j.respol.2008.08.015.

Nguyen, T. V., N. T. B. Le, and S. E. Bryant. 2013. "Sub-national Institutions, Firm Strategies, and Firm Performance: A Multilevel Study of Private Manufacturing Firms in Vietnam." *Journal of World Business* 48 (1): 68–76. doi:10.1016/j.jwb.2012.06.008.

North, D. C. 1990. *Institutions, Institutional Change, and Economic Performance*. New York: Cambridge University Press.

Ozgen, E., and R. A. Baron. 2007. "Social Sources of Information in Opportunity Recognition: Effects of Mentors, Industry Networks, and Professional Forums." *Journal of Business Venturing* 22 (2): 174–192. doi:10.1016/j.jbusvent.2005.12.001.

Peng, M. W., and Y. Luo. 2000. "Managerial Ties and Firm Performance in a Transition Economy: The Nature of a Micro-macro Link." *Academy of Management Journal* 43 (3): 486–501.

Peng, M. W., D. Y. L. Wang, and Y. Jiang. 2008. "An Institution-based View of International Business Strategy: A Focus on Emerging Economies." *Journal of International Business Studies* 39 (5): 920–936. doi:10.1057/palgrave.jibs.8400377.

Raudenbush, S. W. 1988. "Educational Applications of Hierarchical Linear Models: A Review." *Journal of Educational Statistics* 13: 85–116. doi:10.3102/10769986013002085.

Rong, M. A., and O. Shenkar. 2011. "Social Networks and Opportunity Recognition: A Cultural Comparison between Taiwan and the United States." *Strategic Management Journal* 32 (11): 1183–1205. doi:10.1002/smj.933.

Roundy, P. T., D. A. Harrison, S. Khavul, L. Pérez-Nordtvedt, and J. E. McGee. 2017. "Entrepreneurial Alertness as a Pathway to Strategic Decisions and Organizational Performance." *Strategic Organization*. doi:10.1177/1476127017693970.

Roussanov, N. 2010. "Diversification and Its Discontents: Idiosyncratic and Entrepreneurial Risk in the Quest for Social Status." *Journal of Finance* 65 (5): 1755–1788. doi:10.1111/j.1540-6261.2010.01593.x.

Sarasvathy, S., N. Dew, S. Velamuri, and S. Venkataraman. 2003. "Three Views of Entrepreneurial Opportunity." In *Handbook of Entrepreneurship Research*, edited by Z. J. Acs and D. B. Audretsch, 141-160. New York: Springer.

Sarasvathy, S. D. 2001. "Causation and Effectuation: Toward a Theoretical Shift from Economic Inevitability to Entrepreneurial Contingency." *Academy of Management Review* 26 (2): 243–263. doi:10.5465/amr.2001.4378020.

Schumpeter, J. A. 1934. *A Theory of Economic Development*. Cambridge, UK: Harvard University Press.

Scott, W. R. 2008. *Institutions and Organizations: Ideas and Interests*. Thousand Oaks, CA: Sage.

Shane, S., and J. Eckhardt. 2003. "The Individual-Opportunity Nexus." In *Handbook of Entrepreneurship Research: An Interdisciplinary Survey and Introduction (vol. 1)*. edited by Z. J. Acs and D. B. Audretsch, 161–191. New York: Springer.

Shane, S., and S. Venkataraman. 2000. "The Promise of Entrepreneurship as a Field of Research." *Academy of Management Review* 25 (1): 217–226.

Sharma, P., and J. J. Chrisman. 1999. "Toward a Reconciliation of the Definition in the Field of Corporate Entrepreneurship." *Entrepreneurship Theory and Practice* 23 (3): 11–27. doi:10.1177/104225879902300302.

Shi, W., L. Markóczy, and C. Stan. 2015. "The Continuing Importance of Political Ties in China." *Academy of Management Executive* 28 (1): 57–75.

Shi, W., S. L. Sun, and M. W. Peng. 2012. "Sub-national Institutional Contingencies, Network Positions, and IJV Partner Selection." *Journal of Management Studies* 49 (7): 1221–1245. doi:10.1111/joms.2012.49.issue-7.

Short, J. C., D. J. Ketchen, C. L. Shook, and R. D. Ireland. 2010. "The Concept of "opportunity" in Entrepreneurship Research: Past Accomplishments and Future Challenges." *Journal of Management* 36 (1): 40–65. doi:10.1177/0149206309342746.

Simsek, Z., and C. Heavey. 2011. "The Mediating Role of Knowledge-based Capital for Corporate Entrepreneurship Effects on Performance: A Study of Small- to Medium-sized Firms." *Strategic Entrepreneurship Journal* 5 (1): 81–100. doi:10.1002/sej.v5.1.

Su, J., Q. Zhai, and H. Landström. 2015. "Entrepreneurship Research in China: Internationalization or Contextualization?" *Entrepreneurship & Regional Development* 27 (1–2): 50–79. doi:10.1080/08985626.2014.999718.

Sun, P., and M. Wright. 2012. "The Contingent Value of Corporate Political Ties." *Academy of Management Perspectives* 26 (3): 68–82. doi:10.5465/amp.2011.0164.

Tang, J., K. M. Kacmar, and L. Busenitz. 2012. "Entrepreneurial Alertness in the Pursuit of New Opportunities." *Journal of Business Venturing* 27 (1): 77–94. doi:10.1016/j.jbusvent.2010.07.001.

Valliere, D. 2013. "Towards a Schematic Theory of Entrepreneurial Alertness." *Journal of Business Venturing* 28 (3): 430–442. doi:10.1016/j.jbusvent.2011.08.004.

Vanacker, T., V. Collewaert, and S. A. Zahra. 2017. "Slack Resources, Firm Performance, and the Institutional Context: Evidence from Privately Held European Firms." *Strategic Management Journal* 38 (6): 1305–1326. doi:10.1002/smj.2017.38.issue-6.

Venkataraman, S. 1997. "The Distinctive Domain of Entrepreneurship Research." In *Advances in Entrepreneurship, Firm Emergence, and Growth (Vol. 3)*, edited by J. A. Katz, 119–138. Oxford, UK: JAI Press.

Wang, H., J. Feng, X. Liu, and R. Zhang. 2011. "What Is the Benefit of TMT's Governmental Experience to Private-owned Enterprises? Evidence from China." *Asia Pacific Journal of Management* 28 (3): 555–572. doi:10.1007/s10490-009-9167-y.

Wang, X., G. Fan, and J. Yu (2017). *Marketization index of China's provinces: NERI Report 2016*. Beijing: China Social Sciences Academic Press.

Whyte, M. K. 1999. "Danwei: The Changing Chinese Workplace in Historical and Comparative Perspective, by Xiaobo Lu; Elizabeth J. Perry." *The China Journal* 28 (41): 182–183. doi:10.2307/2667597.

Wiersema, M. F., and K. A. Bantel. 1992. "Top Management Team Demography and Corporate Strategic Change." *Academy of Management Journal* 35 (1): 91–121.

Wooldridge, J. M. 2010. *Econometric Analysis of Cross Section and Panel Data*. Boston MA: MIT Press.

Xing, Y., Y. Liu, and S. C. L. Cooper. 2018. "Local Government as Institutional Entrepreneur: Public–Private Collaborative Partnerships in Fostering Regional Entrepreneurship." *British Journal of Management*. doi:10.1111/1467-8551.12282.

Yang, K. 2002. "Double Entrepreneurship in China's Economic Reform: An Analytical Framework." *Journal of Political & Military Sociology* 30 (1): 134–147.

Yang, K. 2004. "Institutional Holes and Entrepreneurship in China." *Sociological Review* 52 (3): 371–389. doi:10.1111/j.1467-954X.2004.00485.x.

Yang, K. 2007. *Entrepreneurship in China*. Hampshire, UK: Ashgate Publishing Limited.

Yiu, D. W., and C. M. Lau. 2008. "Corporate Entrepreneurship as Resource Capital Configuration in Emerging Market Firms." *Entrepreneurship Theory and Practice* 32 (1): 37–57. doi:10.1111/j.1540-6520.2007.00215.x.

Zahra, S. A., and J. G. Covin. 1995. "Contextual Influences on the Corporate Entrepreneurship-performance Relationship: A Longitudinal Analysis." *Journal of Business Venturing* 10 (1): 43–58. doi:10.1016/0883-9026(94)00004-E.

Zahra, S. A., and D. M. Garvis. 2000. "International Corporate Entrepreneurship and Firm Performance: The Moderating Effect of International Environmental Hostility." *Journal of Business Venturing* 15 (5–6): 469–492. doi:10.1016/S0883-9026(99)00036-1.

Zahra, S. A., and J. C. Hayton. 2008. "The Effect of International Venturing on Firm Performance: The Moderating Influence of Absorptive Capacity." *Journal of Business Venturing* 23 (2): 195–220. doi:10.1016/j.jbusvent.2007.01.001.

Zhang, Y., and H. Li. 2010. "Innovation Search of New Ventures in a Technology Cluster: The Role of Ties with Service Intermediaries." *Strategic Management Journal* 31 (1): 88–109. doi:10.1002/smj.v31:1.

Zhao, H., and J. Lu. 2016. "Contingent Value of Political Capital in Bank Loan Acquisition: Evidence from Founder-controlled Private Enterprises in China." *Journal of Business Venturing* 31 (2): 153–174. doi:10.1016/j.jbusvent.2015.12.002.

Zhou, W. 2011. "Regional Deregulation and Entrepreneurial Growth in China's Transition Economy." *Entrepreneurship & Regional Development* 23 (9–10): 853–876. doi:10.1080/08985626.2011.577816.

Zhou, W. 2013. "Political Connections and Entrepreneurial Investment: Evidence from China's Transition Economy." *Journal of Business Venturing* 28 (2): 299–315. doi:10.1016/j.jbusvent.2012.05.004.

Should I stay or should I go? Job demands' push and entrepreneurial resources' pull in Chinese migrant workers' return-home entrepreneurial intention

Jinyun Duan, Juelin Yin, Yue Xu and Daoyou Wu

ABSTRACT

This study explores how the push factor of job demands and the pull factor of entrepreneurial resources influence the intention of Chinese migrant workers to return to their hometown and engage in entrepreneurial activities. Data were collected from 302 Chinese migrant workers. The main findings are as follows: a) job demands can increase the return-home entrepreneurial intention of migrant workers through the mediation of job burnout; b) entrepreneurial resources can positively influence the return-home entrepreneurial intention of migrant workers through the mediation of entrepreneurial conviction; c) generation positively moderates the job demands – job burnout – entrepreneurial intention relationship and negatively moderates the entrepreneurial resources – entrepreneurial conviction – entrepreneurial intention relationship. This study reveals the importance of examining push and pull factors concurrently, and emphasizes the intergenerational differences in explaining the return-home entrepreneurial intention of Chinese migrant workers.

1. Introduction

Growing self-employment in non-agricultural sectors is a striking feature of many rural regions in developing countries (Brünjes and Diez 2013). China is also witnessing such a trend in recent years, behind which is an increasing number of migrant workers who migrate from the city back home and choose to become self-employed. Particularly with the release of national policy supporting mass entrepreneurship and innovation by the Chinese Premier, the implementation of the Rise of Central and Western China Plan, and a nationwide targeted poverty-alleviation campaign aimed at reviving rural China, more entrepreneurial opportunities have emerged for local laborers in rural China (Lin 2015). According to the statistics provided by the Ministry of Agriculture, the number of Chinese migrant workers returning home and beginning a new venture is now over 4.5 million, accounting for 68.5% of the total population of return workers engaging in entrepreneurial activities in their rural hometown (China Economic Net 2017). In addition, in the past five years, the increase in the number of migrant workers returning home has remained at more than 10% and the annual number of migrant workers returning home is 3.1 times higher than it was in the 1990s (www.gov.cn 2016).

Return migration is one of the important channels through which migration can contribute to the regional development of the home regions (Démurger and Xu 2011; Lianos and Pseiridis 2009). For instance, Zhao (2002) argues that return migrants can be carriers of capital, technology, and entrepreneurship, all of which contribute to the development of their home regions and native communities. Migrants carrying a working experience from the city to return to rural areas might accumulate more diverse human, social and financial capital than local peasants, which enables them to be more likely to start their own businesses upon return, and benefit their home region and native community (Démurger and Xu 2011). While the reasons for out-migration in China (i.e. rural-to-urban) have been relatively well researched (e.g. Zhao 1999a, 1999b; Zhang and Song 2003; Seto 2011), the increasing trend of return migration and the rise of new entrepreneurs in rural China is a relatively new phenomenon that merits attention (Démurger and Xu 2011). Preliminary justifications for such return migration include failure to find a good paying job in the city, higher returns to the human or financial capital accumulated in the destination areas at home, and lower living costs at home (Zhao 2002). However, return migration is not simply the mirror image of out-migration (Zhao 2002). The differences between returning migrants and those who have never migrated are reflected in qualities such as having a more diverse labor-market experience, more capital, and different expectations about future career moves (Zhao 2002).

Moreover, research on migration and entrepreneurship has indicated that returning migrants have a higher propensity to engage in entrepreneurial activities (Gubert and Nordman ; Wahba and Zenou 2012). Though many factors have been identified in the literature to explain China's migration, such as economic reforms and rural–urban income gaps (Zhang and Song 2003), very few studies have investigated the individual-level socio-psychological determinants (e.g. Baron 2004; Keh, Foo, and Lim 2002) of migrant workers' occupational choices (e.g. self-employment in the hometown) (Wang and Yang 2013). As Démurger and Xu (2011) note, research on reasons of return migration in China remains rather limited despite a mounting interest on the issue. Understanding the motivations behind the entrepreneurial intention of returning migrant workers from a psychological and socio-cognitive perspective has significant theoretical and policy implications, and therefore merits research attention (Zhu et al. 2010).

The current literature generally outlines two counteracting arguments explaining the motivation of entrepreneurship, and divides the factors that motivate individuals to begin their own businesses into push factors (e.g. dissatisfaction with current position, difficulties of looking for a new job, unfair workplace treatment and low wages) and pull factors (e.g. desire for independence, self-actualization, wealth and other personal benefits) (Amit and Muller 1995; Brünjes and Diez 2013; Gilad and Levine 1986; Kirkwood 2009; Schjoedt and Shaver 2007). In the context of Chinese migrant workers, their decision making to leave their urban job (and leaving the city to return home) and choosing to become self-employed in their hometown (among other career choices) is influenced by the combined effects of push factors in urban areas and pull factors from the rural hometown (Zhao 2002). On the push side, many migrant workers working in small and medium enterprises make a living through cheap labor, and are usually obligated to undertake dull, demanding, and dangerous work that urban workers do not want to undertake (Cai, Park, and Zhao 2008). The labor intensity, long working hours and high job requirements (Ngai and Chan 2012) push migrant workers to leave their current job. Since the Chinese *Hukou* system has denied rural migrants permanent urban residence rights and associated social benefits, migrant workers are constantly presented the dilemma whether to leave the city and return home (Hu, Xu, and Chen 2011). On the pull side, the business experience, skills, knowledge, information, and capital accumulated through the years of working in the city, as well as the expanding business opportunities and favorable policies in their hometowns, not only improve the migrant workers' entrepreneurial willingness, but also enhance their entrepreneurial confidence and chances of success.

To explain the decision making of Chinese migrant workers to return to their hometown and seek self-employment opportunities, we apply and adapt the Job Demands – Resources (JD-R) model (Bakker and Demerouti 2007; Demerouti et al. 2001) to the entrepreneurial context. This model argues that every occupation may have its own specific risk factors associated with job stress, which can be classified into job demands and job resources. Job demands refer to the physical, psychological, social, or organizational aspects of a job that require sustained physical and/or psychological efforts or skills (e.g. high-level work pressure, unfavorable physical environ- ments, and emotional exhaustion) (Demerouti et al. 2001). Job resources include the physical, psychological, social, and organizational aspects of the job that may a) be functional in achieving work goals; b) reduce job demands and the associated physiological and psychological costs; and c) stimulate personal growth and development (Demerouti et al. 2001). While there is sufficient research on applying the JD-R model to salaried workers, studies on the group of entrepreneurs are quite few (Dijkhuizen et al. 2016). What is more, the JD-R model has been widely used to explain job attitudes and performance, yet with limited attention to how factors in the JD-R model may influence entrepreneurial intention of individuals.

We specifically focus on job demands as the push factors that affect Chinese migrant workers' decision to leave their urban job (i.e. the health-impairment process) and entrepreneurial resources as the pull factors that increase Chinese migrant workers' intention to seek self-employment as a career choice in their hometown (i.e. the motivational process) (Xanthopoulou et al. 2007). Further, given the significant economic, political, and social changes in transitional China and the effect of these changes on the work-value orientation of different generations of workers (Dou, Wang, and Zhou 2006; Egri and Ralston 2004; Ralston et al. 1999), we attempt to discover whether there is any discrepancy in the antecedents of entrepreneurial intention between the 'new' and 'old' generations of migrant workers in China.

The theoretical contributions of this paper are as follows. First, it reveals the decision-making mechanisms motivating Chinese migrant workers (who are largely ignored in the existing entrepre- neurship literature) to return to their hometown and engage in entrepreneurial activities. Second, while prior research has generally either examined the push or pull factors influencing entrepreneurial intention, very few studies have examined their effects together (Dawson and Henley 2012; Schjoedt and Shaver 2007). Adapting the JD-R model to the context of entrepreneurial intention, we find that urban push factors are not sufficient to encourage migrant workers to return to their hometown to engage in entrepreneurial activities. Resource endowments and the resource environment in their hometown are also pull factors influencing them to return home to pursue entrepreneurial opportu- nities. Third, implications for policy makers and managers could be derived by the more detailed explanation on how different job and environmental characteristics shape entrepreneurial intention between different generations of Chinese migrant workers.

The remainder of the paper is structured as follows. Section 2 presents a literature review on job demands and entrepreneurial resources, and outlines the mediating role of job burnout and entrepreneurial conviction, as well as the moderating role of generation in the process. Section 3 presents the methodology and data. Section 4 present the empirical analyses and Section 5 presents the discussion of the results and the implications of the findings.

2. Literature review and research hypothesis

2.1. Entrepreneurship of Chinese returning migrant workers

Migrant workers have been the engine of China's rapid economic growth over the past four decades, but they remain socially, economically, and legally marginalized, and are subject to institutionalized discrimination (Chan 2010; Pun and Chan 2013; Wong et al. 2007).[1] In addition to receiving a lower income and delayed payment of income, they are also bound by institutional barriers and restrictions such as the household-registration system known as the *Hukou* system (Shi 2008). Most of these migrants seldom have a permanent contract with their employers and are ineligible to receive welfare services in the city (Ning and Qi 2017). Thus, the job mobility of migrant workers in China is much higher than that of urban Chinese workers (Knight and Yueh 2004; Qin, Hom, and Xu 2018). The current economic situation in cities makes it more difficult for these migrants to find stable and well-paid jobs (Démurger and Xu 2011; Murphy 1999). Having to move back and forth between their home and cities, migrant workers are constantly faced with the choice of staying in the city or returning home. For migrant workers who have not been fully assimilated into urban work and cannot settle down permanently in cities due to the restrictions of the household-registration system and unaffordable living costs (Chan 2001; Démurger and Xu 2011; Hu, Xu, and Chen 2011; Zhao 1999b; Zhang 2018), leaving their urban job and making a living in their hometown is becoming increasingly attractive, particularly for those who have accumulated several years of capital and related experience through working in urban areas (China Economic Net 2015).

Self-employment seems to be a popular career choice for returning migrants in China (Zhang et al. 2006; Zhang 2018). Recently, central and local Chinese governments have introduced 'Back to the Countryside' policies aimed at encouraging migrants who have moved from rural areas to the cities to return to their hometowns and begin businesses[2] because of the positive link of small business with economic growth (Koellinger and Thurik 2012). In addition, empirical evidence in several countries confirms that migrants with more diverse work experience and skills are more likely to begin a business (see Orazem et al. for a review). That is, migrants carrying a working experience from the city to return to rural areas might accumulate more diverse human, social and financial capital than local peasants, which enables them to be more likely to start their own businesses upon return, and benefit their home region and native community (Démurger and Xu 2011). Returning migrant workers are also found to have more savings and therefore face less severe credit constraints than people who have never left rural areas to work (Zhao 2002).

2.2. Job demands and Chinese returning migrant workers' entrepreneurial intention

Job demands refer to the degree to which a work environment contains stimuli that peremptorily require attention and a response (Jones and Fletcher 1996). Specifically, they refer to the physical, psychological, social, and organizational aspects of a job (e.g. cognitive or emotional stress and work requirements) that consume the physical and mental resources of employees (Demerouti et al. 2001). Although job demands are not necessarily negative, they often cause physical and psychological loss, which leads to employee job burnout, and results in employee absenteeism and turnover behavior (Bakker, Demerouti, and Verbeke 2004; Hakanen, Bakker, and Schaufeli 2006).

All job and work environments have different job requirements, which can be divided into skill requirement, physical requirement, psychological requirement and job insecurity. Cavanaugh et al. (2000) argue that excessive job demands such as heavy workload and job insecurity impede individual achievement of work objectives and make employees feel out of control. In such circumstances, even if employees work hard, they are unable to meet the job requirements, and the resulting resentment toward their job renders them more willing to cease exerting effort on their work tasks, thus resulting in negative work outcomes such as low productivity and resignation (Lepine, Podsakoff, and Lepine 2005).

The level of working conditions and workplace treatment faced by Chinese migrant workers are generally lower than those faced by urban Chinese workers (Cai, Park, and Zhao 2008). The high level of work intensity, repetitive mechanical work, little break time, and lack of a social-security system mean that migrant workers are under constant high level of work pressure. In addition, the strict division between urban and rural household-registration systems makes it difficult for migrant workers to achieve steady career development in the cities (Gallagher 2015). Even if they change from one urban job to another, the work pressure is not much likely to improve. The constant high-level work pressure, unsatisfactory work conditions, moving from one urban position of employment to another, often being away from family, and facing discrimination mean that some migrant workers prefer to leave the city permanently and return to rural hometown.

Self-employment has been found to be one of the most popular career choices for the returning migrants. Self-employment can mean greater freedom to make decisions about what type of work to engage in, as well as how and when to perform the work (Hessels, Rietveld, and van der Zwan 2017). Although self-employment sometimes means longer working hours (which contribute to job demand), self-employed people have been found to face fewer job demands because they do not operate within organizational hierarchies and perform the monotonous tasks that migrant workers often do in urban employment (Benz and Frey 2008). In addition, as argued from the perspective of social exclusion theory (Silver 1994), when migrant workers feel excluded from their urban employ-ment, they tend to return home to advance their career development by beginning a business. This move not only improves their work autonomy, but also helps them to achieve the recognition of others, which is difficult to win from their urban job. Entrepreneurship research finds that work-related stress tends to be lower for self-employed workers than for wage workers because of the higher level of job control enjoyed by the self-employed (Hessels, Rietveld, and van der Zwan 2017). We argue that Chinese migrant workers' entrepreneurial intention when returning home is not an accidental phenomenon, but the result of the ingrained rural–urban divide reflected in the discrimi-nation of urban residents against rural immigrant workers, and of the pressure of the barriers to career development, and the uncertainty of having to change occupations frequently in the city. Pressured by the high level of job demand, migrant workers who cannot see any opportunity for career advancement feel it a better choice to return to their hometown and become self-employed. Therefore, we propose the following hypothesis:

Hypothesis 1: Job demands are positively related to return-home entrepreneurial intention.

A basic assumption of the JD-R model is that job demands lead to job strain, and in extreme cases, to burnout. Job burnout is a symptom of emotional exhaustion, a disintegration of personality, and a reduction in individual accomplishment in a professional field (Maslach and Jackson 1986). The first aspect of exhaustion is an extreme form of fatigue as a consequence of intense physical, affective and cognitive stress due to prolonged exposure to specific working conditions. The second aspect of disengagement represents an extensive and intensive reaction in terms of an emotional, cognitive and behavioral rejection of the job. Over time, workers experiencing burnout lose the capacity to accomplish fruitful work results and to maintain an intense involvement that has a meaningful impact at work (Bakker, Demerouti, and Verbeke 2004; Schaufeli, Leiter, and Maslach 2009).

Compared with their urban counterparts, the majority of Chinese migrant workers are employed in low-paid labor-intensive jobs characterized by working long overtime hours, low levels of job security, and experiencing ill treatment in the workplace (Cheo 2017). Those who experience job burnout become tired of work, lose work enthusiasm, and have low levels of subjective wellbeing and life satisfaction in big cities (Shen and Huang 2012). Research has indicated that a high level of burnout usually leads to negative work-output results such as employee dissatisfaction, low productivity and high turnover rates (Bakker, Demerouti, and Schaufeli 2003; Cheo 2017). Due to restrictions of the household-registration system and other discriminatory policies and state control regime, migrant workers experience greater difficulty than urban residents in obtaining progressive career development (e.g. promotions to management positions) in urban employment. Therefore, choosing to leave the urban job and seeking self-employment opportunities back home may become a coping mechanism for the migrant workers to escape from, or compensate for the experienced burnout in the city work circumstances. We thus propose the second hypothesis:

Hypothesis 2: Job burnout mediates the positive relationship between job demands and return-home entrepreneurial intention.

2.3. *Entrepreneurial resources and Chinese returning migrant workers' entrepreneurial intention*

While the first psychological process of the JD-R model focuses on the health-impairment process of urban employment that results in job burnout and job turnover, the second psychological process of the JD-R is motivation driven and focuses on the availability of resources that lead to organizational conviction and work engagement (Bakker and Demerouti 2007; Davidsson 1995; Schaufeli and Bakker 2004). In the context of deciding to engage in self-employment, the availability of resources in the environment is an important external factor in stimulating individual entrepreneurial intention and behavior (Erikson 2002; Greene, Brush, and Brown 2015; Kibler 2013; Tang 2008). Each new entrepreneurial-resource combination can consist of three forms of capital: human, financial and social capital (Davidsson and Honig 2003; Firkin 2001). Human capital refers to the individual's education, prior work experience, and related knowledge and skills (Becker 1993; Schultz 1959). Financial capital refers to the financial benefits that can be directly obtained by the entrepreneur (Bourdieu 1986). Social capital refers to the bonds, bridges, and linkages that connect members of society and may be transformed into other forms of capital (Davidsson and Honig 2003). The value of social capital depends on the size of the relationship network and the amount of resources held by the relationship members.

Entrepreneurial resources play a key role in the formation of individuals' entrepreneurial cognition and intention, and the lack of these resources is considered a principal constraint of entrepreneurial motivation and success. We argue that the importance of entrepreneurial resources has particularly significant implications for the often resource-deprived migrant workers when considering pursuing entrepreneurial opportunities in their hometown for the following reasons. First, entrepreneurial resources provide knowledge, funding, and policy support to the individual, helping the individual to overcome resource constraints and enhancing their expectations of business success. For example, migrant workers with a relatively high level of education are better able to learn the legal, operational, and managerial knowledge required for entrepreneurship. Training can also cultivate the ability to perceive entrepreneurial opportunities and broaden entrepreneurial thinking, so that returning migrant workers are more likely to realize potential business opportunities (Davidsson and Honig 2003). Further, the work experience gained in urban employment differentiates returning migrant workers from local farmers in that returning migrants have greater entrepreneurial confidence, vision, and skills.

Second, financial resources can alleviate the financial burdens of returning migrant workers and help them overcome one of the greatest barriers to entrepreneurship, that is, accessing the initial financial capital. Favorable policies by local Chinese governments have given rural entrepreneurs financial benefits in relation to business registration, taxation, and financing, which means that returning migrant workers should have less resistance to entrepreneurship and greater willingness to begin their own business (Blanchflower 2000; Fonseca, Lopez-Garcia, and Pissarides 2001).

Third, social capital facilitates the identification, collection, and allocation of scarce resources. For returning migrant workers, beginning a business in their hometown is not related only to their own financial survival and development, but also to the fate of their entire family. When returning migrant workers face great financial and social pressure, receiving financial assistance and obtaining emotional support from family and friends, who may become their business partners, can enhance their entrepreneurial confidence and strengthen their entrepreneurial intention. Moreover, informal social networks in the hometown have been found to be associated with high levels of trust and interaction, which further enhances the utility of social capital (Paxton 1999). Therefore, we propose the following hypothesis:

Hypothesis 3: Entrepreneurial resources are positively related to return-home entrepreneurial intention.

As stated, entrepreneurial resources may instigate a motivational process leading to self-employment-related learning, work engagement, and conviction (Bakker and Demerouti 2007; Davidsson 1995). We argue that a returning migrant worker is more convinced of and committed to the idea of self-employment when their entrepreneurial resources enable them to see and exploit the potential of entrepreneurial opportunities. Entrepreneurial conviction is the degree to which an entrepreneur identifies with and is sure to engage in activities for new business creation (Davidsson 1995; Tang 2008). It refers to the self-conviction or self-expectation of entrepreneurial behavior, including the emotions, intelligence, and physical strength implied in the direction of intention, constituting a bridge to entrepreneurial intention (Erikson 2002).

The ability to recognize and exploit business opportunities differentiates migrant workers who are committed to entrepreneurial activities from those who are not because entrepreneurial resources enable them to be better prepared to search for useful information and knowledge and take advantage of the available resources required to pursue an entrepreneurial opportunity. Following Erikson (2002), who demonstrates that the availability of entrepreneurial resources is positively related to entrepreneurial commitment, this study suggests that migrant workers who own more entrepreneurial resources are more likely to form a positive evaluation of entrepreneurial success and develop greater conviction to entrepreneurship, thus leading to increased intention to engage in entrepreneurial activities in their hometown. Therefore, we propose the following hypothesis:

Hypothesis 4: Entrepreneurial conviction mediates the positive relationship between entrepreneurial resources and return-home entrepreneurial intention.

2.4. Moderating role of intergenerational differences

The concept of a 'generation' is often broadly defined as 'an identifiable group that shares birth years, age, location and significant life events at critical developmental stages' (Kupperschmidt 2000, 66). According to generational cohort theory (Inglehart 2015), each generation, as one type of societal subculture, has a different set of values and attitudes, which reflects the unique growth experience and historical background the specific grouping of individuals shares within the group (Egri and Ralston 2004; Parry and Urwin 2011). Generational cohort theory (Inglehart 1997) argues that intergenerational value dynamics are based on the socialization hypothesis and the scarcity hypothesis: the former proposes that adults' basic values reflect the socioeconomic conditions of their childhood and adolescence; the latter argues that the greatest subjective value is derived from socioeconomic environmental aspects that are in short supply during a generation's childhood and adolescence.

Significant economic, political, and social changes in transitional China in the past decades have had significant effects on the work values of different generations of Chinese people (Dou, Wang, and Zhou 2006; Egri and Ralston 2004; Ralston et al. 1999). The older and younger generations of migrant workers have had very different experiences in their growth environments, work participation, value orientation, and entrepreneurial spirit. Compared with the older generation, who were usually born before the 1980s and moved from rural areas to work in the newly industrialized urban China, migrant workers born and raised in the reform period (in the 1980s and 1990s) have been described as the new generation of 'rights awakening' (Franceschini, Siu, and Chan 2016). As Deng Xiaoping's modernization policies ushered in the Social Reform Era (since 1978), societal values in China have placed greater emphasis on individual achievement, materialism, economic efficiency, and entrepreneurship (Tian 1998). As a result, Chinese migrant workers who have grown up during the Social Reform Era may be more individualistic, materialistic, and entrepreneurial than Chinese migrant workers who grew up before this era (Egri and Ralston 2004). Research has also found a higher rate of job turnover and less job loyalty among the new generation of migrant workers because the rapid economic growth in the Social Reform Era has shaped a social structure in which the new generation faces even greater rural–urban divide, income inequality, and social exclusion despite an improvement in general working and living conditions in China (Egri and Ralston 2004; Pun and Lu 2010; Park and Wang 2010). Some research argues that the new generation of migrant workers is less tolerant of arduous job demands than the older generation, and feels greater frustration when encountering job difficulties (Franceschini, Siu, and Chan 2016). Once the new generation of migrant workers becomes disillusioned with the gap between their expectations in becoming urban worker–citizens and the reality of the employment conditions, they are more likely than the older generation to leave their job. In this study, we refer migrant workers born before 1980s (i.e. before the Social Reform Era) as the older generation of migrant workers and those born in the 1980s and 1990s as the new generation of migrant workers (Pun and Lu 2010). We propose that:

Hypothesis 5a: Intergeneration positively moderates the mediating relationships among job demands, job burnout, and return-home entrepreneurial intention.

Although we argue that the new generation of migrant workers is more likely to develop entrepreneurial intention when experiencing high job demands and job burnout in their urban employment, research demonstrates that the majority of Chinese returning migrant workers are aged in their 40s (i.e. the older generation). This is partly because this generation of migrant workers has acquired professional skills, and wealth and management experience after working in urban employment for many years. When the older generation of migrant workers sees an opportunity to begin their own business in their hometown, they are more likely to develop entrepreneurial conviction and act on the entrepreneurial idea. In contrast, the members of the new generation of migrant workers (who were exposed to contemporary ideas, information, and knowledge related to individualism and wealth accumulation much earlier in their life) have been characterized as having a greater disposition toward individualism and urban culture, being less constrained by economic circumstances, being more inclined to pursue personal development and freedom, and having a cosmopolitan outlook (Egri and Ralston 2004; Franceschini, Siu, and Chan 2016; Pun and Lu 2010). Thus, the decision of the new generation of migrant workers to return home and engage in entrepreneurial activities may be derived less from resource endowments and environment, and more from their desire for economic independency, career development, and social achievement. Therefore, we propose the following hypothesis:

Hypothesis 5b: Intergeneration negatively moderates the mediating relationships among entrepreneurial resources, entrepreneurial conviction, and return-home entrepreneurial intention.

Based on the stated hypotheses, the following research model (see Figure 1) is proposed:

3. Methods

3.1. Sample and procedure

We conducted a survey during the 2016 Spring Festival in China, when the world's largest urban migration occurs. We recruited research assistants to distribute questionnaires to Chinese migrant workers who were returning home for the Spring Festival holiday (Cheo 2017). Data were obtained from 390 migrant workers in the provinces of Jiangsu, Shandong, and Anhui where a large number of Chinese migrant workers have been migrating from. We first invited the migrant worker participants to report job demands, job burnout, entrepreneurial resources, entrepreneurial conviction, and control variables such as achievement motive and risk

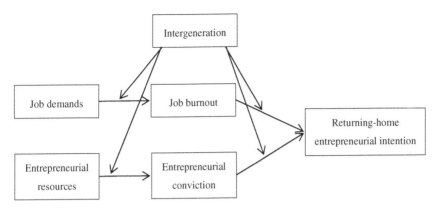

Figure 1. Hypothesized model.

propensity, as well as their demographic information. We attempted to avoid common method bias by inserting extraneous variables between the independent and mediation variables, and disrupting the order of the items. Three days after filling the first part of questionnaire, every participant was asked to report their intention to return home and begin a new business venture. We obtained 367 responses, representing a response rate of 94.10%. After excluding incomplete responses and unpaired questionnaires, we retained 302 usable questionnaires (usable response rate of 82.29%). Of the participants, 63.2% were male, with an average age of 33.48 (SD = 7.63) and an average work tenure of 11.53 years (SD = 7.77).

3.2. Measures

All items were rated on a Likert scale ranging from '1 = strongly disagree to 5 = strongly agree' unless otherwise indicated.

3.2.1. Job demands

We used the well-validated Job Content Questionnaire to measure job demands (Li et al. 2004; Karasek 1978). This questionnaire elicits information on different aspects of job demands such as psychological demands, physical demands, and job insecurity. Sample items include 'My work requires working very hard' and 'My job involves a lot of repetitive work'. The Cronbach's alpha for this measure is 0.91.

3.2.2. Job burnout

We adopted the 15-item job burnout scale from the Maslach Burnout Inventory – General Survey (MBI-GS) (Li and Shi 2003; Schaufeli, Leiter, and Maslach et al. 1996). A sample item is 'work makes me feel physically and mentally exhausted'. The Cronbach's alpha for this measure is 0.83.

3.2.3. Entrepreneurial resources

We adapted the entrepreneurial resource scale from Huang (2016). It measures three forms of entrepreneurial capital: financial, human, and social. Sample items include 'when developing a business venture, I will prepare the funds needed for investment' and 'I have work experience matching the field of the business venture'. The Cronbach's alpha for this measure is 0.76.

3.2.4. Entrepreneurial conviction

We adopted Davidsson's (1995) five-item entrepreneurial conviction scale to measure migrant workers' entrepreneurial conviction. A sample item is 'I think I am capable enough to start my business'. The Cronbach's alpha for this measure is 0.85.

3.2.5. Return-home entrepreneurial intention

We adapted Chen, Greene, and Crick (1998) five-item scale to measure entrepreneurial intention of rural migrant workers, and revised the expression in every term to highlight the entrepreneurial context of the returning migrant workers. Sample items include 'I have considered returning my hometown and setting up my own business'. The Cronbach's alpha for this measure is 0.87.

3.2.6. Control variables

We controlled for the following participant characteristics that could affect key relationships in our model: gender, age, marriage, household annual income, and personal monthly income. Gender and marriage were dummy coded, with male and married respondents separately coded as '1'. Age was self-reported by years. Family annual income was reported by 10,000 yuan and personal monthly income was reported by yuan. In addition, we controlled for the respondents' achievement motive and risk propensity because these factors can influence entrepreneurial intention. Achievement motive was measured using Man, Nygard, and Gjesme (1994) four-item scale and risk propensity was measured using Miner's (1990) three-item scale. The Cronbach's alpha for these two measures was 0.80 and 0.81, respectively.

4. Results

4.1. CFA

Before testing our hypotheses, we conducted confirmatory factor analysis (CFA) procedures to examine the fit of the measurement model and the distinctiveness among the key variables. As recommended by Podsakoff and Organ (1986), we first performed Harman's one-factor test, which includes all variable measures in a single-factor analysis. The results indicated that neither a single factor nor a general factor could account for the majority of the covariance in the variables (the eigenvalue of the first factor was 12.31; the percentage of variance explained by the first factor was 22.39; the total variance was 66.86). We then conducted a series of CFAs to compare our hypothesized five-factor model with alternative models. Table 1 presents the details of the CFA results. The results demonstrated that the hypothesized five-factor model provided the best fit to the data, with $x^2 = 351.22$, $df = 125$, $x^2/df = 2.8$, CFI = 0.90, TLI = 0.88, RMSEA = 0.08.

Table 1. The results of CFA (N = 302).

Model	x^2	df	x^2/df	CFI	TLI	RMSEA
Five-factor model	351.22	125	2.8	0.90	0.88	0.08
Four-factor model[a]	379.88	129	2.94	0.86	0.83	0.08
Four-factor model[b]	374.73	129	2.90	0.86	0.83	0.09
Three-factor model[c]	403.38	132	3.06	0.85	0.82	0.08
One-factor model[d]	813.01	135	6.02	0.61	0.56	0.13

Note: The five factors are job demands, job burnout, entrepreneurial resources, entrepreneurial conviction and entrepreneurial intention.
[a]Combined job demands and job burnout into one factor
[b]Combined entrepreneurial resources and entrepreneurial conviction into one factor
[c]Combined a and b respectively in one model
[d]Combined all variables into one factor

4.2. Descriptive statistics

Table 2 presents the means, standard deviations, and Pearson correlations of all key variables. As presented in Table 2, the variables job demands and entrepreneurial resources were both positively correlated with returning migrant workers' entrepreneurial intention ($r = 0.30$, $p < 0.001$; $r = 0.32$, $p < 0.001$). In addition, the variable job demands was positively correlated with job burnout ($r = 0.24$, $p < 0.001$), and job burnout was positively correlated with entrepreneurial intention ($r = 0.20$, $p < 0.001$). Similarly, entrepreneurial conviction was positively correlated with entrepreneurial resources ($r = 0.54$, $p < 0.001$) and entrepreneurial intention ($r = 0.47$, $p < 0.001$).

4.3. Hypotheses testing

Hierarchical linear regression was used to test for Hypotheses 1 and 3. Specifically, to test Hypotheses 1 and 3, we regressed return-home entrepreneurial intention on job demands and entrepreneurial resources respectively. As presented in Table 3, there was a significant positive relationship between job demands and entrepreneurial intention ($\beta = 0.28$, $p < .001$, Model 12), as well as between entrepreneurial resources and entrepreneurial intention ($\beta = 0.30$, $p < .001$, Model 13). These results support Hypotheses 1 and 3.

In Hypotheses 2 and 4, we propose that job burnout mediates the relationship between job demands and entrepreneurial intention, and entrepreneurial conviction mediates the relationship between entrepreneurial resources and entrepreneurial intention. We also conducted a bootstrap analysis following Preacher, Rucker, and Hayes (2007). The results demonstrated that the indirect effect of job demands on entrepreneurial intention through job burnout is significant at the 99% confidence interval (indirect effect = 0.06, CI = [0.02, 0.11], Boot SE = 0.02, Sobel test: $Z = 2.69$, $p < 0.01$), and the indirect effect of entrepreneurial resources on entrepreneurial intention via entrepreneurial conviction is also significant at the 99% confidence interval (indirect effect = 0.38, CI = [0.26, 0.52], Boot SE = 0.07, Sobel test: $Z = 6.29$, $p < 0.001$). These results support Hypotheses 2 and 4.

Finally, we conducted moderated path analysis (Edwards and Lambert 2007) to test Hypotheses 5a and 5b, bootstrapping 1000 samples to compute bias-corrected confidence intervals. The results presented in Table 4 indicate that intergenerational differences positively moderated the relationship between job burnout and entrepreneurial intention (new: $r = 0.60$, $p < 0.001$; older: $r = -0.24$, $p < 0.01$; $\Delta r = 0.84$, $p < 0.001$) but did not moderate the relationship between job demands and job burnout ($\Delta r = 0.00$, n.s.), which means the moderation effect mainly worked in the second stage. In addition, the indirect effect of job demands on entrepreneurial intention via job burnout was higher for the new generation ($r = 0.13$, $p < 0.001$) than for the older generation ($r = -0.05$, $p < 0.005$). The intergenerational difference between these indirect effects was significant ($\Delta r = 0.18$, $p < 0.001$). These results support Hypothesis 5a, which indicates that the indirect effect of job demands on entrepreneurial intention through job burnout is significantly moderated by intergenerational differences, with the effect being stronger for the new generation of migrant workers than it is for the older generation of migrant workers.

As presented in Table 5, the variable intergenerational differences negatively moderates the relationship between entrepreneurial resources and entrepreneurial conviction (new: $r = 0.58$, $p < 0.001$; older: $r = 0.88$, $p < 0.001$; $\Delta r = -0.30$, $p < 0.001$) and the relationship between entrepreneurial conviction and entrepreneurial intention (new: $r = 0.33$, $p < 0.001$; older: $r = 0.71$, $p < 0.001$; $\Delta r = -0.38$, $p < 0.001$). In addition, the results in Table 5 demonstrate that the indirect effect of entrepreneurial resources on entrepreneurial intention via entrepreneurial conviction is greater for the older generation ($r = 0.63$, $p < 0.001$), and the difference in the indirect effect was significant at the 99% confidence interval ($\Delta r = -0.44$, $p < 0.001$). These results support Hypothesis 5b, which proposes that intergenerational differences negatively moderate the relationship between entrepreneurial resources and entrepreneurial intention, and that the mediation effect

Table 2. Means, standard deviations and correlations (N = 302).

	M	SD	1	2	3	4	5	6	7	8	9	10	11	12	13
1. Gender	1.37	0.48													
2. Age	33.48	7.63	-0.10+												
3. Marriage	1.19	0.38	0.06	0.55***											
4. Family annual income	13.17	86.02	-0.05	-0.02	-0.02										
5. Personal monthly income	2.15	0.99	-0.27***	-0.09	-0.00	-0.04									
6. Achievement motive	3.36	0.98	0.01	-0.04	0.15*	-0.05	0.15**	0.80							
7. Risk propensity	2.81	0.70	-0.02	-0.05	0.19**	0.05	0.13*	0.13*	0.81						
8. Job demands	3.34	0.69	-0.11+	0.13*	-0.20***	-0.02	-0.07	0.10+	-0.09	0.91					
9. Entrepreneurial resources	3.3	0.59	-0.04	0.09	-0.10+	0.02	0.13*	0.23***	0.11*	0.40***	0.76				
10. Job burnout	2.87	0.58	-0.02	-0.10+	-0.14*	0.00	-0.20***	-0.25***	-0.24***	0.24***	-0.12*	0.83			
11. Entrepreneurial conviction	3.56	0.81	-0.13*	-0.03	0.05	-0.02	0.14*	0.22***	0.06	0.44***	0.54***	0.04	0.85		
12. Intergeneration	0.67	0.47	0.05	-0.77***	0.34***	0.05	0.13*	0.04	0.01	-0.11+	0.07	0.07	0.03		
13. Return-home entrepreneurial intention	3.46	0.91	0.00	0.16**	-0.19***	0.01	-0.04	0.05	0.11+	0.30***	0.32***	0.20***	0.47***	0.04	0.87

Note: M = mean, SD = Standard deviation. *** $p < 0.001$, ** $p < 0.01$, * $p < 0.05$, + $p < 0.10$.
Gender: 1 = male, 2 = female; marriage: 1 = married, 2 = unmarried; intergeneration: 0 = older generation, 1 = new generation.
Cronbach's alpha in italics.

Table 3. Results of hierarchical regression (N = 302).

	Return-home entrepreneurial intention		
	M11	M12	M13
Gender	0.01	0.05	0.01
Age	0.07	0.07	0.05
Marriage	−0.19**	−0.13[+]	−0.15*
Family annual income	−0.00	0.01	−0.01
Personal monthly income	−0.06	−0.03	−0.09
Achievement motive	0.07	0.03	0.01
Risk propensity	0.14*	0.16**	0.11*
Job demands		0.28***	
Entrepreneurial resources			0.30***
Adjusted R^2	0.04	0.11	0.13
$\triangle R^2$		0.07	0.09
F	2.99**	5.75***	6.48***

Note: *** $p < 0.001$, ** $p < 0.01$, * $p < 0.05$, [+]$p < 0.10$.

Table 4. Results of moderated-mediation analysis (N = 302).

	Job demands (X) → job burnout (M) → entrepreneurial intention (Y)				
	First stage	Second stage	Direct effect	Indirect effect	Total effect
Moderator	P_{MX}	P_{YM}	P_{YX}	$P_{YM} P_{MX}$	$P_{YX} + P_{YM} P_{MX}$
Older generation	0.21***	−0.24*	0.37***	−0.05**	0.32***
New generation	0.21***	0.60***	0.33***	0.13***	0.46***
Difference	0.00	0.84***	−0.04	0.18***	0.14

Note: *$p < 0.01$, **$p < 0.005$, ***$p < 0.001$.

Table 5. Results of moderated-mediation analysis (N = 302).

	Entrepreneurial resources(X) → entrepreneurial conviction (M) → entrepreneurial intention (Y)				
	First stage	Second stage	Direct effect	Indirect effect	Total effect
Moderator	P_{MX}	P_{YM}	P_{YX}	$P_{YM} P_{MX}$	$P_{YX} + P_{YM} P_{MX}$
Older generation	0.88***	0.71***	−0.04	0.63***	0.59***
New generation	0.58***	0.33***	0.22	0.19***	0.41***
Difference	−0.30***	−0.38***	0.26	−0.44***	−0.18

Note: *$p < 0.01$, **$p < 0.005$, ***$p < 0.001$.

of entrepreneurial conviction is stronger for the older generation of migrant workers than it is for new generation.

To further determine the nature of the moderating effect of intergenerational differences, we used Preacher, Curran, and Bauer (2006) procedure to plot the interaction by computing simple slopes for the new and older generation of migrant workers. Given that the moderation effect only worked on the second stage of 'job demands–job burnout–entrepreneurial intention', we did not further examine the simple-slope analysis to the push line. Figure 2 demonstrates that the variable entrepreneurial resources is more positively related to entrepreneurial intention for the older generation ($\beta = 0.44$, $p < 0.001$) than for the new generation ($\beta = 0.27$, $p < 0.001$).

5. Discussion and conclusion

Growing self-employment and small-business ownership in many less-developed regions globally has stirred significant debate over the factors fueling this increase. The entrepreneurship literature has drawn on different models to explain the formation of entrepreneurial intention (Krueger, Reilly, and Carsrud 2000). A strong argument suggests that there are factors that either *pull* individuals toward creating new businesses or *push* them into doing this (Kirkwood 2009;

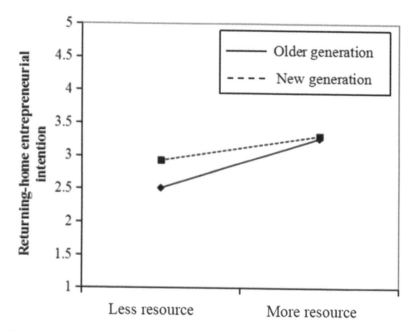

Figure 2. Moderating effect of intergeneration on entrepreneurial resources and return-home entrepreneurial intention.

Schjoedt and Shaver 2007). It is often asked whether individuals are pulled into self-employment by the attraction of entrepreneurial opportunities and the desire for independence and autonomy or whether they are pushed into entrepreneurial activities due to negative events such as unemployment, restructuring, and downsizing. Although there is a growing trend of returning migrant workers engaging in entrepreneurial activities in rural China, little research has investigated whether these migrant workers are attracted to self-employment as an emancipatory route to pursue opportunities in their hometown, or whether they are marginalized workers forced into self-employment as a job of last resort to overcome barriers created by job dissatisfaction and discrimination in urban employment.

Applying and adapting the JD-R model (Bakker and Demerouti 2007; Demerouti et al. 2001) to the context of the entrepreneurial intention of migrant workers, this study finds that job demands (as the push factor) and entrepreneurial resources (as the pull factor) together influence Chinese migrant workers' return-home entrepreneurial intention. First, when the requirements of the urban job become a significant burden, migrant workers are pushed to consider returning to their hometown to engage in entrepreneurial activities. According to the two-dimensional structural models of sources of work pressure (Cavanaugh et al. 2000), job requirements are categorized as obstructive (job hindrance) or challenging (job challenge). The obstructive job requirements usually lead to negative outcomes (Lepine, Podsakoff, and Lepine 2005). That is, the excessive level of job demands that is typically experienced in the urban employment undertaken by Chinese migrant workers represents obstructive job requirements that lead to these migrant workers leaving urban employment to return to their hometown. In addition, the push of job demands can be mediated by job burnout. Echoing the study of Bakker and Demerouti (2007) and Ten Brummelhuis et al. (2011), we demonstrate that job demands leads to physical or emotional exhaustion, a disintegration of personality, and a reduction in individual accomplishment, which further affect employees' work behavior such as turnover.

Second, if push force represents the dissatisfaction of migrant workers with their current urban employment propelling them away from this employment, then it is the 'pulling force' of entrepreneurial resources that instils in returning Chinese migrant workers a conviction to embracing self-employment opportunities in their hometown. We also tested the pull factor of entrepreneurial resources and found a positive effect of entrepreneurial resources on migrant workers' entrepreneurial intention in their hometown. In the entrepreneurial process, resources are the key elements for the development of business opportunities and the creation of new ventures (Huang 2016). That is, entrepreneurial resources directly provide the individual with the monetary, social, or policy support required to embark on entrepreneurial ventures, and having such resources can also enhance the confidence of an individual to achieve entrepreneurial success, thus strengthening entrepreneurial conviction. Therefore, entrepreneurial conviction functions as a bridge between migrant workers' entrepreneurial resources and their attitudes toward entrepreneurial behavior, which means that migrant workers become more committed to self-employment and are more likely to pursue entrepreneurial opportunities when their entrepreneurial resources enable them to identify and exploit the potential of entrepreneurial opportunities.

Third, the different moderation effects of generation on the relationship between job demands and entrepreneurial intention, and on the relationship between entrepreneurial resources and entrepreneurial intention suggests the importance of considering intergenerational differences when examining entrepreneurial attitudes and behaviors (Zhu 2010). The older generation of Chinese migrant workers has endured great difficulty due to the long working hours, high level of labor intensity, underpayment, and discriminatory treatment experienced in urban employment. However, the new generation of Chinese migrant workers (born in the 1980s and 1990s) is less tolerant of the hardship and discrimination than the older generation due to expanded worker rights and changed social dynamics (Franceschini, Siu, and Chan 2016). As a result, the new generation of migrant workers struggling with job burnout is more likely to develop the idea of leaving their urban employment to return to their hometown. In addition, the trait of desiring personal development and freedom of the members of the new generation of migrant workers can also mean they consider entrepreneurship to represent self-expression, while the members of the older generation of workers are more conservative when analyzing their personal circumstances, which may lead them to decide against self-employment as a career choice. The new generation may be attracted to entrepreneurship due to the influence of the social atmosphere, and the desire for entrepreneurial success, even if they lack experience and resources. However, the older generation decides to pursue entrepreneurial opportunities in their hometown only when they have accumulated employment experience and entrepreneurial resources.

This study contributes to the entrepreneurship and migration literature in the following ways. First, Chinese migrant workers, as a growing group of nascent entrepreneurs, have largely been ignored in the extant entrepreneurship literature. While prior research has examined parts or all of the relationships in the JD-R model among the salaried employees in different occupations, very limited research has applied it to the entrepreneur group (Dawson and Henley 2012; Dijkhuizen et al. 2016; Kirkwood 2009; Schjoedt and Shaver 2007). Moreover, while the JD-R model has often been adopted to explain job attitudes and performance, such as absence, turnover, work engagement and life satisfaction, limited attention has been devoted to how factors in the JD-R model may influence entrepreneurial intention of individuals.

Given that Chinese returning migrant workers are an important group of nascent entrepreneurs, we find that this model to a large extent can also be applied to explain entrepreneurial decision-making, at least among migrant group who are constantly drawn between the push of leaving (the city) and the pull of going back (to rural hometown). While the urban 'push' of job demands may drive migrant workers away from the city to the hometown (through the job burnout mechanism); it is the resource endowments and the resource environment in the hometown that increase returning migrant workers' conviction to pursuing entrepreneurial opportunities in their hometown (through the entrepreneurial conviction mechanism). Further, we highlight the generation-contingent mechanisms of the JD-R perspective in examining the entrepreneurial intention of Chinese returning migrant workers.

Second, it complements prior research on migration and entrepreneurship, which may be primarily focused on the linkage between the two in the Western context such as North American and European regions (Aliaga-Isla and Rialp 2013). Among the limited research on migration in China researchers mostly examine the determinants and consequences of out-migration (rural-to-urban) from a macro-level economic perspective. We reveal the socio-cognitive mechanisms motivating Chinese migrant workers to return to their hometown and engage in entrepreneurial activities, thus offering a fresh explanation for return migration in China.

Chinese migrant workers returning home to engage in entrepreneurial activities presents important implications for rural–urban integration and rural development. By revealing the entre-preneurial motivations behind the rising trend of Chinese returning migrant workers, our study presents the following implications for policymakers in China, particularly those in the rural regions who are enthusiastic about promoting local rural economic development through self-employment and entrepreneurship. First, local governments should aim to formulate policies that provide initial funds and offer entrepreneurial training and technical support for returning migrant workers, so that nascent entrepreneurs are better prepared and more committed to pursuing an entrepreneur-ial career in their local region. Second, it is important to provide tailor support and services to the different generational cohorts of migrant workers because they exhibit different motivational and behavioral characteristics in relation to entrepreneurial decision making. For example, while the new generation of migrant workers is better educated, has a more cosmopolitan outlook, is more independent, and more entrepreneurial than the older generation, it is not as experienced and does not hold as many resources as the older generation, and thus would require different types of training and support.

This study also has implications for business managers, especially the employers in the city who need to retain high-caliber migrant workers. Even though self-employment and entrepreneurship can contribute to regional economic development and vitality, it may not necessarily be a blessing for the employers in the big cities. As reports show, in recent years many manufacturing businesses in China's coastal regions are suffering from a shortage of labor, partly due to the high turnover rate of migrant workers as well as the rising trend of return migration. To minimize the costs resulting from labor shortage or loss, managers first of all need to reduce job demands as well as burnout experienced by the migrant workers, particularly for the new generation of migrant workers. For example, as workers express their increasing expectations, firms need to be responsive to them and treat them better through changing management style, investing in higher quality talent for longer-term conviction, and allowing for career path training and development to support ambitious migrant workers. Furthermore, for migrant workers with relatively more abun-dant financial, intellectual and social capital, if they exhibit greater entrepreneurial conviction, managers may consider offering opportunities of intrapreneurship within their current businesses or even choose to support and invest in the migrant workers' entrepreneurial ideas and activities. Last but not least, while some business operations may still need to be maintained on the east coast, relocation and investment into western, central, and northern China is getting more feasible as the regions continue to develop infrastructure, supply chain, transport systems, and reduced costs and as the migrant workers prefer working close to hometown.

Our study has several limitations that should be addressed in future research. First, while we focused on the push of job demands and the pull of entrepreneurial resources in predicting the entrepreneurial intention of returning migrant workers, there are other push and pull factors both in the hometown and in the city that can influence entrepreneurial decision making. Future research should include other relevant factors in examining the entrepreneurial behavior of migrant workers to present a more complete understanding of this phenomenon. Second, although we adopted different measures such as inserting extraneous variables in between the independent, mediation, and dependent variables, as well as disrupting the order of items, and separating the time of filling in the independent and dependent variables, the study may suffer from common method bias because all the questions for each questionnaire were answered by the same respondent. Future research should prolong the time gap between multiple waves of data collection and analyze objective data together with the survey data. Third, the research sample comprises migrant workers in the provinces of Jiangsu, Shandong, and Anhui. Future research should increase the sample size and the regional representativeness. Fourth, while we provide a framework to explain the entrepreneurial intention of returning migrant workers in China, the results may not be generalized to explain internal migration in the context of other countries. It would be valuable to replicate our study in other countries and regions, particularly in those with contextual features similar to China's such as a wide rural–urban divide, incomplete social welfare, and discriminatory employment policies that disadvantage migrant workers.

Notes

1. See reports such as Foxconn's suicides http://www.bbc.com/news/10182824 https://www.cbsnews.com/news/what-happened-after-the-foxconn-suicides/. More reports on the migration pattern as well as unique challenges and problems facing Chinese migrant workers can be found from sources such as Shi (2008).
2. These policy guidelines direct local governments to encourage migrant workers (as well as university graduates and discharged soldiers) to use the capital, skills, and experience they have acquired in urban areas to engage in entrepreneurship in underdeveloped rural areas. They are an important step toward reducing rural–urban disparity and rejuvenating rural areas in China. See links such as https://www.cfr.org/blog/guest-post-chinas-back-countryside-policy-step-toward-reducing-rural-urban-disparity.

Disclosure statement

No potential conflict of interest was reported by the authors.

Funding

We fully acknowledge the funding support from the National Science Foundation of China (No.71672146, 71672196, 71772025), as well as the Fundamental Research Funds for the Central Universities (No.2019ECNU-HWFW020).

References

Aliaga-Isla, R., and A. Rialp. 2013. "Systematic Review of Immigrant Entrepreneurship Literature: Previous Findings and Ways Forward." *Entrepreneurship & Regional Development* 25 (9–10): 819–844. doi:10.1080/08985626.2013.845694.
Amit, R., and E. Muller. 1995. "'push' and 'pull' Entrepreneurship." *Journal of Small Business & Entrepreneurship* 12 (4): 64–80. doi:10.1080/08276331.1995.10600505.
Bakker, A., and E. Demerouti. 2007. "The Job Demands-resources Model: State of the Art." *Journal of Managerial Psychology* 22 (3): 309–328. doi:10.1108/02683940710733115.
Bakker, A., E. Demerouti, and W. Schaufeli. 2003. "Dual Processes at Work in a Call Centre: An Application of the Job Demands-resources Model." *European Journal of Work and Organizational Psychology* 12 (4): 393–417. doi:10.1080/13594320344000165.
Bakker, A. B., E. Demerouti, and W. Verbeke. 2004. "Using the Job Demands-resources Model to Predict Burnout and Performance." *Human Resource Management* 43 (1): 83–104. doi:10.1002/(ISSN)1099-050X.
Baron, R. A. 2004. "The Cognitive Perspective: A Valuable Tool for Answering Entrepreneurship's Basic Why Questions." *Journal of Business Venturing* 19 (2): 221–239. doi:10.1016/S0883-9026(03)00008-9.
Becker, G. 1993. *Human Capital*. Chicago, IL: University of Chicago Press.
Benz, M., and B. S. Frey. 2008. "Being Independent Is a Great Thing: Subjective Evaluations of Self-employment and Hierarchy." *Economica* 75 (298): 362–383. doi:10.1111/j.1468-0335.2007.00594.x.
Blanchflower, D. G. 2000. "Self-employment in OECD Countries." *Labour Economics* 7 (5): 471–505. doi:10.1016/S0927-5371(00)00011-7.
Bourdieu, P. 1986. *The Forms of Capital*. UK: Blackwell Publishers.
Brünjes, J., and J. R. Diez. 2013. "'recession Push' and 'prosperity Pull' Entrepreneurship in a Rural Developing Context." *Entrepreneurship & Regional Development* 25 (3–4): 251–271. doi:10.1080/08985626.2012.710267.
Cai, F., A. Park, and Y. Zhao. 2008. "*The Chinese Labor Market in the Reform Era*." In *China's Great Economic Transformation*, edited by L. Brandt and T. Rawski. Cambridge: Cambridge University Press.
Cavanaugh, M. A., W. R. Boswell, M. V. Roehling, and J. W. Boudreau. 2000. "An Empirical Examination of Self-reported Work Stress among U.S. Managers." *Journal of Applied Psychology* 85 (1): 65–74.

Chan, K. W. 2010. "The Global Financial Crisis and Migrant Workers in China: 'there Is No Future as a Labourer; Returning to the Village Has No Meaning'." *International Journal of Urban and Regional Research* 34 (3): 659–677. doi:10.1111/j.1468-2427.2010.00987.x.

Chen, C. C., P. G. Greene, and A. Crick. 1998. "Does Entrepreneurial Self-efficacy Distinguish Entrepreneurs from Managers?" *Journal of Business Venturing* 13 (4): 295–316. doi:10.1016/S0883-9026(97)00029-3.

Cheo, R. 2017. "Migrant Workers and Workplace Bullying in Urban China." *Social Indicators Research* 132 (1): 87–115. doi:10.1007/s11205-015-1214-0.

China Economic Net. 2015 June 20. "Migrant workers return home for better job prospects." Accessed 10 June 2017. http://en.ce.cn/main/latest/201506/20/t20150620_5698247.shtml

China Economic Net. 2017 November 3. "Providing ample space for returning migrant workers to pursue entrepreneurship: pilot sites have increased to 341." Accessed 10 June 2017. http://m.sohu.com/a/201954987_120702

Davidsson, P. 1995. "Determinants of Entrepreneurial Intentions." Paper presented at: RENT Conference, Piacenza, Italy, November 23–24.

Davidsson, P., and B. Honig. 2003. "The Role of Social and Human Capital among Nascent Entrepreneurs." *Journal of Business Venturing* 18 (3): 301–331. doi:10.1016/S0883-9026(02)00097-6.

Dawson, C., and A. Henley. 2012. "'push' versus 'pull' Entrepreneurship: An Ambiguous Distinction?" *International Journal of Entrepreneurial Behavior & Research* 18 (6): 697–719. doi:10.1108/13552551211268139.

Demerouti, E., A. B. Bakker, F. Nachreiner, and W. B. Schaufeli. 2001. "The Job Demands-resources Model of Burnout." *Journal of Applied Psychology* 86 (3): 499–512. doi:10.1037/0021-9010.86.3.499.

Démurger, S., and H. Xu. 2011. "Returning Migrants: The Rise of New Entrepreneurs in Rural China." *World Development* 39 (10): 1847–1861. doi:10.1016/j.worlddev.2011.04.027.

Dijkhuizen, J., M. Gorgievski, M. van Veldhoven, and R. Schalk. 2016. "Feeling Successful as an Entrepreneur: A Job Demands—Resources Approach." *International Entrepreneurship and Management Journal* 12 (2): 555–573. doi:10.1007/s11365-014-0354-z.

Dou, W., G. Wang, and N. Zhou. 2006. "Generational and Regional Differences in Media Consumption Patterns of Chinese Generation X Consumers." *Journal of Advertising* 35 (2): 101–110. doi:10.1080/00913367.2006.10639230.

Edwards, J. R., and L. S Lambert. 2007. "Methods for Integrating Moderation and Mediation: a General Analytical Framework Using Moderated Path Analysis." *Psychological Methods* 12 (1): 1. doi:10.1037/1082-989X.12.1.1.

Egri, C. P., and D. A. Ralston. 2004. "Generation Cohorts and Personal Values: A Comparison of China and the United States." *Organization Science* 15 (2): 210–220. doi:10.1287/orsc.1030.0048.

Erikson, T. 2002. "Entrepreneurial Capital: The Emerging Venture's Most Important Asset and Competitive Advantage." *Journal of Business Venturing* 17 (3): 275–290. doi:10.1016/S0883-9026(00)00062-8.

Firkin, P. 2001. *Entrepreneurial Capital: A Resource-based Conceptualisation of the Entrepreneurial Process.* Labour Market Dynamics Research Programme, Massey University.

Fonseca, R., P. Lopez-Garcia, and C. A. Pissarides. 2001. "Entrepreneurship, Start-up Costs and Employment." *European Economic Review* 45 (4–6): 692–705. doi:10.1016/S0014-2921(01)00131-3.

Franceschini, I., K. Siu, and A. Chan. 2016. "The 'rights Awakening' of Chinese Migrant Workers: Beyond the Generational Perspective." *Critical Asian Studies* 48 (3): 422–442. doi:10.1080/14672715.2016.1189838.

Gallagher, M. E. 2015 September 29. "The Future of Work: China's Own Migrant Challenge." *Pacific Standard.* Accessed 24 May 2017. https://psmag.com/economics/the-future-of-work-chinas-own-migrant-challenge

Gilad, B., and P. Levine. 1986. "A Behavioral Model of Entrepreneurial Supply." *Journal of Small Business Management* 24: 45–54.

Greene, P. G., C. G. Brush, and T. E. Brown. 2015. "Resources in Small Firms: An Exploratory Study." *Journal of Small Business Strategy* 8 (2): 25–40.

Gubert, F., and C. J. Nordman. 2011. "Return Migration and Small Enterprise Development in The Maghreb." *Diaspora for Development in Africa* 3: 103-126.

Hakanen, J. J., A. B. Bakker, and W. B. Schaufeli. 2006. "Burnout and Work Engagement among Teachers." *Journal of School Psychology* 43 (6): 495–513. doi:10.1016/j.jsp.2005.11.001.

Hessels, J., C. A. Rietveld, and P. van der Zwan. 2017. "Self-employment and Work-related Stress: The Mediating Role of Job Control and Job Demand." *Journal of Business Venturing* 32 (2): 178–196. doi:10.1016/j.jbusvent.2016.10.007.

Hu, F., Z. Xu, and Y. Chen. 2011. "Circular Migration, or Permanent Stay? Evidence from China's Rural–Urban Migration." *China Economic Review* 22 (1): 64–74. doi:10.1016/j.chieco.2010.09.007.

Huang, H. C. 2016. "Entrepreneurial Resources and Speed of Entrepreneurial Success in an Emerging Market: The Moderating Effect of Entrepreneurship." *International Entrepreneurship and Management Journal* 12 (1): 1.

Inglehart, R. 1997. *Modernization and Postmodernization: Cultural, Economic, and Political Change in 43 Societies.* Princeton, NJ: Princeton University Press.

Inglehart, R. 2015. *The Silent Revolution: Changing Values and Political Styles among Western Publics.* Princeton, NJ: Princeton University Press.

Jones, F., and B. C. Fletcher. 1996. "Job Control and Health." In *Handb Work and Health Psychol*, edited by M. J. Schabracq, J. A. M. Winnubst, and C. L. Cooper, 33–50. Chichester: Wiley.

Karasek, R. A. 1978. "The Job Content Questionnaire (JCQ): An Instrument for Internationally Comparative Assessments of Psychosocial Job Characteristics." *Journal of Occupational Health Psychology* 11 (22): 56.

Keh, H. T., M. D. Foo, and B. C. Lim. 2002. "Opportunity Evaluation under Risky Conditions: The Cognitive Processes of Entrepreneurs." *Entrepreneurship Theory and Practice* 27 (2): 125–148. doi:10.1111/1540-8520.00003.

Kibler, E. 2013. "Formation of Entrepreneurial Intentions in a Regional Context." *Entrepreneurship & Regional Development* 25 (3–4): 293–323. doi:10.1080/08985626.2012.721008.

Kirkwood, J. 2009. "Motivational Factors in a Push-pull Theory of Entrepreneurship." *Gender in Management: An International Journal* 24 (5): 346–364.

Knight, J., and L. Yueh. 2004. "Job Mobility of Residents and Migrants in Urban China." *Journal of Comparative Economics* 32 (4): 637–660. doi:10.1016/j.jce.2004.07.004.

Koellinger, P. D., and A. R. Thurik. 2012. "Entrepreneurship and the Business Cycle." *Review of Economics and Statistics* 94 (4): 1143–1156. doi:10.1162/REST_a_00224.

Krueger, N. F., M. D. Reilly, and A. L. Carsrud. 2000. "Competing Models of Entrepreneurial Intentions." *Journal of Business Venturing* 15 (5): 411–432. doi:10.1016/S0883-9026(98)00033-0.

Kupperschmidt, B. R. 2000. "Multigeneration Employees: Strategies for Effective Management." *The Health Care Manager* 19 (1): 65–76.

Lepine, J. A., N. P. Podsakoff, and M. A. Lepine. 2005. "A Meta-analytic Test of the Challenge Stressor-hindrance Stressor Framework: An Explanation for Inconsistent Relationships among Stressors and Performance." *Academy of Management Journal* 48 (5): 764–775. doi:10.5465/amj.2005.18803921.

Li, C., and K. Shi. 2003. "The Influence of Distributive Justice and Procedural Justice on Job Burnout." *Acta Psychologica Sinica* 35 (5): 677–684. Chinese.

Li, J., W. Yang, P. Liu, Z. Xu, and S. I. Cho. 2004. "Psychometric Evaluation of the Chinese (mainland) Version of Job Content Questionnaire: A Study in University Hospitals." *Industrial Health* 42 (2): 260–267. doi:10.2486/indhealth.42.260.

Lianos, T., and A. Pseiridis. 2009. "On the Occupational Choices of Return Migrants." *Entrepreneurship & Regional Development* 21 (2): 155–181. doi:10.1080/08985620802176187.

Lin, Y. 2015. "Mass Entrepreneurship and Innovation Will Keep the Chinese Economy Soaring." Accessed 1 May 2017. http://english.counsellor.gov.cn/html/2015-07/76.html

Man, F., R. Nygard, and T. Gjesme. 1994. "The Achievement Motives Scale (AMS): Theoretical Basis and Results from a First Try-out of a Czech Form." *Scandinavian Journal of Educational Research* 38 (3–4): 209–218. doi:10.1080/0031383940380304.

Maslach, C., and S. E. Jackson. 1986. *MBI: Maslach Burnout Inventory*. Manual Research Edition. ed. Palo Alto (CA): University of California.

Miner, J. B. 1990. "Entrepreneurs, High-growth Entrepreneurs, and Managers: Contrasting and Overlapping Motivational Patterns." *Journal of Business Venturing* 5: 221–234. doi:10.1016/0883-9026(90)90018-O.

Murphy, K. J. 1999. "Executive Compensation." *Handbook of Labor Economics* 3: 2485–2563.

Ngai, P., and J. Chan. 2012. "Global Capital, the State, and Chinese Workers: The Foxconn Experience." *Modern China* 38 (4): 383–410. doi:10.1177/0097700412447164.

Ning, G., and W. Qi. 2017. "Can Self-employment Activity Contribute to Ascension to Urban Citizenship? Evidence from Rural-to-urban Migrant Workers in China." *China Economic Review* 45: 219-231. doi:10.1016/j.chieco.2017.07.007.

Park, A., and D. Wang. 2010. "Migration and Urban Poverty and Inequality in China." *China Economic Journal* 3 (1): 49–67. doi:10.1080/17538963.2010.487351.

Parry, E., and P. Urwin. 2011. "Generational Differences in Work Values: A Review of Theory and Evidence." *International Journal of Management Reviews* 13 (1): 79–96. doi:10.1111/ijmr.2011.13.issue-1.

Paxton, P. 1999. "Is Social Capital Declining in the United States? A Multiple Indicator Assessment." *American Journal of Sociology* 105 (1): 88–127. doi:10.1086/210268.

Podsakoff, P. M., and D. W. Organ. 1986. "Self-reports in Organizational Research: Problems and Prospects." *Journal of Management* 12 (4): 531–544.

Preacher, K. J., D. D. Rucker, and A. F. Hayes. 2007. "Addressing Moderated Mediation Hypotheses: Theory, Methods, and Prescriptions." *Multivariate Behavioral Research* 42 (1): 185–227. doi:10.1080/00273170701341316.

Preacher, K. J., P. J. Curran, and D. J. Bauer. 2006. "Computational Tools for Probing Interactions in Multiple Linear Regression, Multilevel Modeling, and Latent Curve Analysis." *Journal of Educational and Behavioral Statistics* 31 (4): 437–448. doi:10.3102/10769986031004437.

Pun, N., and H. Lu. 2010. "Unfinished Proletarianization: Self, Anger, and Class Action among the Second Generation of Peasant-workers in Present-day China." *Modern China* 36 (5): 493–519. doi:10.1177/0097700410373576.

Pun, N., and J. Chan. 2013. "The Spatial Politics of Labor in China: Life, Labor, and a New Generation of Migrant Workers." *South Atlantic Quarterly* 112 (1): 179–190. doi:10.1215/00382876-1891332.

Qin, X., P. W. Hom, and M. Xu. 2018. "Am I a Peasant or a Worker? an Identity Strain Perspective on Turnover among Developing-world Migrants." *Human Relations*. doi:10.1177/0018726718778097.

Ralston, D. A., C. P. Egri, S. Stewart, R. H. Terpstra, and Y. Kaicheng. 1999. "Doing Business in the 21st Century with the New Generation of Chinese Managers: A Study of Generational Shifts in Work Values in China." *Journal of International Business Studies* 30 (2): 415–427. doi:10.1057/palgrave.jibs.8490077.

Schaufeli W, Leiter MP, Maslach C, et al. 1996. *MBI – General Survey*. Palo Alto (CA): Consulting Psychologists Press.

Schaufeli, W. B., and A. B. Bakker. 2004. "Job Demands, Job Resources, and Their Relationship with Burnout and Engagement: A Multi-sample Study." *Journal of Organizational Behavior* 25 (3): 293–315. doi:10.1002/(ISSN)1099-1379.

Schaufeli, W. B., M. P. Leiter, and C. Maslach. 2009. "Burnout: 35 Years of Research and Practice." *Career Development International* 14 (3): 204–220. doi:10.1108/13620430910966406.

Schjoedt, L., and K. G. Shaver. 2007. "Deciding on an Entrepreneurial Career: A Test of the Pull and Push Hypotheses Using the Panel Study of Entrepreneurial Dynamics Data." *Entrepreneurship Theory and Practice* 31 (5): 733–752. doi:10.1111/etap.2007.31.issue-5.

Schultz, T. W. 1959. "Investment in Man: An Economist's View." *Social Service Review* 33 (2): 109–117. doi:10.1086/640656.

Seto, K. C. 2011. "Exploring the Dynamics of Migration to Mega-delta Cities in Asia and Africa: Contemporary Drivers and Future Scenarios." *Global Environmental Change* 21: S94–S107. doi:10.1016/j.gloenvcha.2011.08.005.

Shen, H., and C. Huang. 2012. "Domestic Migrant Workers in China's Hotel Industry: An Exploratory Study of Their Life Satisfaction and Job Burnout." *International Journal of Hospitality Management* 31 (4): 1283–1291. doi:10.1016/j.ijhm.2012.02.013.

Shi, L. 2008. *Rural Migrant Workers in China: Scenario, Challenges and Public Policy*. Geneva: ILO.

Silver, H. 1994. "Social Exclusion and Social Solidarity: Three Paradigms." *International Labour Review* 133 (5): 531–578.

Tang, J. 2008. "Environmental Munificence for Entrepreneurs: Entrepreneurial Alertness and Commitment." *International Journal of Entrepreneurial Behavior & Research* 14 (3): 128–151. doi:10.1108/13552550810874664.

Ten Brummelhuis, L. L., C. L. Ter Hoeven, A. B. Bakker, and B. Peper. 2011. "Breaking through the Loss Cycle of Burnout: The Role of Motivation." *Journal of Occupational and Organizational Psychology* 84 (2): 268–287. doi:10.1111/j.2044-8325.2011.02019.x.

Tian, X. 1998. *Dynamics of Development in an Opening Economy: China since 1978*. Hauppauge, NY: Nova Science Publishers.

Wahba, J., and Y. Zenou. 2012. "Out Of Sight, out Of Mind: Migration, Entrepreneurship and Social Capital." *Regional Science and Urban Economics* 42 (5): 890-903. doi:10.1016/j.regsciurbeco.2012.04.007.

Wang, Z. C., and W. G. Yang. 2013. "Self-employment or Wage-employment? on the Occupational Choice of Return Migration in Rural China." *China Agricultural Economic Review* 5 (2): 231–247. doi:10.1108/17561371311331115.

Wong, K., D. Fu, C. Y. Li, and H. X. Song. 2007. "Rural Migrant Workers in Urban China: Living a Marginalised Life." *International Journal of Social Welfare* 16 (1): 32–40. doi:10.1111/ijsw.2007.16.issue-1.

Xanthopoulou, D., A. B. Bakker, E. Demerouti, and W. B. Schaufeli. 2007. "The Role of Personal Resources in the Job Demands-resources Model." *International Journal of Stress Management* 14 (2): 121–141. doi:10.1037/1072-5245.14.2.121.

Zhang, H. 2018 March 5. "Migrant Workers Returning for Entrepreneurship: What Customized Support They Need?." *China City News*. Accessed 5 March 2018. http://paper.people.com.cn/zgcsb/html/2018-03/05/content_1839968.htm

Zhang, J., L. Zhang, S. Rozelle, and S. Boucher. 2006. "Self-employment with Chinese Characteristics: The Forgotten Engine of Rural China's Growth." *Contemporary Economic Policy* 24 (3): 446–458. doi:10.1093/cep/byj034.

Zhang, K. H., and S. Song. 2003. "Rural–Urban Migration and Urbanization in China: Evidence from Time-series and Cross-section Analyses." *China Economic Review* 14 (4): 386–400. doi:10.1016/j.chieco.2003.09.018.

Zhao, Y. 1999a. "Labor Migration and Earnings Differences: The Case of Rural China." *Economic Development and Cultural Change* 47 (4): 767–782. doi:10.1086/452431.

Zhao, Y. 1999b. "Leaving the Countryside: Rural-to-urban Migration Decisions in China." *American Economic Review* 89 (2): 281–286. doi:10.1257/aer.89.2.281.

Zhao, Y. 2002. "Causes and Consequences of Return Migration: Recent Evidence from China." *Journal of Comparative Economics* 30: 376–394. doi:10.1006/jcec.2002.1781.

Zhu, H. G., L. Y. Kang, Z. L. Weng, and X. C. Liu. 2010. "An Empirical Study about the Influences of Migrant Workers' Returning-home Entrepreneurial Intention from a Labor-exporting Province." *China Rural Survey* 5: 38–47. Chinese.

Zhu, Y. 2010. "China's New Generation of Migrant Workers: Characteristics, Problems and Countermeasures." *Journal of Population Research* 32 (2): 31–56. Chinese.

International networking and knowledge acquisition of Chinese SMEs: the role of global mind-set and international entrepreneurial orientation

Zhibin Lin (ID), Xuebing Cao (ID) and Ed Cottam (ID)

ABSTRACT

Chinese small and medium-sized enterprises (SMEs) are increasing their international networking and knowledge acquisition activities. This paper attempts to explain this phenomenon by examining the joint influence of leader global mind-set and firms' international entrepreneurial orientation on those two internationalisation activities. A conceptual model was developed and tested with data from a sample of 208 SMEs in China. The results indicate that both leader global mind-set and firm's international entrepreneurial orientation have a direct impact on Chinese SMEs' international networking and knowledge acquisition activities; in addition, leader global mind-set has an indirect effect through the mediation of firms' international entrepreneurial orientation. The findings of this study provide important theoretical and practical implications.

1. Introduction

The rapid development of China's small and medium-sized enterprises (SMEs) is one of the major drivers of the country's dramatic economic growth in recent decades. As the world's largest emerging economy, China has benefited from the rapid development of an internationally oriented growth for decades. Furthermore, the fast growth of its private sector has produced a large number of entrepreneurial owner-managers (Atherton and Newman 2017). Entrepreneurial activities in China are supported by an improved institutional environment for private ownership and the personal attributes of would-be entrepreneurs (Lu and Tao 2010). It has been suggested that China has entered the golden era of mass entrepreneurship development (He, Lu, and Qian 2018). Furthermore, the Chinese Government has promoted the 'Belt and Road Initiative' to nurture a new wave of global economic growth, and Chinese SMEs are expected to be actively engaged in their business activities in countries across Asia and Europe (Atherton and Newman 2017).

Entrepreneurship in China is embedded in the country's unique social networks and institutional context (He, Lu, and Qian 2018). To develop internationally, SMEs use networks to access important social capital and to overcome resource/capability limitations and liabilities of smallness (Huggins and Johnston 2010; Leppäaho and Pajunen 2018). SMEs often lack manufacturing capabilities, marketing channels and are impeded by smaller scale of markets. Such weaknesses mean SMEs, particularly in emerging economies, need to create a collaboration network in order to innovate and develop (Colombo, Piva, and Rossi-Lamastra 2014). There has been a well-documented discussion about the Chinese version of networking, guanxi, which refers to the interpersonal relationship that is linked to social exchanges (Batjargal 2010). Established through social ties and networking, guanxi is an essential method used by Chinese SMEs to develop their global business, helping them to access resources and maintain growth momentum (Guo and Miller 2010).

Knowledge acquisition helps firms respond to an increasingly uncertain and changing market situation and aids international expansion (Martin and Javalgi 2016). Both internationalization process theory (Johanson and Vahlne 1977) and international new venture research (Oviatt and McDougall 1994) recognize the role of learning and knowledge accumulation in SMEs' internationalization. Firms can formally collect foreign market information and proactively combine knowledge residing in people, firms or wider networks to build and update their knowledge (Casillas et al. 2009). However, despite the growing recognition of the significance of Chinese SMEs internationalisation in the literature (Tang 2011; Zhang et al. 2016), there is little research into the factors that drive Chinese SMEs' international networking and knowledge acquisition activities.

For a firm to succeed in international venturing, both leaders' global mind-set and firm-level international entrepreneurial orientation are important. Global mind-set refers to a business leader's competence and mentality that can handle the cognitive complexity combined with a certain holistic view of the world, characterized by openness and collaboration with multiple cultures and realities (Levy et al. 2007). A global mind-set is particularly relevant for SMEs, as their leaders' cognition and mentality about the domestic versus foreign markets will have a significant impact on the firm's strategies in an international environment (Weaver et al. 2002). A firm is considered to be entrepreneurially orientated if it has the disposition like that of an entrepreneur (Miller 2011). Firm international entrepreneurial orientation enables the discovery and exploitation of business opportunities in foreign markets (Etemad 2015; Martin and Javalgi 2016), and their future development (Oviatt and McDougall 2005; Wang, Chung, and Lim 2015). Constrained by limited resources, the internationalisation for SMEs is both complex and costly, involving both new product lines and new geographic markets (Wang, Chung, and Lim 2015). Only those SMEs with high international entrepreneurial orientation are likely to succeed by diversifying their activities, expanding into an uncertain international market, and improving international performance (Brouthers, Nakos, and Dimitratos 2015; Jantunen et al. 2005; Knight 2000).

Previous studies have examined the link between individual and firm-level global mind-set (Andresen and Bergdolt 2017) and the influence of individual leadership on the development of firm-level international entrepreneurial orientation (e.g. Ling et al. 2008; Jung, Wu, and Chow 2008; Engelen et al. 2015; Simsek, Heavey, and Veiga 2010). However, little attention has been paid to examining the linkage between leader global mind-set and firm entrepreneurial orientation. Following the upper echelons view of the firm that the characteristics of a leader directly influence the firm's business orientation (Hambrick and Mason 1984), we argue that investigating the linkage would provide a better understanding of the factors and the mechanism influencing Chinese SMEs' internationalisation behaviours.

This study therefore attempts to examine the joint influence of leader global mind-set and firm international entrepreneurial orientation on driving Chinese SMEs' internationalisation activities. Specifically, the study aims to address the following questions: Does firm international entrepreneurial orientation drive Chinese SMEs' international networking and knowledge acquisition activities? How does individual SME leaders' global mind-set influence firm-level entrepreneurial orientation? How do leaders' global mind-set and firm international entrepreneurial orientation jointly influence Chinese SMEs' international networking and knowledge acquisition activities? To address these questions, we develop and test a conceptual model with several hypotheses using data collected from a sample of 208 Chinese SMEs that are actively involved with international business.

The findings of this study contribute to the entrepreneurship literature in three ways. First, the study contributes to our understanding of the two prominent activities of Chinese SMEs' internationalisation, i.e. networking and knowledge acquisition, by focusing on two major explanatory factors: leader global mind-set and firm entrepreneurial orientation. The results show that both factors show a significant and positive impact on Chinese SMEs' internationalisation activities. Second, the study uncovers the mechanism of the joint effect of leader global mind-set and firm international entrepreneurial orientation above and beyond their individual effects: leader global mind-set has an indirect effect on the firm's internationalisation activities through the mediation of firm entrepreneurial orientation. Third, the study results further reveal that SME leader's global mind-set influences firm-level entrepreneurial orientation. This finding expands the stream of research into the role of business leaders in shaping organisation-wide entrepreneurial orientation, behaviours and subsequent firm performance (Engelen et al. 2015; Simsek, Heavey, and Veiga 2010; Miller and Le Breton–Miller 2011).

2. Literature review and hypotheses

2.1. International networking and knowledge acquisition activities

International networking helps build inter-firm relationships, so that organizations can create and exploit social capital and access external resources (Barney 1991; Peng and Luo 2000; Danso et al. 2016). These resources can help SMEs to identify and exploit new opportunities. Moreover, network relationships are also conduits of valuable information that can inform decision-making, reduce uncertainty, and reduce risk and fuel success. Furthermore, smaller firms are often attracted to collaborative scale opportunities (Bergman 2009).

International knowledge acquisition plays a key part in firm internationalization (Stoian, Dimitratos, and Plakoyiannaki 2018; Gulanowski, Papadopoulos, and Plante 2018). Internationalising firms need to access new knowledge to succeed (Fernhaber, Mcdougall-Covin, and Shepherd 2009). Entrepreneurs can effectively obtain foreign market knowledge by actively pursuing entrepreneurial opportunities abroad (Zhou 2007). People's informal networks are important conduits of local market knowledge during early internationalization (Harris and Wheeler 2005). Moreover, such networked learning enhances a firm's' ability to manage future relationships (Johanson and Vahlne 2003). The learning from firms' diverse, international market experiences also helps them build new business networks (Blomstermo et al. 2004).

2.2. Global mind-set

There is no agreed definition of a global mind-set in the literature (Andresen and Bergdolt 2017). A global mind-set can be studied at an individual level or firm level. At the individual level, Levy et al. (2007) suggest an integrative definition that addresses both strategic and cultural realities: a global mind-set is a cognitive structure that is characterised by openness to multiple strategic and cultural realities on both home market and abroad, and a cognitive ability to mediate and integrate across different environments. A global mind-set enables one to gain insights into the local market needs and build cognitive bridges between these needs and the firms' own global experiences and capabilities (Gupta and Govindarajan 2002).

At the firm level, Paul (2000) suggests that a global mind-set is about how the firm sees the world, which reflects the structural characteristics of the firm, the individual mind-set of the leaders, administrative heritage and industry forces. In other words, firm-level global mind-set is seen as a function of the interaction of individual mind-set and other factors of, and surrounding, the firm. Begley and Boyd (2003) emphasise that firm-level global mind-set is demonstrated through individual managers' and employees' global mind-sets. It is evident that individual global mind-sets have a positive effect on a firm-level global mind-set. However, it is less clear whether individual global mind-sets influence firm-level entrepreneurial orientation, an essential characteristic for SMEs to succeed in a foreign market where there are different consumer needs, competition, economic and technological conditions (Knight 2000). This paper investigates individual, rather than firm level, global mind-sets to address calls for enhancing our understanding of the role of managers' cognitive attributes within organizations (Felício, Caldeirinha, and Ribeiro-Navarrete 2015). Also, SME managers tend to have high control and decision making power owing partially to enhanced likelihood of an ownership stake in the firm and the informal manage-ment style of smaller companies (Willard, Krueger, and Feeser 1992; Mintzberg 1989; Matzler et al. 2008). These features could intensify the role of individual managerial characteristics in informing SMEs' business orientation.

2.3. International entrepreneurial orientation

International entrepreneurial orientation characterises a firm's opportunity-seeking behaviour in the international markets. Boso, Oghazi, and Hultman (2017) define international entrepreneurial orientation as 'the processes that firms use to exploit entrepreneurial opportunities to create new products and services abroad' (p.6). They consider international entrepreneurial orientation as a strategic posture of a firm in the international markets (Boso, Oghazi, and Hultman 2017). The construct has been operationalised as either a single or multi-dimensional construct in the previous studies (Covin and Lumpkin 2011). For example, McDougall and Oviatt (2000) define the construct specifically as 'a combination of innovative, proactive, and risk-seeking behaviour that crosses national borders' (p.903). International innovativeness refers to a tendency to introduce new product or service into foreign markets (Boso, Oghazi, and Hultman 2017). International proactive-ness refers to a tendency to identify and exploit market opportunities ahead of competitors in foreign markets (Boso, Oghazi, and Hultman 2017). International risk-taking is an inclination to take risks and bold actions in uncertain environments within foreign markets (Covin and Miller 2014). This multi-dimensional definition has been adopted to examine Chinese SMEs' internationalisation in previous work (e.g. Zhang et al. 2016). In this study, we conceptualise international entrepre-neurial orientation as a second-order, composite construct that incorporates the three sub-dimensions of innovativeness, pro-activeness and risk taking across national borders (Miller 1983).

In contrast to the individual-level definition of global mind-set, international entrepreneurial orientation is often studied at the firm level rather than referring to an entrepreneur who takes risks, is innovative, and is quick to spot and take an opportunity (Randerson 2016; Covin and Lumpkin 2011). An international entrepreneurial orientation enables a firm to take a posture like an entrepreneur toward opportunities in the market (Lumpkin and Dess 1996). An international entrepreneurial orientation helps SMEs adapt to the changing international context (Swoboda and Olejnik 2016). They need to acquire key resources to develop a sustainable competitive advantage. In this respect, international entrepreneurial orientation can be regarded as a critical resource for SMEs to nurture innovation, production and market management (Rangone 1999).

2.4. Hypotheses

There is a growing interest in identifying the factors that foster firm-level entrepreneurial orientation, given its importance for a firm's performance in a competitive environment (Cao, Simsek, and Jansen 2015). The key determinants revealed are associated with the characteristics of the leader (Ling et al. 2008; Simsek, Heavey, and Veiga 2010), the firm context (Covin, Green, and Slevin 2006), and the industry lifecycle and business environment (Lumpkin and Dess 2001). A particular stream of research focuses on the individual characteristics of the leaders in shaping firm-level entrepreneurial orientation, such as their personality, leadership style, and social ties and others (Cao, Simsek, and Jansen 2015). The upper echelons view of the firm argues that leaders' interpretation of the business environment and strategic decision about innovation, market expansion are influenced by their personal experience and background, as such the characteristics of leaders directly impact firm orientation and subsequent performance (Hambrick and Mason 1984). Consistent with this perspective, studies show that leader-ship could have an impact on several firm-level outcomes (Ling et al. 2008). Specifically, they show that a transformational leader will influence the different facets of the firm's entrepreneurial orientation, such as organizational innovation (Jung, Wu, and Chow 2008), top management teams' risk propensity and consequently corporate entrepreneurship (Ling et al. 2008).

The mind-set of the leaders of an SME directly influences their decision-making approach, the business process and practices of the firm. Individuals with a global mind-set have a strong interest in developing international business (Felício, Caldeirinha, and Rodrigues 2012). Levy et al. (2007) argue that global mind-set is necessary although not sufficient for firms to become effective in global expansion. Moreover, Gaffney et al. (2014) indicate that a leader's global mind-set drives firm-level strategic orientation and subsequently leads to accelerated internationalisation. Individuals with a global mind-set are open to diversified cultures and markets in the global environment (Rogers and Blonski 2010) and are able to formulate and implement strategies to take opportunities available in an international arena (Levy et al. 2007). This existing research highlights a global mind-set can help exploit international opportunities that are central to an international entrepreneurial orientation (Boso, Oghazi, and Hultman 2017).Thus, we propose:

H1: Leaders' global mind-set has a positive effect on a firm's international entrepreneurial orientation.

Leaders with a global mind-set are curious about foreign cultures and committed to foreign markets, they are keen to learn both the foreign cultures and the operation of the foreign market environment and other institutions (Gupta and Govindarajan 2002). Furthermore, as argued in the upper echelons view of the firm (Hambrick and Mason 1984), a leader's global mind-set will influence the firm's actions, and we may conceptualise these actions to include firm's venturing behaviours in foreign markets. Networks are important sources of resources and knowledge for SMEs as their experience, knowledge and resource limitations place them at a disadvantage to large firms whilst internationalizing (Bell, Murray, and Madden 1992; Etemad 1999). Therefore, their managers' interest and willingness to socialise and engage with foreign cultures can be a key ingredient of internationalization success. Felício, Caldeirinha, and Rodrigues (2012) suggest that global mind-set is one of the key determinants of internationalisation behaviours. Specifically, global mind-set was positively associated with networking events that facilitated knowledge and resource acquisition and helped establish and maintained relationships with customers and suppliers (Felício, Caldeirinha, and Rodrigues 2012). Therefore, we propose the following:

H2a: Leader global mind-set has a positive effect on international networking activities.

H2b: Leader global mind-set has a positive effect on international knowledge acquisition activities.

To develop international business, entrepreneurs need to discover, evaluate and exploit new cross-border opportunities. SMEs need to weight the potential short-term financial loss and long-term gain (Wang, Chung, and Lim 2015). Compared with larger firms, SMEs often confront more difficulties in obtaining the resources needed to develop international markets (Fernhaber, Gilbert, and McDougall 2014). Entrepreneurially orientated firms can leverage marketing strategies and respond to complicated cross-country environments, as well as apply innovative strategies in response to overseas demands (Knight 2000). International entrepreneurial orientation helps the firm to develop key capabilities (Lee, Lee, and Pennings 2001) for better utilizing internal and external resources for overseas expansion (Wiklund and Shepherd 2003).

The attention-based view of the firm argues that firm behaviours are dependent on the decision makers' attention, and the firm's norms and rules (Ocasio 1997). Following the logic of the attention-based view, we argue that a firm with international entrepreneurial orientation has the norm or rule to seek opportunities proactively. When faced with unfamiliar foreign market environments, the entrepreneurially orientated firm has the propensity to focus their attention on identifying new business partners, and acquire new knowledge. Previous studies have shown that international entrepreneurial orientation is associated with different resource seeking behaviours.

For example, Sapienza, De Clercq, and Sandberg (2005) found that international entrepreneurial orientation has a positive influence on firms' domestic and international learning activities.

Similarly, Keh, Nguyen, and Ng (2007) show that international entrepreneurial orientation positively affects firms' market information acquisition and utilization. Given international entrepreneurial orientation facilitates international learning activities and information acquisition and utilization, the same mechanism may also lead firms to establish business relationships that permit access to further resources and knowledge crucial for internationalization (Lavie 2006; Lee et al. 2012). Neergaard (2005) outlines networking activity as a crucial source of resources and as such will likely attract the attention of SMEs high in international entrepreneurial orientation as they seek to offset their knowledge and resource deficits (Bell, Murray, and Madden 1992; Etemad 1999).

In summary, the prior section has outlined how international entrepreneurial orientation is associated with international learning activities, market information acquisition and international networking activities. Given these complementary findings, it is reasonable to assume entrepreneurial orientation has a positive effect on both international networking activities and international knowledge acquisition activities. Thus we propose:

H3a: Firm's international entrepreneurial orientation has a positive effect on international networking activities.

H3b: Firm's international entrepreneurial orientation has a positive effect on international knowledge acquisition activities.

Combining Hypothesis 1, which states that leaders' global mind-set has a positive effect on a firm's entrepreneurial orientation, with Hypothesis 3, which further posits that firm international entrepreneurial orientation has a positive effect on: a) international networking activities and b) international knowledge acquisition activities, we can postulate that there is a potential mediation effect of firm international entrepreneurial orientation (Baron and Kenny 1986):

H4a: The effect of leader global mind-set on international networking activities is partially mediated through firm's international entrepreneurial orientation.

H4b: The effect of leader global mind-set on international knowledge acquisition activities is partially mediated through firm's international entrepreneurial orientation.

A research model of this study has been developed to reflect the above hypotheses (Figure 1).

3. Research method

The empirical data for this study were collected through a questionnaire survey, which was first developed in English, then translated into Chinese by a bilingual scholar of business studies, and translated back into English by another bilingual scholar in the same subject area. Minor adjustments were made following the discussion of the two scholars and the authors.

3.1. Sample and data collection

We developed an online questionnaire hosted by 'Sojump.com' (a large scale commercial survey website in China, similar to Survey Monkey) to collect empirical data and test our hypotheses. The target population for this study consisted of owners or key leaders of Chinese SMEs (Fabian and Molina 2009; Zhang et al. 2016). We approached a nation-wide SME trade association (with approx. 2000 members) and secured its collaboration in recruiting survey participants. The SME trade association sent out invitations to its member organizations via a social network application, specifically WeChat's group function. The use of social media WeChat is justified because it has been widely used by Chinese SME owners/managers to communicate with each other, exchange commercial information, and build social

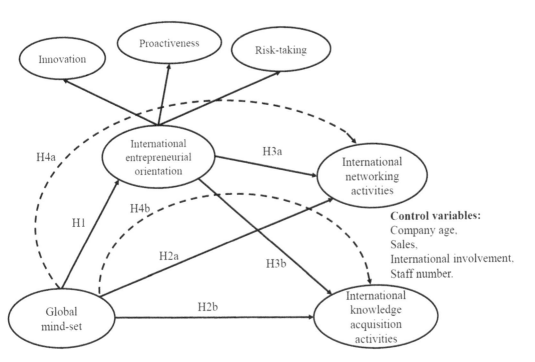

Figure 1. Research model.

networks. Furthermore, compared with the traditional tools such as postal or drop-and-collect surveys, social media is a highly efficient and effective means to reach and engage with potential research participants. Following the definition of SME by the European Union (European Commission Small Business, 2009), to be included in the study, the respondent's company should have fewer than 250 employees (Brouthers, Nakos, and Dimitratos 2015). The use of the European definition facilitates comparison with previous studies. Although a Chinese definition of SME (maximum 2000 employees) (Zhang, Ma, and Wang 2012) would seem more logical, it would be difficult to compare across international studies. SMEs by European definition are a subset of those by a Chinese one; hence the sample in our study is still SMEs by Chinese definition, although they are much smaller in size.

The survey started from 26 February and lasted until 7 March 2017. We received 208 valid responses. Because participant invitation was through social media, the exact response rate is unknown; however, given that the population of the trade association was around 2000 members, the minimal response rate was about 10.4%, assuming that all of the members had received the survey invitation message. There is a likelihood of non-response bias in a survey. To test the bias, we compared early responses with late ones (Armstrong and Overton 1977). A t-test of the two groups' mean responses showed no significant differences between early and late responses, thus non-response bias is not a concern, and the sample was deemed as representative of the target population.

3.2. Construct measures

The construct measures in the questionnaire were based on sources from the extant literature. Global mind-set was measured by 3 items selected from the behavioural dimension of individual global mind-set in Felício, Caldeirinha, and Ribeiro-Navarrete (2015): see the world as single, vast market (glob1); internationalisation as a means to achieve growth objectives (glob2); and lead the firm into the international market (glob3).

For entrepreneurial orientation, we followed Zhang et al. (2016) and adopted the commonly used nine items developed by Covin and Slevin (1989) and Zahra and Garvis (2000a) to measure a firm's innovativeness (3 items), proactiveness (3 items) and risk-taking (3 items). The three items measuring innovativeness were: changes in product lines (inn1); new products (inn2); and new processes (inn3). The three items measuring proactiveness were about: engagement with competitors proactively (pro1), innovation introduction when engaging with competitors (pro2); and long-term goals and strategies (pro3). The three items measuring risk-taking were: a proclivity for high-risk projects (risk1); reward calculated risks (risk2), and taking bold actions (risk3).

The measures of international networking activities were adapted from Felício, Caldeirinha, and Ribeiro-Navarrete (2015) and Bai, Holmström Lind, and Johanson (2016): explore foreign market resources (network1); engage in social interactions with foreign clients (network2); and create/maintain relationship with foreign business partners (network3). The measures of international knowledge acquisition activities were adapted from Bai, Holmström Lind, and Johanson (2016): participate in activities to acquire foreign marketing knowledge (know1); foreign business opportunities and ideas (know2); and foreign new technological ideas (know3).

In addition to the construct measures, the questionnaire also requests participating firms' demographic variables, annual sales, geographic coverage of business activities, and the major mode of international business involved.

4. Results

4.1. Sample profile

Within the sample, the average number of countries that each sample SME has a business relationship with is 5.14, the average staff number is 123, and the average sale is 142 million Chinese Yuan. Other company demographic variables are listed in Table 1. The age of the sample companies is mostly between 6–15 years, while the majority of them are in the electronics and textile industries. The most common type of international involvement is export (74%).

4.2. Measurement model results

We use Partial Least Squares Structural Equation Modelling (PLS-SEM) to test our model. International entrepreneurial orientation as a second-order reflective construct, with the first-order features being innovation (0.850), proactiveness (0.843), risk-taking (0.729), and the loadings were well above the recommended threshold of 0.7.

Table 1. Company profile (n = 208).

	Frequency	percentage
Company age		
1–5 years	28	13.5
6–10 years	67	32.2
11–15 years	76	36.5
16–20 years	22	10.6
20 and above	15	7.2
Industry		
Textile and garment	50	24
Chemical, rubber and plastic products	37	17.8
Metal and machinery	37	17.8
Electronic, optical, electrical products	73	35.1
Others	11	5.3
Involvement		
Export	154	74
Strategic alliance	29	13.9
Joint venture	18	8.7
Direct investment/Subsidiary	7	3.4

Table 2 shows the average variance extracted (AVE), composite reliability (CR) and Cronbach's Alpha for each first-order construct. According to Hair, Ringle, and Sarstedt (2011), Cronbach's Alpha is not a suitable criterion in PLS-SEM. Therefore we focused on assessing the values of AVE and CR. The recommended level of AVE is 0.5 and the recommended level of CR is 0.7 (Hair, Ringle, and Sarstedt 2011). The results as shown in Table 2 meet the requirements because they are all above the 0.5 and 0.7 thresholds respectively. Thus the convergent validity of the measures was verified.

To test discriminant validity, one needs to examine cross-loadings and compare the square roots of the AVE (Hair, Ringle, and Sarstedt 2011) and the correlations between latent variables (Fornell and Larcker 1981). As shown in Table 3, each indicator loads higher on its respective construct than on others. Table 4 shows that the square roots of the AVEs exceed the correlations between every pair of latent variables. Thus, discriminant validity can be confirmed.

To reduce common method variance, we followed Podsakoff et al.'s (2003) guidelines, by first using proximal separation of the items that measure different constructs and then employing a statistical procedure to test the potential of common method bias. A commonly used method in PLS-SEM is the full collinearity assessment approach proposed by Kock (2015). The results of the test (Table 5) show that none of our inter-construct variance inflation factors (VIFs) is greater than 3.3, the threshold level for a model to be considered as contaminated by common method bias (Kock 2015), indicating that common method bias is not an issue of concern in our model.

4.3. Structural model results

Figure 2 presents the structural model results, which indicate that the aggregate path coefficients are statistically significant. R^2 values for networking, knowledge acquisition activities and international entrepreneurial orientation were 57.1%, 51.6% and 34% respectively, indicating adequate explanatory power (Hair, Ringle, and Sarstedt 2011).

Table 2. Convergent validity.

	AVE	Composite Reliability	Cronbach's Alpha
Global mind-set	0.640	0.842	0.718
Innovation	0.575	0.802	0.629
Pro-activeness	0.517	0.762	0.533
Risk-taking	0.681	0.865	0.767
Networking activities	0.562	0.794	0.614
Knowledge acquisition activities	0.616	0.828	0.688

Note: AVE = average variance extracted.

Table 3. Cross-loadings.

	Global mind-set	Innovation	Knowledge acquisition	networking	Pro-activeness	Risk-taking
glob1	**0.791**	0.528	0.473	0.548	0.454	0.090
glob2	**0.779**	0.469	0.556	0.532	0.487	0.147
glob3	**0.828**	0.454	0.491	0.554	0.517	0.150
inn1	0.56	**0.801**	0.437	0.487	0.516	0.275
inn2	0.452	**0.746**	0.411	0.437	0.473	0.323
inn3	0.354	**0.725**	0.324	0.486	0.404	0.316
know1	0.408	0.393	**0.773**	0.415	0.467	0.306
know2	0.501	0.379	**0.816**	0.548	0.545	0.332
know3	0.574	0.443	**0.764**	0.580	0.422	0.241
network1	0.579	0.574	0.549	**0.779**	0.513	0.348
network2	0.504	0.382	0.490	**0.733**	0.407	0.182
network3	0.436	0.416	0.438	**0.736**	0.313	0.292
pro1	0.353	0.356	0.315	0.346	**0.683**	0.367
pro2	0.521	0.515	0.537	0.455	**0.755**	0.270
pro3	0.430	0.447	0.453	0.398	**0.718**	0.282
risk1	−0.024	0.259	0.175	0.222	0.219	**0.772**
risk2	0.206	0.411	0.384	0.404	0.450	**0.885**
risk3	0.184	0.302	0.333	0.266	0.345	**0.816**

Table 4. Correlations and the square root of AVEs.

	Global mind-set	Innovation	Knowledge acquisition	Pro-activeness	Risk-taking	Networking
Global mind-set	**0.800**					
Innovation	0.605	**0.758**				
Knowledge acquisition	0.635	0.517	**0.785**			
Pro-activeness	0.608	0.614	0.610	**0.719**		
Risk-taking	0.162	0.401	0.372	0.423	**0.825**	
Networking	0.681	0.620	0.661	0.558	0.371	**0.750**

Note: Boldface numbers on the diagonal are the square root of the average variance extracted.

Table 5. Common method variance test: inter-construct variance inflation factors.

	International entrepreneurial orientation	Global mind-set	Knowledge acquisition	Networking
International entrepreneurial orientation	–	1.914	1.776	1.747
Global mind-set	2.092	–	1.973	1.835
Knowledge acquisition	1.955	2.033	–	2.009
Networking	2.227	2.132	2.249	–

The results indicate that there was a positive relationship between global mind-set and international entrepreneurial orientation ($\beta = 0.583$, $t = 13.667$), supporting H1.

Hypotheses 2a and H2b state that global mind-set has a positive effect on international networking (H2a) and knowledge acquisition activities (H2b). This set of hypotheses received statistical support: $\beta s = 0.446$ (H2a) and 0.406 (H2b) respectively ($ps<0.001$).

Hypotheses 3a and 3b state that there is a positive effect of international entrepreneurial orientation on international networking (H3a) and knowledge acquisition activities (H3b). This set of hypotheses received statistical support too: $\beta s = 0.369$ (H3a) and 0.406 (H3b) respectively, ($ps<0.001$).

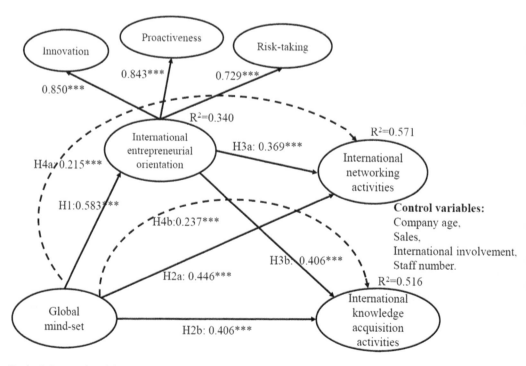

Figure 2. Structural model results.

To test the mediation hypotheses of H4a and H4b, we ran two sets of mediation analysis using the bootstrapping procedure with 1000 resamples. The results indicate that international entrepreneurship orientation mediates the relationships between global mind-set and international networking (indirect effect = 0.215, t-value = 5.054, 95% confidence interval = [0.133, 0.302]) and knowledge acquisition activities (indirect effect = 0.237, t-value = 4.515, 95% confidence interval = [0.147, 0.348]). Given that there are significant direct effects of global mind-set on international networking and knowledge acquisition activities, the mediation effects are considered as partial. Thus, H4a and H4b were supported. The results of all the hypotheses testing are summarised in Table 6.

5. Discussion

International networking activities for Chinese SMEs, most frequently shown as guanxi in the Chinese culture, can provide alternative access to resources (Peng and Luo 2000). International business knowledge acquisition helps the Chinese SMEs' entrepreneurial venturing at the international stage (Alvarez and Busenitz 2001). This study examines two important antecedents of such behaviours by considering both the direct effect and the joint influence of leader global mind-set and the firm's international entrepreneurial orientation. The empirical results show that a) leaders' global mind-set directly influences firm-level international entrepreneurial orientation and international networking and knowledge acquisition activities; b) firm-level international entrepreneurial orientation drives Chinese SMEs' international networking and knowledge acquisition activities; c) leaders' global mind-set has an indirect effect on Chinese SMEs' international networking and knowledge acquisition activities through the mediation of firm entrepreneurial orientation. The empirical results have both theoretical and practical implications.

5.1. Theoretical implications

This study contributes to the literature on firms' international expansion behaviours, specifically the social capital creation and knowledge acquisition behaviours (e.g. Felício, Caldeirinha, and Rodrigues 2012; Swoboda and Olejnik 2016; Levy et al. 2007; García-Villaverde, Parra-Requena, and Molina-Morales 2018). Our findings show that Chinese SMEs' engagement with international networking and international knowledge acquisition activities is driven by the two major factors: leader global mind-set and firm international entrepreneurial orientation. The significant effect of leader global mind-set is consistent with expectations derived from the upper-echelon view of the firm (Hambrick and Mason 1984), while that of international entrepreneurial orientation provides evidence to support the attention-based view of the firm (Ocasio 1997) in that Chinese SMEs with international entrepreneurial orientation tend to focus their attention on building international business networks and acquiring new knowledge. Moreover, according to resource-based view (Barney 1991), both leaders' global mind-set and firm-level international entrepreneurial orientation are intangible resources, which facilitate the firm and its employees to participate in networking and knowledge acquisition activities so as to deal with the complex environments and cultural

Table 6. Results of hypothesis testing.

Hypotheses	Supported?
H1 Global mind-set → International entrepreneurial orientation	Yes
H2a Global mind-set → International networking activities	Yes
H2b Global mind-set → International knowledge acquisition activities	Yes
H3a International entrepreneurial orientation → International networking activities	Yes
H3b Entrepreneurial orientation→ International knowledge acquisition activities	Yes
H4a Global mind-set → International entrepreneurial orientation → International networking activities	Yes
H4b Global mind-set → International entrepreneurial orientation → International knowledge acquisition activities	Yes

diversity overseas (Levy et al. 2007). The findings are particularly useful because, despite the rapid growth in recent years, most Chinese SMEs are still in the early stage of development and are constrained by limited resources with regard to international market knowledge and social capital development (Atherton and Newman 2017).

This study provides greater insights and sophistication than what was reported in the previous studies, which implied simple, direct effects of global mind-set (Felício, Caldeirinha, and Rodrigues 2012; Gaffney et al. 2014) and international entrepreneurial orientation (Zhang, Ma, and Wang 2012) on international networking and knowledge acquisition activities. Our study reveals that, in addition to its direct effect, leader global mind-set has indirect effects on international networking and knowledge acquisition activities through the mediation of firm-level international entrepreneurial orientation. The additional mediating role of international entrepreneurial orientation implies that for SMEs, being entrepreneurially orientated is central to transferring the leader's global mind-set at the firm level in driving both social capital and knowledge resources creating activities. In other words, international entrepreneurial orientation is likely to augment the leader's efforts in creating international social networks and accumulating market knowledge.

The study's results extend the upper echelons perspective of the firm (Hambrick and Mason 1984) by investigating the role of SME leaders' global mind-set and firm-level international entrepreneurial orientation in influencing Chinese SMEs' internationalisation activities. The emprical evidence of this study shows that SME leaders' global mind-set influences firm-level entrepreneurial orientation. To the best of our knowledge, this is among the first studies that test the linkage between leader global mind-set and firm entrepreneurial orientation. This finding further enriches the literature on the role of business leaders in shaping organisation-wide entrepreneurial behaviours (Engelen et al. 2015; Simsek, Heavey, and Veiga 2010; Miller and Le Breton–Miller 2011).

5.2. Managerial implications

The findings suggest that in the sampled Chinese SMEs, global mind-set and international entrepreneurial orientation have a direct impact on the firm's international venturing behaviours, especially their engagement with the networking and knowledge acquisition activities. A policy implication is that although the Chinese government has attempted to promote the development of SMEs, more could be done to support them in developing global mind-set, and international entrepreneurial orientation, including innovation, pro-activeness and risk-taking, which are critical for SMEs to venture into foreign markets. The cultivation of global mind-set depends on the level of curiosity about and commitment to foreign markets, comprehension of existing mind-set, diversity orientation, and readiness to learn (Gupta and Govindarajan 2002). Governments should promote more opportunities for SME leaders to engage in international networking and knowledge acquisition activities. Public sector organizations can be excellent relationship brokers and channels into foreign markets given their superior network and resource position. Particular opportunities for SMEs to pursue, and for policymakers to facilitate, are matchmaking services for foreign firms and SMEs, and participation in bilateral trade missions and exhibitions. Additionally, firms can develop their network by reaching out to international business associations and trade offices.

The findings of this study indicate that global mind-set and international entrepreneurial orientation are two key drivers for international networking and learning activities, in addition to market opportunities and ultimately firm performance, as reported in the literature (e.g. Wang, Chung, and Lim 2015; Saeed, Yousafzai, and Engelen 2014; Peng and Luo 2000; Zahra and Garvis 2000b; Lumpkin and Dess 2001; Danso et al. 2016). SME leaders should train themselves to be global minded, by examining their own cultural values, world view, and compare with those in other country markets. They should also invest in developing an international entrepreneurial orientation at the firm level. SMEs should be proactive in international networking and acquiring knowledge in international markets. SMEs with international entrepreneurial orientation could first evaluate their own network capabilities and, if necessary, implement development programmes and training to cultivate this skill internally. Moreover, resource limited SMEs may benefit from focusing their efforts on those few crucial partners who can provide the best business opportunities and capabilities. This approach is particularly effective when rapid internationalization is required (Casillas and Moreno-Menéndez 2014). SMEs could pursue international partnerships with firms possessing complementary capabilities to help establish mutual benefit, these can make strategic alliances easier to form and enhance performance (Rothaermel 2001).

Chinese entrepreneurs naturally tend to put guanxi and building a network of relationships as a priority in their daily business practices, but it is useful for entrepreneurs to engage with international knowledge acquisition activities in addition to international networking activities. Nevertheless, it should be noted that the two activities are not mutually exclusive, and entrepreneurs could use their international networks for the purpose of knowledge acquisition. Collaborating with major, well-connected organizations is particularly helpful here given their large networks enable SMEs to access more geographically distant and diverse knowledge. Additionally, formal contracts can be used to help structure knowledge sharing, codify prior experience, coordinate exchanges and formalize specifications. SMEs can significantly enhance knowledge absorption by utilising both relational and contractual mechanisms.

5.3. Limitations and further research

The study is constrained by several limitations. First, the data used for the study were collected from the same source at one point in time; as such the correlations between variables could be inflated. Our sample is limited to a pool of 2,000 Chinese SMEs in a nation-wide trade association. Therefore, caution should be taken when interpreting the results. Second, when sampling participating firms, we followed the European Union's definition for SME (maximum of 250 employees) that helps cross-research context comparison; future research could adopt a definition that is widely accepted in China to examine Chinese SMEs. Third, our conceptual model is limited to the four constructs investigated, future research could examine other factors that may drive SME internationalisation activities, such as different leadership style and firm-level characteristics. Future studies could test the consequences of firms' social networks and knowledge acquisition on firm performance variables such as product innovation, sales growth and profitability.

6. Conclusion

The current paper advances the international entrepreneurship research by conceptualizing the effect of leader global mind-set and firm international entrepreneurial orientation on the internationalisation activities of Chinese SMEs, acknowledging the unique Chinese culture in understanding firms' global expansion. It responds to the calls for more studies of entrepreneurship in China (e.g. Batjargal 2010; Dimitratos et al. 2016; Lu and Tao 2010; Su, Zhai, and Landström 2015; Zhang, Ma, and Wang 2012; Zhang et al. 2016), with special focus on the country-specific variables and the contextual nature of China's emerging economy (Zhang et al. 2016). Our study suggests that global mind-set and international entrepreneurial orientation are essential in driving Chinese SMEs' international knowledge and social capital acquisition activities, and SME leaders may need to develop a global mind-set and foster an international entrepreneurial orientation in their organization to strategically guide their internationalisation activities.

Disclosure statement

No potential conflict of interest was reported by the authors.

ORCID

Zhibin Lin (iD) http://orcid.org/0000-0001-5575-2216
Xuebing Cao (iD) http://orcid.org/0000-0001-9392-2554
Ed Cottam (iD) http://orcid.org/0000-0001-7309-4405

References

Alvarez, S. A., and L. W. Busenitz. 2001. "The Entrepreneurship of Resource-based Theory." *Journal of Management* 27 (6): 755–775. doi:10.1177/014920630102700609.

Andresen, M., and F. Bergdolt. 2017. "A Systematic Literature Review on the Definitions of Global Mindset and Cultural Intelligence–Merging Two Different Research Streams." *The International Journal of Human Resource Management* 28 (1): 170–195. doi:10.1080/09585192.2016.1243568.

Armstrong, J. S., and T. S. Overton. 1977. "Estimating Nonresponse Bias in Mail Surveys." *Journal of Marketing Research* 14 (3): 396–402. doi:10.1177/002224377701400320.

Atherton, A., and A. Newman. 2017. *Entrepreneurship in China: The Emergence of the Private Sector*. London: Routledge.

Bai, W., C. Holmström Lind, and M. Johanson. 2016. "The Performance of International Returnee Ventures: The Role of Networking Capability and the Usefulness of International Business Knowledge." *Entrepreneurship & Regional Development* 28 (9–10): 657–680. doi:10.1080/08985626.2016.1234003.

Barney, J. 1991. "Firm Resources and Sustained Competitive Advantage." *Journal of Management* 17 (1): 99–120. doi:10.1177/014920639101700108.

Baron, R. M., and D. A. Kenny. 1986. "The Moderator–Mediator Variable Distinction in Social Psychological Research: Conceptual, Strategic, and Statistical Considerations." *Journal of Personality and Social Psychology* 51 (6): 1173–1182.

Batjargal, B. 2010. "Network Dynamics and New Ventures in China: A Longitudinal Study." *Entrepreneurship & Regional Development* 22 (2): 139–153. doi:10.1080/08985620802628864.

Begley, T. M., and D. P. Boyd. 2003. "The Need for a Corporate Global Mind-set." *MIT Sloan Management Review* 44 (2): 25.

Bell, J., M. Murray, and K. Madden. 1992. "Developing Expertise: An Irish Perspective." *International Small Business Journal* 10 (2): 37–53. doi:10.1177/026624692010000203.

Bergman, E. M. 2009. "Embedding Network Analysis in Spatial Studies of Innovation." *The Annals of Regional Science* 43 (3): 559–565. doi:10.1007/s00168-008-0250-y.

Blomstermo, A., K. Eriksson, A. Lindstrand, and D. D. Sharma. 2004. "The Perceived Usefulness of Network Experiential Knowledge in the Internationalizing Firm." *Journal of International Management* 10 (3): 355–373. doi:10.1016/j.intman.2004.05.004.

Boso, N., P. Oghazi, and M. Hultman. 2017. "International Entrepreneurial Orientation and Regional Expansion." *Entrepreneurship & Regional Development* 29 (1–2): 4–26. doi:10.1080/08985626.2016.1255430.

Brouthers, K. D., G. Nakos, and P. Dimitratos. 2015. "SME Entrepreneurial Orientation, International Performance, and the Moderating Role of Strategic Alliances." *Entrepreneurship Theory and Practice* 39 (5): 1161–1187. doi:10.1111/etap.2015.39.issue-5.

Cao, Q., Z. Simsek, and J. J. Jansen. 2015. "CEO Social Capital and Entrepreneurial Orientation of the Firm: Bonding and Bridging Effects." *Journal of Management* 41 (7): 1957–1981. doi:10.1177/0149206312469666.

Casillas, J. C., A. M. Moreno, F. J. Acedo, M. A. Gallego, and E. Ramos. 2009. "An Integrative Model of the Role of Knowledge in the Internationalization Process." *Journal of World Business* 44 (3): 311–322. doi:10.1016/j.jwb.2008.08.001.

Casillas, J. C., and A. M. Moreno-Menéndez. 2014. "Speed of the Internationalization Process: The Role of Diversity and Depth in Experiential Learning." *Journal of International Business Studies* 45 (1): 85–101. doi:10.1057/jibs.2013.29.

Colombo, M. G., E. Piva, and C. Rossi-Lamastra. 2014. "Open Innovation and Within-industry Diversification in Small and Medium Enterprises: The Case of Open Source Software Firms." *Research Policy* 43 (5): 891–902. doi:10.1016/j.respol.2013.08.015.

Covin, J. G., K. M. Green, and D. P. Slevin. 2006. "Strategic Process Effects on the Entrepreneurial Orientation–Sales Growth Rate Relationship." *Entrepreneurship Theory and Practice* 30 (1): 57–81. doi:10.1111/etap.2006.30.issue-1.

Covin, J. G., and G. T. Lumpkin. 2011. "Entrepreneurial Orientation Theory and Research: Reflections on a Needed Construct." *Entrepreneurship Theory and Practice* 35 (5): 855–872. doi:10.1111/etap.2011.35.issue-5.

Covin, J. G., and D. Miller. 2014. "International Entrepreneurial Orientation: Conceptual Considerations, Research Themes, Measurement Issues, and Future Research Directions." *Entrepreneurship Theory and Practice* 38 (1): 11–44. doi:10.1111/etap.12027.

Covin, J. G., and D. P. Slevin. 1989. "Strategic Management of Small Firms in Hostile and Benign Environments." *Strategic Management Journal* 10 (1): 75–87. doi:10.1002/(ISSN)1097-0266.

Danso, A., S. Adomako, J. O. Damoah, and M. Uddin. 2016. "Risk-taking Propensity, Managerial Network Ties and Firm Performance in an Emerging Economy." *The Journal of Entrepreneurship* 25 (2): 155–183. doi:10.1177/0971355716650367.

Dimitratos, P., T. Buck, M. Fletcher, and N. Li. 2016. "The Motivation of International Entrepreneurship: The Case of Chinese Transnational Entrepreneurs." *International Business Review* 25 (5): 1103–1113. doi:10.1016/j.ibusrev.2016.01.012.

Engelen, A., V. Gupta, L. Strenger, and M. Brettel. 2015. "Entrepreneurial Orientation, Firm Performance, and the Moderating Role of Transformational Leadership Behaviors." *Journal of Management* 41 (4): 1069–1097. doi:10.1177/0149206312455244.

Etemad, H. 1999. "Globalization and the Small and Medium-sized Enterprises: Search for Potent Strategies." *Global Focus* 11: 85–104.

Etemad, H. 2015. "Entrepreneurial Orientation-performance Relationship in the International Context." *Journal of International Entrepreneurship* 13 (1): 1. doi:10.1007/s10843-015-0150-z.

Fabian, A. P. F., and H. Molina. 2009. "Understanding Decisions to Internationalize by Small and Medium-sized Firms Located in an Emerging Market." *Management International Review* 49 (5): 537–563. doi:10.1007/s11575-009-0007-6.

Felício, J. A., V. R. Caldeirinha, and B. Ribeiro-Navarrete. 2015. "Corporate and Individual Global Mind-set and Internationalization of European SMEs." *Journal of Business Research* 68 (4): 797–802. doi:10.1016/j.jbusres.2014.11.031.

Felício, J. A., V. R. Caldeirinha, and R. Rodrigues. 2012. "Global Mindset and the Internationalization of Small Firms: The Importance of the Characteristics of Entrepreneurs." *International Entrepreneurship and Management Journal* 8 (4): 467–485. doi:10.1007/s11365-012-0232-5.

Fernhaber, S. A., B. A. Gilbert, and P. P. McDougall. 2014. "International Entrepreneurship and Geographic Location: An Empirical Examination of New Venture Internationalization." In *Location of International Business Activities*, edited by J. Cantwell, 94–136. London: Palgrave Macmillan .

Fernhaber, S. A., P. P. Mcdougall-Covin, and D. A. Shepherd. 2009. "International Entrepreneurship: Leveraging Internal and External Knowledge Sources." *Strategic Entrepreneurship Journal* 3 (4): 297–320. doi:10.1002/sej.v3:4.

Fornell, C., and D. F. Larcker. 1981. "Evaluating Structural Equation Models with Unobservable Variables and Measurement Error." *Journal of Marketing Research* 18 (1): 39–50. doi:10.1177/002224378101800104.

Gaffney, N., D. Cooper, B. Kedia, and J. Clampit. 2014. "Institutional Transitions, Global Mindset, and EMNE Internationalization." *European Management Journal* 32 (3): 383–391.

García-Villaverde, P. M., G. Parra-Requena, and F. X. Molina-Morales. 2018. "Structural Social Capital and Knowledge Acquisition: Implications of Cluster Membership." *Entrepreneurship & Regional Development* 30 (5–6): 530–561.

Gulanowski, D., N. Papadopoulos, and L. Plante. 2018. "The Role of Knowledge in International Expansion: Toward an Integration of Competing Models of Internationalization." *Review of International Business and Strategy* 28 (1): 35–60.

Guo, C., and J. K. Miller. 2010. "Guanxi Dynamics and Entrepreneurial Firm Creation and Development in China." *Management and Organization Review* 6 (2): 267–291.

Gupta, A. K., and V. Govindarajan. 2002. "Cultivating a Global Mindset." *The Academy of Management Executive* 16 (1): 116–126.

Hair, J. F., C. M. Ringle, and M. Sarstedt. 2011. "PLS-SEM: Indeed a Silver Bullet." *The Journal of Marketing Theory and Practice* 19 (2): 139–152.

Hambrick, D. C., and P. A. Mason. 1984. "Upper Echelons: The Organization as a Reflection of Its Top Managers." *Academy of Management Review* 9 (2): 193–206.

Harris, S., and C. Wheeler. 2005. "Entrepreneurs' Relationships for Internationalization: Functions, Origins and Strategies." *International Business Review* 14 (2): 187–207.

He, C., J. Lu, and H. Qian. 2018. "Entrepreneurship in China." *Small Business Economics,* 52(3): 1–10.

Huggins, R., and A. Johnston. 2010. "Knowledge Flow and Inter-Firm Networks: The Influence of Network Resources, Spatial Proximity and Firm Size." *Entrepreneurship & Regional Development* 22 (5): 457–484.

Jantunen, A., K. Puumalainen, S. Saarenketo, and K. Kyläheiko. 2005. "Entrepreneurial Orientation, Dynamic Capabilities and International Performance." *Journal of International Entrepreneurship* 3 (3): 223–243.

Johanson, J. 2003. "Business Relationship Learning and Commitment in the Internationalization Process." *Journal of International Entrepreneurship* 1 (1): 83–101.

Johanson, J., and J.-E. Vahlne. 1977. "The Internationalization Process of the Firm-a Model of Knowledge Development and Increasing Foreign Market Commitments." *Journal of International Business Studies* 8 (1): 23–32.

Jung, D. D., A. Wu, and C. W. Chow. 2008. "Towards Understanding the Direct and Indirect Effects of CEOs' Transformational Leadership on Firm Innovation." *The Leadership Quarterly* 19 (5): 582–594.

Keh, H. T., T. T. M. Nguyen, and H. P. Ng. 2007. "The Effects of Entrepreneurial Orientation and Marketing Information on the Performance of SMEs." *Journal of Business Venturing* 22 (4): 592–611.

Knight, G. 2000. "Entrepreneurship and Marketing Strategy: The SME under Globalization." *Journal of International Marketing* 8 (2): 12–32.

Kock, N. 2015. "Common Method Bias in PLS-SEM: A Full Collinearity Assessment Approach." *International Journal of e-Collaboration (ijec)* 11 (4): 1–10.

Lavie, D. 2006. "The Competitive Advantage of Interconnected Firms: An Extension of the Resource-based View." *Academy of Management Review* 31 (3): 638–658.

Lee, C., K. Lee, and J. M. Pennings. 2001. "Internal Capabilities, External Networks, and Performance: A Study on Technology-based Ventures." *Strategic Management Journal* 22 (6–7): 615–640.

Lee, H., D. Kelley, J. Lee, and S. Lee. 2012. "SME Survival: The Impact of Internationalization, Technology Resources, and Alliances." *Journal of Small Business Management* 50 (1): 1–19.

Leppäaho, T., and K. Pajunen. 2018. "Institutional Distance and International Networking." *Entrepreneurship & Regional Development* 30 (5–6): 502–529.

Levy, O., S. Beechler, S. Taylor, and N. A. Boyacigiller. 2007. "What We Talk about When We Talk about 'global Mindset': Managerial Cognition in Multinational Corporations." *Journal of International Business Studies* 38 (2): 231–258.

Ling, Y., Z. Simsek, M. H. Lubatkin, and J. F. Veiga. 2008. "Transformational Leadership's Role in Promoting Corporate Entrepreneurship: Examining the CEO-TMT Interface." *Academy of Management Journal* 51 (3): 557–576.

Lu, J., and Z. Tao. 2010. "Determinants of Entrepreneurial Activities in China." *Journal of Business Venturing* 25 (3): 261–273.

Lumpkin, G. T., and G. G. Dess. 1996. "Clarifying the Entrepreneurial Orientation Construct and Linking It to Performance." *Academy of Management Review* 21 (1): 135–172.

Lumpkin, G. T., and G. G. Dess. 2001. "Linking Two Dimensions of Entrepreneurial Orientation to Firm Performance: The Moderating Role of Environment and Industry Life Cycle." *Journal of Business Venturing* 16 (5): 429–451.

Martin, S. L., and R. R. G. Javalgi. 2016. "Entrepreneurial Orientation, Marketing Capabilities and Performance: The Moderating Role of Competitive Intensity on Latin American International New Ventures." *Journal of Business Research* 69 (6): 2040–2051.

Matzler, K., E. Schwarz, N. Deutinger, and R. Harms. 2008. "The Relationship between Transformational Leadership, Product Innovation and Performancein SMEs." *Journal of Small Business & Entrepreneurship* 21 (2): 139–151.

McDougall, P. P., and B. M. Oviatt. 2000. "International Entrepreneurship: The Intersection of Two Research Paths." *Academy of Management Journal* 43 (5): 902–906.

Miller, D. 2011. "Miller (1983) Revisited: A Reflection on EO Research and Some Suggestions for the Future." *Entrepreneurship Theory and Practice* 35 (5): 873–894.

Miller, D. 1983. "The Correlates of Entrepreneurship in Three Types of Firms." *Management Science* 29 (7): 770–791.

Miller, D., and I. Le Breton–Miller. 2011. "Governance, Social Identity, and Entrepreneurial Orientation in Closely Held Public Companies." *Entrepreneurship Theory and Practice* 35 (5): 1051–1076.

Mintzberg, H. 1989. "The Structuring of Organizations." In *Readings in Strategic Management*, edited by D. Asch and C. Bowman, 322–352. London: Palgrave. .

Neergaard, H. 2005. "Networking Activities in Technology-based Entrepreneurial Teams." *International Small Business Journal* 23 (3): 257–278.

Ocasio, W. 1997. "Towards an Attention-based View of the Firm." *Strategic Management Journal* 18: 187–206.

Oviatt, B. M., and P. P. McDougall. 1994. "Toward a Theory of International New Ventures." *Journal of International Business Studies* 25 (1): 45–64.

Oviatt, B. M., and P. P. McDougall. 2005. "Defining International Entrepreneurship and Modeling the Speed of Internationalization." *Entrepreneurship Theory and Practice* 29 (5): 537–554.

Paul, H. 2000. "Creating a Global Mindset." *Thunderbird International Business Review* 42 (2): 187–200.

Peng, M. W., and Y. Luo. 2000. "Managerial Ties and Firm Performance in a Transition Economy: The Nature of a Micro-macro Link." *Academy of Management Journal* 43 (3): 486–501.

Podsakoff, P. M., S. B. MacKenzie, J.-Y. Lee, and N. P. Podsakoff. 2003. "Common Method Biases in Behavioral Research: A Critical Review of the Literature and Recommended Remedies." *Journal of Applied Psychology* 88 (5): 879–903.

Randerson, K. 2016. "Entrepreneurial Orientation: Do We Actually Know as much as We Think We Do?" *Entrepreneurship & Regional Development* 28 (7–8): 580–600.

Rangone, A. 1999. "A Resource-based Approach to Strategy Analysis in Small-medium Sized Enterprises." *Small Business Economics* 12 (3): 233–248.

Rogers, E. M., and D. Blonski. 2010. "The Global Leadership Mindset." *Chief Learning Officer*, 9 (6): 18–21.

Rothaermel, F. T. 2001. "Complementary Assets, Strategic Alliances, and the Incumbent's Advantage: An Empirical Study of Industry and Firm Effects in the Biopharmaceutical Industry." *Research Policy* 30 (8): 1235–1251.

Saeed, S., S. Y. Yousafzai, and A. Engelen. 2014. "On Cultural and Macroeconomic Contingencies of the Entrepreneurial Orientation–Performance Relationship." *Entrepreneurship Theory and Practice* 38 (2): 255–290.

Sapienza, H. J., D. De Clercq, and W. R. Sandberg. 2005. "Antecedents of International and Domestic Learning Effort." *Journal of Business Venturing* 20 (4): 437–457.

Simsek, Z., C. Heavey, and J. F. Veiga. 2010. "The Impact of CEO Core Self-evaluation on the Firm's Entrepreneurial Orientation." *Strategic Management Journal* 31 (1): 110–119.

Stoian, M.-C., P. Dimitratos, and E. Plakoyiannaki. 2018. "SME Internationalization beyond Exporting: A Knowledge-based Perspective across Managers and Advisers." *Journal of World Business* 53 (5): 768–779.

Su, J., Q. Zhai, and H. Landström. 2015. "Entrepreneurship Research in China: Internationalization or Contextualization?" *Entrepreneurship & Regional Development* 27 (1–2): 50–79.

Swoboda, B., and E. Olejnik. 2016. "Linking Processes and Dynamic Capabilities of International SMEs: The Mediating Effect of International Entrepreneurial Orientation." *Journal of Small Business Management* 54 (1): 139–161.

Tang, Y. K. 2011. "Influence of Networking on the Internationalization of SMEs: Evidence from Internationalized Chinese Firms." *International Small Business Journal* 29 (4): 374–398.

Wang, Y.-K. M., C. C. Chung, and D. S. Lim. 2015. "The Drivers of International Corporate Entrepreneurship: CEO Incentive and CEO Monitoring Mechanisms." *Journal of World Business* 50 (4): 742–753.

Weaver, K. M., P. H. Dickson, B. Gibson, and A. Turner. 2002. "Being Uncertain: The Relationship between Entrepreneurial Orientation and Environmental Uncertainty." *Journal of Enterprising Culture* 10 (02): 87–105.

Wiklund, J., and D. Shepherd. 2003. "Knowledge-based Resources, Entrepreneurial Orientation, and the Performance of Small and Medium-sized Businesses." *Strategic Management Journal* 24 (13): 1307–1314.

Willard, G. E., D. A. Krueger, and H. R. Feeser. 1992. "In Order to Grow, Must the Founder Go: A Comparison of Performance between Founder and Non-founder Managed High-growth Manufacturing Firms." *Journal of Business Venturing* 7 (3): 181–194.

Zahra, S. A., and D. M. Garvis. 2000a. "International Corporate Entrepreneurship and Firm Performance: The Moderating Effect of International Environmental Hostility." *Journal of Business Venturing* 15 (5): 469–492.

Zahra, S. A., and D. M. Garvis. 2000b. "International Corporate Entrepreneurship and Firm Performance: The Moderating Effect of International Environmental Hostility." *Journal of Business Venturing* 15 (5–6): 469–492.

Zhang, X., X. Ma, and Y. Wang. 2012. "Entrepreneurial Orientation, Social Capital, and the Internationalization of SMEs: Evidence from China." *Thunderbird International Business Review* 54 (2): 195–210.

Zhang, X., X. Ma, Y. Wang, X. Li, and D. Huo. 2016. "What Drives the Internationalization of Chinese SMEs? the Joint Effects of International Entrepreneurship Characteristics, Network Ties, and Firm Ownership." *International Business Review* 25 (2): 522–534.

Zhou, L. 2007. "The Effects of Entrepreneurial Proclivity and Foreign Market Knowledge on Early Internationalization." *Journal of World Business* 42 (3): 281–293.

Index

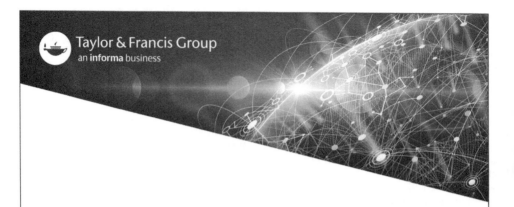